A God Called Father

One Woman's Recovery from Incest and Multiple Personality Disorder

By

Judith Machree

ISBN: 0-7596-6146-4

All scriptures quoted are from the New Living Translation of the Bible

This book is printed on acid free paper.

Dutch translation: "Ik zal een Vader voor je zijn…"

Cover design by Erik Houwer.

1stBooks – rev. 3/8/02

Dedication

To my therapist "Jan" —
You invested your time, energy and wisdom,
believing in me when I didn't believe in myself.
I'll never forget what I learned from you.

To my beloved children —
You paid a price in your childhood
for the legacy of pain that was passed down to me.
May the cycle be broken in your generation.

To my husband and my hero —
You invested your heart and soul in our marriage,
faithfully and loyally refusing to give up on me,
no matter how often I pushed you away in my fear,
no matter how hard and long my journey to wholeness.
May you find the reward has been worth the wait.

To my Lord Jesus Christ —
You paid the highest price of all,
death on the cross,
that I might be adopted into your family,
becoming a beloved child of a God called Father.
You are my Comforter, Healer and Deliverer
and the Author of my resurrection story.

Preface

Sometimes I wish I didn't know anything about sexual abuse, incest or Dissociative Identity Disorder (DID, formerly called Multiple Personality Disorder). I wish I was singularly unqualified to write this book on the painful and challenging process of recovery and healing. In 1991 when, as a Christian missionary in Holland, I "hit the wall" with depression and burnout and could no longer see my way forward in life, I didn't know anything about these subjects— or so I thought.

If you had asked me, I probably would have told you that incest is "when cousins marry" and it only happens in the hills of backwoods southern states. Asked about DID, I would have said, "Huh?" and if you asked my opinion about multiple personalities, I would have mentioned that I had seen half of the movie "Sybil" on television one night. I figured it was either a make-believe Hollywood illness or at least extremely rare.

Less than three years later, I began the slow process of becoming an unwilling "expert" on these subjects as I navigated the rough seas of recovery from my own long-buried history of incest and struggled to create some unity in the diversity of fourteen different identities who lived within my body. These identities or "alters" had remained relatively dormant since the day I turned my will and my life over to the care of Jesus Christ back in 1981.

By the grace of God, I was given ten stable years to grow in my knowledge and understanding of the Lord and His ways before I had to face the fact that my "glittering image" as a strong, invincible Christian woman and missionary was not all it was cracked up to be. That ten year "grace period" allowed me to begin to understand something of what it meant to belong to a supportive family, the body of Christ, His church, and something of what it meant to feel loved—things I had failed to learn in my family of origin. But my awareness of God's overwhelming love was limited by my image of God the Father, an image which closely resembled the dark side of my own father—demanding, judging, distant, unreachable, and never, ever satisfied. Jesus was my friend and Savior but God the Father? Well, I didn't know Him and frankly, He scared me.

I could see in His Word, the Bible, and in the sacrifice of His Son that He loved me. I could say "He loves you" to others with sincere conviction, but I couldn't sense His love deeply for myself. Deep down inside, I believed that I was unlovable, that there was something really wrong with me, and that He could never love me, though God knows, I tried desperately to earn His love.

This book is the story of a little girl severely betrayed by her earthly father and a woman who must learn at last to trust in a heavenly Father to find the love and safety she always longed for but never knew. There are no easy answers here. No formulas to follow. The path I traveled to recovery was not neatly groomed and manicured nor well sign-posted. It often seemed that I traveled in circles and inadvertently doubled-back along the trail to cross territory I was sure I had already covered. This is not a step-by-step, how-to book. It's a frightening, frustrating and sometimes seemingly impossible journey into and through a tomb of darkness and despair to find at the very darkest place at the back of the tomb a fountain of life and joy. It's my own resurrection story.

Incest is ugly. The incest I suffered was severe and spanned many years of my childhood. Each new traumatic occurrence became attached to and intertwined with the scars left by the traumas that came before. The damage to body, soul and spirit was extensive. The ability to dissociate from the terrifying experiences of my childhood was a gift from God that allowed me to survive. But when combined with a creative child's ability to pretend the abuse was happening to someone else, it also fostered the development of separate identities within me. This made life as an adult confusing and stressful and the path to recovery even more complex.

In this book, I openly expose the ugliness and the confusion I have experienced. I do not pretend, but tell the whole truth about my failures and about my pain. I also share the beauty and the clarity that came over time and I tell the holy truth about my victories and my joy. If you have been a victim, whether you specifically remember the abuse or not, you may find yourself being triggered by the images of sexual and emotional betrayal in this book. Take a break, breathe deeply, set the book aside for a while and call a friend. Don't force yourself to read on. Wait until you're ready. You have a right to set your own pace. You deserve to be treated gently and with respect.

If you have been abused, whether sexually, physically or emotionally, I hope my story will be a signpost along your path to healing. If you are a supportive friend, family member or counselor of an abused person (and given current statistics of abuse, you are!) I hope my story will deepen your understanding of the challenges survivors face in coming to terms with a God called Father.

Note: It is with regret that I must publish under a pen name and must change certain names, details and locations in my story in order to protect myself and other innocent people from the damage of being associated with the perpetrator of the crimes. My regret comes mostly from a concern that you, the reader, would misunderstand this necessity, thinking I have hidden my identity because I am ashamed. I am not ashamed. What happened to me was not my fault. I am not to blame. I am proud to be able to say I have recovered from incest and Multiple Personality Disorder. It means I am no longer a victim. I have won the decisive victory by deciding to get well. I have nothing to hide. And if you are a victim fighting to reclaim your life, neither do you. Give the shame back to the perpetrator and stand tall and proud. You deserve a place in this world!

Introduction

☐ November 27, 1995 — She curled up in a ball, knees to her chest, hands held in tight fists in front of her mouth, mewing like a kitten and crying out "I want my Mommy! I want my Mommy!"

An agony of longing knotted her stomach. Fear and panic caused her arm muscles to tense painfully and her hands to tremble. She was two-and-a-half years old. Shivering on the floor of a dark room, she hurt everywhere, inside and out. So little, so alone, so lost and confused and so longing to be rescued, she desperately needed comforting arms to enfold her and soothing words to reassure her. Her mind struggled to understand: "Where is Mommy? Why did Daddy do this to me?"

As terrifying images filled her mind, jagged-edged sobs spilled over one another in an endless cry of despair. She had no words to describe her sense of rejection and abandonment. She could only feel—and what she felt was unbearable. Her hands reached up to cover her eyes and she shook her head "no" in an effort to chase away the face of her attacker from her mind...

Seeing the panic in her eyes, Jan reminded her, "The bad man is long gone now. It will never happen again." His words wrapped around her like loving arms.

"You're safe now. You're here with me. It's just a memory. You were a very brave girl."

She followed his soothing voice back to the present, to the room with the couch and the kind man she was beginning to trust. Slowly her breathing returned to normal and she began to relax. She was six years old again, though she lived in the body of a 43-year-old woman. She admitted she wanted him to adopt her and take her home to his house. He helped her to see that it wasn't possible for him to make up for the past—that he could help her but he couldn't be her Daddy. He told her only God could be her Daddy now.

She wrestled with her feelings of fear and anger as he reminded her that God would always be with her, too. She need never be alone again.

Listening to a voice within, dropping her eyes, she nodded her head and was gone. In her place, I appeared. Touching my face with my fingertips to ground myself to my surroundings, I sat in silent reflection, allowing the feelings and the memories to rise within me. The overwhelming desire for a loving father, and the grief in knowing that desire must go unfulfilled in the human realm, flooded over my body, soul and spirit. Racking sobs rose in my throat and I let them come without resistance. I faced the feelings and I owned them. The deep well of rejection and abandonment, of love-hunger and endless longing, belonged to me.

There was no running away from it now, no blessed relief of dissociation. The little girl had carried the pain without me for many years, and in recent months, I had been able to feel deep empathy for her, but today it became my burden, my reality. I felt it as deeply as I would have felt it 40 years ago if I hadn't run away in my mind.

Today I stayed. Today I, too, was a brave girl. Today I took one more significant step toward healing and wholeness. Today I began to mourn. As I attend to every painful thought, feeling and sensation, as I look intently into each one, I mourn. I mourn the loss of innocence. I mourn the carefree childhood I never had. I mourn the fantasy mother and father. I mourn the wasted years, the chaos and confusion of my life. I enter the swirling vortex of darkness and pain, embrace the truth I find there, and I mourn.

To my surprise I discover at the farthest corner of the black tomb, beyond the Pit of Loneliness, the Cave of Anger and the River of Shame, is a fountain. Buried behind the layers of previously unacknowledged, unmourned pain is a fountain of life and hope and joy and laughter that also belongs to me—a hidden treasure. Somehow learning how to feel the sadness, to mourn the tragedy in my life, is setting me free to feel the hope and experience the laughter in my life. I can rejoice in the midst of such suffering because I have discovered that joy comes in the mourning. □

Throughout this book you will find that I will follow my healing journey in a chronological format using excerpts from my journals as well as narrative to show the tapestry of my recovery as it was woven over a period of years. I chose, however, to begin with the above passage, which was written when I was quite far along on the path, for two reasons. First, for survivors of abuse who are reading this book, I want you to know there is hope for healing. I want to give you a glimpse of the future "happy ending" to give you sustenance along the way. It will take courage to enter the pain with me, to enter into the darkness of the tomb. This is my way of offering you a glimpse of light in the distance.

Second, I believe the passage fairly accurately illustrates how healing and integration take place within the context of Dissociative Identity Disorder (DID, formerly MPD), a much misunderstood and somewhat mythologized disorder which I feel bears some clarification here before I can proceed with my story.

We can thank the media for many distortions in the public's understanding of DID. You may have seen the movies "The Three Faces of Eve" and "Sybil" and more recently, the made-for-TV movie depicting the story of Truddi Chase, a "multiple" who has chosen to remain highly divided and fragmented, and who can frequently be seen on shows like Oprah. These depictions frustrate me because they are so dramatic and extreme. You may be left with the feeling you'd know a "multiple" instantly if you met one but you hope you never will!

Most of the time, those who struggle with DID do so in much more subtle ways, and many hold highly responsible positions within society and the working world. Your next-door neighbor or your friend could be a multiple without your awareness. I was and no one ever suspected. I appeared to be a woman of solid spiritual maturity and stability, dedicated to serving the Lord, with an effective ministry that involved leading many people to Christ and planting a large and successful church. On one level that was indeed who I was, but there were other unseen levels. No one saw the frightened, lonely little girls inside of me, or the Rebel, or the Wicked Woman—least of all me.

Many who are in treatment for Dissociative Identity Disorder consider the name to be a misnomer. DID is a brilliant defense (as opposed to a disorder) when employed by a child to survive the horrors of abuse. It is a highly functional response to extremely dysfunctional circumstances and events that cannot be contained within the mind of a child who has no way to make sense or meaning out of the experiences forced upon her.

When Daddy tucks his little girl in bed with a story or a song and a kiss on the forehead and then later returns to rape her, being able to pretend the abuse is happening to someone else or is being done by some other little girl's Daddy makes perfect sense for survival. DID becomes dysfunctional only in its effects on the life of the surviving adult who must reclaim the truth of her history in order to reintegrate her split-off emotions, memories and disowned parts to become whole.

So what exactly is DID and how is it created? Dissociation, as it relates to childhood abuse of any kind, is a form of "traumatic forgetting" along with denial and repression. In a way, each of these three psychological mechanisms is a way of pretending that what happened to you never happened to you.

In dissociation, the mind literally cuts off its awareness of some or all aspects of an event at the moment the event is occurring! Then aspects of the overall memory may be stored separately and become very difficult to retrieve or to understand. In DID, which is the most extreme form of dissociation, one or more alter personalities are formed in the mind at the moment of trauma to "take the abuse" or handle the difficult situation. The "other" child is protected from remembering the unbearable truth that the very people she is dependent upon for her life are hurting her.

What about demon possession? Living and working as a missionary on the frontline in Europe where Satan has a powerful stronghold, I have seen him at work and I believe in his power to deceive and to oppress. I also believe that the consummate act of evil on this planet is the abuse of an innocent child. There is no question that Satan and his henchmen are involved in every such act.

But can we dismiss DID and deny its reality by saying it is "demonic"? No, we can't. There is far too much evidence to the contrary and to deny it is to re-victimize those who have been hurt, rejected and abandoned enough already. My prayer is to see the Church become a healing refuge, a place of safety, where survivors with DID will be embraced with love and understanding, not shunned and condemned for their lack of faith when exorcisms and prayers for deliverance don't resolve their dividedness. How then do we understand DID from a spiritual perspective?

Christians view man as an image-bearer of God who Himself is Spirit, Mind, Will and Emotions. Therefore, we have a spirit, a mind, a will and emotions neatly contained within a human body. Sanctification or spiritual growth is the gradual process of aligning our emotions, will, mind and body with the Spirit of Christ that enters our spirit when we believe.

For the person who has suffered severe childhood physical or sexual abuse resulting in DID, the challenge of conforming wholeheartedly to the Spirit of God can seem overwhelming. Frequently only one or two parts of the person have made commitments to follow Christ, while other parts are either ignorant of, apathetic to or antagonistic toward the gospel. The Bible tells us to be single-minded in our obedience, difficult to do in the best of circumstances. For the multiple who is not yet integrated, it is virtually impossible. The consciously Christian part(s) can only be single-minded about eventually being single-minded!

What do I mean by "consciously Christian?" I believe that DID occurs on the level of the soul—where mind, will and emotions reside—not on the level of the spirit. When a person receives Jesus, that transaction takes place on the level of the spirit and the whole spirit is filled up with Christ. The multiple has one spirit, one body, but a divided soul.

The spirit contains the underlying unity of personality, the original blueprint that God had intended, beneath all the divisions of the soul. The spiritual core of the dissociative Christian belongs to Christ. But the soul has been divided into any number of different centers of awareness—each with its own mind, will and emotions. On the soul level, only some of these centers of awareness (or alter personalities) are conscious of this change on a spiritual level—thus, they are "consciously Christian." This is how I began to experience my spirituality after I became aware of my system of alters.

Working together with my Christian therapist and using principles of friendship evangelism, over time I built bridges to those parts who had not been exposed to the gospel or who were in active rebellion against God. Unsanctified alters were treated with love and respect and accepted wherever they were on their spiritual journey. For nearly two years, my internal world was my mission field.

People with DID who are treated with love, acceptance and understanding are empowered to pass on that love to their "people inside" and revolutionary transformation and healing are made possible because of their testimony of love. As each alter recognizes and surrenders to the call of Christ and makes Jesus Lord over his or her mind, will and emotions, integration becomes a natural step as Christian unity brings closer and closer internal harmony.

God understands multiplicity. The ability to dissociate, as a defense against horrible events that could otherwise destroy an innocent child, is truly a gift from God. When He allows the dissociation to occur, He never intends for it to remain that way. He knows the original design, the person He created you to be, His own precious child. He can make the divided person whole again as every part learns to trust and depend on Him, putting spirit, soul and body in alignment with a God called Father.

For a victim of incest it isn't easy to trust a God called Father. Even if it wasn't your father who abused you, it was someone bigger and more powerful than you were, probably someone who had a lot more authority than you did. Broken trust is one of the hardest things to restore, but the resurrection power of Jesus Christ can bring new life to trust that has died. He did it in my life. He can do it in yours. Come walk with me now on my journey to healing and resurrection.

Chapter 1 — Against the Wall

A Crack in the Wall

☐ My First Journal Entry — It has been at least three years since I have practiced the presence of God in my life through a daily time of prayer and meditation. This is the first day of a sabbatical from major ministry responsibilities. I have worked 50-60 hours per week for 3 years planting a new church in Amsterdam. I am depleted emotionally and spiritually. I finally ran out of steam. Why do I do that? That crazy running? Am I trying to prove I am worthy of God's love? I've hit rock bottom spiritually and now I have to try to begin again. Here I am, Lord, broken and on my knees. God help me. ☐

Ten years before those words were written, I had committed my life to Jesus Christ and had thrown myself into His service with all my natural enthusiasm. Within six months I was working full-time in a church and within six years, my husband Paul and I were getting ready to pack up our children and everything we owned to move to Holland as missionary church planters. Never one to do things halfheartedly, I threw myself into the work of the mission, losing all control of appropriate balance and boundaries, and one day I woke up and realized I couldn't go on. Things were out of control and it was time to stop and assess the damage. Life suddenly had no meaning and I could no longer see any future. I was feeling suicidal. I asked for a six-month sabbatical from my role and the mission agency made counseling part of the deal. The journey began.

I was both afraid and excited about the empty days that stretched ahead of me and the opportunity to try to understand the confusion and the drivenness of my life. I was in enough pain to realize I had no choice but to surrender to whatever the Lord was going to show me.

Thank You, Lord, for this great expanse of uncluttered days you have laid before me so I can have time to seek You and know You more. Lord, guide my days one-by-one that I might use them as You would have me use them. Grow me up into maturity and at the same time hold me like a little child in Your arms and be my Father God. My best friend Carolyn said maybe it's time I looked at "Judy, the child.' I think she may be right. I'm willing but scared. Amen.

In talking with my Dutch counselor Jan, I realized memories of my childhood were few. I had almost no memories of my father prior to when I was twelve, which I always attributed to the travelling he did during those early years. I didn't have any memories of my life prior to the age of five-and-a-half when we moved to North Street. We lived there until I was ten and I had elaborate memories of my friends on the street including their first and last names, which house they lived in and the kinds of games we played together. On the other hand, I had no memories at all past the threshold of the door to my own house on North Street. I couldn't remember what the house was like on the inside or where I slept. I had no memories of life inside the house with my parents and brothers and sisters.

Most of the people on our street were poor Irish or Italian working class families, good Catholics, so I remember playing First Holy Communion with my friends and learning how to say the "Hail Mary". We weren't Catholics and didn't attend church but we fit in okay, because by the time we left that street and town, there were six kids in our family—making us honorary Catholics in the eyes of our neighbors.

The oldest was my brother Charles, about 19 months older than I. I was the oldest girl. My sister Jean was born when I was 15 months old and during those North Street years we were almost inseparable friends. Five years after Jean was born, the "little kids" began to arrive. Five more babies were born in quick succession, for a total of four girls and four boys born over a period of thirteen years.

My father worked and traveled a lot. My mother was left on her own with the children to face the challenges of long, cold Vermont winters. She didn't even know how to drive a car. I saw my father as a dragon-slaying hero off in the distance and my mother as a beautiful queen who was much too busy with her brand new babies to notice me. School was a terrifying place where I didn't fit in. My security lay only in the context of my friends on the street. That's where my happy childhood memories were to be found.

When I was ten, that bit of security was lost as we moved to a bigger house in a new town on Riverside Drive. I don't remember anything about the move but I know I entered into a deep loneliness in my life at that time. Later in my process of recovery, I realized that I had no memories of being in school from the time I was 10 until I was 14, fifth through eighth grade.

We lived on Riverside Drive until I was 16 years old. Again the memories inside the house were few and vague, the memories of school almost nonexistent and mostly what I recalled were times when I was by myself down by the river that flowed behind our house—that was my safe place.

One thing I never forgot was the "play yard" my father created with a chain-link fence in the backyard. We lived on two and a half acres of land going down to a small wood and a river, so Dad created a contained place for the little kids to play. But the kids hated it in there and spent all their time clinging to the fence, looking out and crying. Then Mom and Dad found a new use for the play yard. Every day that the weather allowed, they took their drinks and spent the "cocktail hour" in the play yard locking the kids out. My younger brothers and sisters spent their time clinging to the fence, looking in and crying.

I never realized that my parents were alcoholics.

☐ October 19, 1993 — *Father God, could it be that You really do love me? I mean the real me—not the "charming" me I show to the world, but the angry, frightened, hateful, lost me that lives so far under the surface? Could it really be that I could let You see all of me—even the parts that I don't see—and You'd still love me? Okay, God, I'll try. Because I love You, Lord. God, please help me open every door and expose every nook and cranny to Your light, Your grace and Your cleansing power. Even when it's painful, when the wounds are so deep that healing seems impossible, help me to believe in You, to trust You, to obey You. Let me hear Your voice in the darkness, Lord. Amen.*

These words of surrender, these small insights into my childhood, were rising from a hidden place in my heart where the truth of my history was known. Somehow I had begun to recognize and to allow myself to experience the tip of the iceberg of shame that was my heritage. I was given a glimpse of my bondage to the past and a taste of hope for a future freedom. I had no idea then just how deep the shame would go, how black the tomb of loneliness and fear I would enter was going to be. I was hungry. I only knew I wanted to trade the pain of my past for a promise of peace in the future and I began to open myself to God. The defensive barriers I had so long ago established to protect me from the pain began to grow weaker. A crack was beginning to spread in the wall.

The Glittering Image

Still unaware of my history of incest or of my dissociated alters, I began to express myself through writing songs and poems. The songs, the poems, the artwork, all the creative gifts God began to release in me, became tools He used in my healing process. One of the first was a song I wrote called "Glittering Images":

> Glittering images sparkle and shine.
> Little girl's dressed up, looking so fine.
> Playing the grown-up, playing the game,
> Hiding her fear, covering her shame.
> Momma didn't love her, Daddy didn't care.
> When he was around, she had to beware.
> Being a good girl wasn't enough,
> But keeping her glittering image was tough.
>
> She puts on her makeup, she puts on her mask.
> She puts on a show, performing her task.
> Out on the street how she's strutting her stuff.

She's looking for someone who's looking for love.
She's walking the tightrope, she's toeing the line.
In her glittering image how she will shine.
But deep in her heart she sees with such dread
The image is living but inside she is dead.

Who will enter her world of confusion
And shatter at last her tragic illusion?
Wiping away the pain of rejection,
Offering hope and resurrection.
Look past the glitter and see the gold
Refined in the fire of pain untold.
Jesus loves her, this I know,
But who on earth will tell her so?

I know that little ones to Him belong.
They are weak but He is strong.
Yes, Jesus loves her.
Yes, Jesus loves her.
Yes, Jesus loves her.
But who on earth will tell her so?

As I wrote the last line of the lyrics above I doubled over in pain and something within me told me that there was a key in these words that would unlock secrets as yet unknown about myself.

As I began to face and feel the loneliness of my childhood and to acknowledge the needs that had been left unmet, as I began to cry the unshed tears, not only did my own glittering image come crashing down but my glittering images of Mom and Dad began to look less sparkling, too. I started to realize how their weakness, their neglect and their alcoholism had affected me. I saw that carrying the burden of their images as the "hero" and the "saint" was weighing me down. I began the long painful process of letting go of the fantasy me and of the fantasy mother and father I had created—glittering images all.

☐ November 2, 1993 — I had a dream. I was in a large home with my family (though I didn't recognize them as actual family members, just as "family"). "Nazis" came into the house and began rounding everyone up and taking them outside to a big truck. I knew the Nazis were "bad" even though they were smiling. They had a coffin-like box with them and I saw a six-foot hole in the ground outside that matched the shape of the box. There was a little baby in the house and it was up to me to protect and save the baby. I dressed her in extra layers of clothing and took her outside to put her in the vehicle while the Nazis

4

were still in the house. I told the "father" to get in the driver's seat and drive away as quickly as possible because the Nazis would kill them all if they stayed. The "father" took the family and drove away but the Nazis went after them. Later the Nazis told me they had captured the family and killed them all, including the baby I had tried so hard to protect and save. Then they said I would be the next to die. I woke up.

I have been growing emotionally lately, discovering and learning to love the "little girl" in me. I've even given her a name! I'm calling my so-called "inner child" Judy Marie. As I think about this dream, I realize that all my life I've been trying to protect that broken little girl, the "baby" in my dream, and in the process, causing the near annihilation of my own family through my defensive postures and unwillingness to risk emotional intimacy. It has been the very attempts at protection that have been so destructive. I need to lay down my defenses and open my heart—learning to trust. □

The Lord revealed to me that as I shed my own self-constructed armor, He would give me a new set of armor. While my own armor was poor protection, yet at the same time almost impenetrable by love, His armor offered absolute protection but was completely permeable by love. While my defenses were falling, at the same time, I was actually becoming safer!

As the glittering images of my parents began to destabilize, I was beginning to get in touch with feelings of anger. Anger was never acceptable in my family and was firmly held in check. When it was released, it came in a torrent, flooding over me and drowning me in its fury. On those rare occasions when Mom's anger came boiling to the surface she threw things at me, she screamed violently, she erupted like a volcano. This kind of anger, rarely exposed, was very scary. Yet anger was often simmering under the surface in our home. I thought it was my fault.

My own anger had been buried for 40 years. In the dream, the Nazis had a coffin and planned to bury something in the yard. Each time the feelings of rage came close to the surface, my body tensed from head to toe and I wanted to run away and hide. Part of me wanted to release the anger but part of me was terrified. The Nazis were saying "It's wrong to feel anger and anger is dangerous... We could kill you if you show any anger!"

□ November 11, 1993 — I'm angry. I was just an innocent child and I deserved to be properly cared for and loved. I was a victim! A victim of extreme neglect! I tried so hard to get the message across that I needed—I needed! It should have been obvious to any parent who cared that something was very wrong. I sucked my thumb 'til I was ten! I wet my bed 'til I was eleven! I gave out signals of distress—SOS. But no one stopped to look and listen. No one seemed to even notice. I was knocking but nobody was home.

It was not right that I had to survive and cope so independently when I wasn't really ready for it. Mom and Dad both failed to protect me when I was very vulnerable. It's no wonder I was angry at them and that I eventually rebelled. I shouldn't feel guilty or ashamed for my feelings toward them. They were the only people in the world I could count on and they let me down. Their absence made me feel invisible and worthless and their obvious disappointment in me made me feel incompetent as well. It made sense that I was angry at them. When I was a child these feelings brought fear and guilt so I buried them away from my consciousness.

You screwed up, Mom and Dad. I grew up feeling worthless, lonely, isolated, incompetent, ugly and stupid. Why? Well, if my parents didn't notice me, why would anyone else? The straight A's didn't matter. Being a good girl didn't matter. Eventually in my teens I found out I could get attention from other people—especially boys, if I played my cards right. You didn't like that much either, did you? But I gave up on trying to please you because nothing I did was working. □

That's as far as I got. As I tried to understand what the anger was about, I was able to legitimize it with a long list of painful losses in my childhood. But none of them, individually or combined, seemed to really explain the degree of fury I sensed would be unleashed if I dared to really crack open that Pandora's Box. My fear was too great. I buried the anger again, reviving a segment of my glittering image to cover it up.

At the same time that I tuned out my anger I tuned into a growing sense of hope that brought me comfort. The little girl whose pain and loneliness was so long denied also held a key to laughter and joy and spontaneity. Since I had set her free from her prison of silence and allowed her to express herself, I had discovered her child's joie de vivre, confidence and courage, and especially her laughter. I felt the life force beginning to pulse within me again.

The Bad Seed

□ November 22, 1993 — Today has been a tough day. I tried to pray this morning and I just couldn't focus. My mind kept on wandering off and my prayers just seemed to hit the ceiling and fall back down on top of me. I've been struggling to look at my feelings about Mom but my struggles with Paul keep pushing their way into my thoughts instead. I'm angry at myself because I tell Paul I want to be held and nurtured and loved and given lots of affection, but when he comes up to me to hug me, I pull away. I say I want intimacy, I want us to be closer and to know each other more completely, but when he starts to draw near I run in the opposite direction. What is wrong with me? I'm really frustrated!

During counseling today, Jan said that maybe, because I grew up with parents that seemed to be so great, except to me; who gave me a taste of what I wanted, but never a full and satisfying portion, that I came to believe there was something really wrong with me. Therefore, now I am afraid if I let anyone get too close, they'll discover my fatal flaw. They'll see what I'm really like, who I really am, the unacceptable one that doesn't deserve their love and attention. When he spoke those words, at the core of me I knew they were true. I feel like I am a bad seed. I feel there is something dark and disgusting deep in my heart. I'm afraid to look and I don't dare let anyone else see it!

I want so much to be loved, but deep in my heart I know I don't deserve to be loved. And if Paul or anyone else sees me as I am, I'll be abandoned. ☐

This was a painful revelation, almost too much truth to bear. Emotional chaos descended on me and I found myself unable to even write in my journal. One aspect of my response to this insight was anger at my therapist Jan for helping me to see it.

☐ December 3, 1993 — Just came back from a week in Scandinavia. No time to write for the past almost two weeks! There has been a lot going on in my mind. I feel as though I have two totally separate lives going on simultaneously. On the surface, I am competently doing my work for the mission, training and equipping the Oslo church-planting team, sharing with a Norwegian pastor some principles of programming for a high-impact church, visiting with our Swedish friends. Even as I am relating to Paul it is part of the superficial persona of normalcy. Inside all is in great turmoil. The discovery of the "bad seed" has created a sense of chaos in my soul.

I have a vivid and shocking fantasy life going on just under the surface and I think it's me trying to prove just how bad I really am. Judy Marie, that precious child within me, has gone into hiding and another side of myself is emerging— the Wicked Woman. I have been obsessing about exactly how I'd like to introduce Jan to this very wicked woman by verbally seducing him. I was supposed to have an appointment with him today but my car refused to start. Could this be God's protection, preventing me from following through on this self-destructive bent I'm on right now?

At this point, all I know is I feel all agitated and ready to do almost anything. What is going on? I don't know. Am I angry at Jan for showing me something about myself that I don't want to see? Do I want to gain control? Do I want to test him to see if he can accept even this wicked part of me? Do I really want to break down his professional reserve and get some kind of reaction from him that's more personal? I don't know what I want! I just know I'm in the mood to create some excitement and take major risks with my emotional welfare. ☐

These aspects of myself, Judy Marie and the Wicked Woman, were very much making themselves heard and influencing my life in dramatic ways. Judy Marie had shown herself in therapy, appearing as regressive emotional states and expressions of pain and loneliness. Now the Wicked Woman was making her presence known. The "Nazis" within me, those harsh defenders against the truth, were losing their power to contain the dissociated realities of my life.

At my next appointment I confessed to Jan that I was obsessed with fantasies about him. I felt the Wicked Woman in me trying to push herself forward with a desire to act in a seductive way, but I managed to maintain control and behave appropriately. Jan suggested that I stop the fantasies. He viewed them as just a diversion from the real work which needed to be done. I accepted his assessment and advice and pushed the Wicked Woman and her fantasies out of my consciousness, shutting the door firmly behind her. That done, I felt much more calm and rolled up my sleeves to get ready to do some hard work.

I figured it all went back to my father. I tried for years to be the good little girl, pliable and sweet, to gain his love and affection. When that didn't work, I tried being the sensual seductress. Of course, I couldn't direct that at Daddy because that was taboo, so I directed it at other boys, and later, men. I gained something from that tactic—lots of male attention—but no love.

Now I was reenacting the same scenario with Jan. I was projecting my childhood longing to be someone special onto him. Being the "little girl" didn't get him to see me as different from the rest of his clients and somehow special, so I thought I'd try being the "seductress". I couldn't accept that I was never going to get what I didn't get as a child. I was still hungering for Daddy's love, attention and approval and I was beginning to hope that Jan could somehow give me what my father never did.

This kind of thinking is known in psychology as transference. It happens quite often in long-term therapeutic relationships and is a natural part of the process of working through issues. The client begins to deal with unresolved past conflicts with parents or others within the context of the counselor/client relationship. Transference began to play a larger role in my search for the truth.

☐ December 9, 1993 — I told Paul about my fear that there is something really wrong with me deep in my inner core. I admitted I was afraid he would see it and be repulsed and realize I am not worthy of his love. He just looked at me and held me and said, "I'm in for the long haul, Judy." And I knew it was true.

Bad seed or not, my husband loved me and the Lord loved me and, for a little while at least, I felt safe. Maybe I wouldn't be abandoned after all! I began to realize that only God could fill my deepest longing. Only He could make me whole.

Lord God, please help me to cast all my cares and struggles and pain at the foot of the Cross where Your Son died for me. Help me to open my heart to Your light and receive Your healing in all my broken places. Thank You for the miracle of healing You have already done. I pray that I will be fully willing to let You complete the work You have begun in me. Search my heart, oh God, and cleanse me of all unrighteousness. Lord, I need Your love and Your grace and Your mercy. Amen. □

The Face of My Father

□ December 12, 1993 — My father was a great and wonderful, though distant, hero to me when I was a little girl. In my eyes, he was handsome and charming, brilliant and humorous, and most of all, he was a great storyteller. I retain a few precious memories of the stories he used to tell of the donut man whose nose was long and strung with donuts; stories of Raggedy Ann and Raggedy Andy; ghost stories that both delighted and frightened me. What a treat were those rare times when Dad was in a story-telling mood. It was thoroughly magical. And when he sang us a song or two before bedtime, I was transported by his beautiful voice into a child's paradise. These, his shining moments, were few and far between. □

It was easy enough to write about the few fond memories. It was tough to write about my disappointments and my father's negative character traits, but I had given myself an assignment to come face to face with him and I was determined to follow through in spite of my strong resistance.

□ December 16, 1993 — Dad was definitely the one in charge in our family—the Boss. He was dominant, and whenever he was home, he was not only in control but the center of attention. My mother was submissive and dependent toward him and treated him like a god—at least that's how she promoted him to us kids. She almost never stood up to him and wouldn't allow anyone to say anything negative about him. Dad was perfect; he was always right and it was clear that he felt superior to just about everyone in the world. He was arrogant and proud and he judged anyone who disagreed with him, mercilessly.

He had tremendous charisma, a great sense of humor and comic delivery and an excellent command of language. When he was in the room, he was in control of every conversation and people looked to him to take the lead, which he did with apparent relish. He was sarcastic and teased his children at times with almost abusive insensitivity, deeply embarrassing especially the most vulnerable and sensitive ones. The whole family revolved around him and he expected and demanded that.

I mostly remember wanting desperately to please and impress him and never knowing how. I tried so many times to say or do just the right thing to win his love and attention. These are the things I remember, the tiny little insignificant things I said, spoken not out of my own truth but out of a desire to get a positive response from him. Invariably, I said the wrong thing and I would feel ashamed. It happened every time... I wanted and needed his validation and love so desperately I was willing to deny my own reality to try to get them, but even that didn't work.

He was generous with criticism, stingy with praise, busy doing his own thing, often absent, and unclear and inconsistent in his discipline of his children. Discipline was directly related to the amount of inconvenience the behavior caused to him personally and to the mood he was in at the moment. I could never really figure out what the rules of the game were. And Dad was a "shoot first and ask questions later" kind of guy.

I don't remember ever feeling I could go to him, or to my mother either for that matter, to talk about a problem or concern I had in my life. In fact there was no one with whom I could share my daily struggles and fears. I always felt I had to face everything on my own. Dad could be charming, but not warm and sensitive; intelligent, but blind to his own children's needs; humorous and appealing, but dangerous and unpredictable. Like my earliest childhood memory, the only one from my toddler days, I reached for a beautiful flower and ended up getting stung by a bee nearly every time I approached him.

December 20, 1993 — I feel loss and deep sadness beyond words. I feel anger and fear. I feel small and powerless and empty. I cry out to God and I get no answers. It's as though I am trying to amputate a part of myself without any anesthesia, as though a gaping hole is being torn open in me and I am left to bleed.

The man who was once a god in my eyes I long ago reshaped and redefined as a "basically harmless eccentric" after I overcame my anger at his affair and his divorce from my mother. I couldn't live with the fallen idol and the hatred I felt toward him, so I refashioned my image of him into something more acceptable. Why is it so hard to let go of that image and grasp a hold of the reality now? What am I afraid of?

December 21, 1993 — I woke up crying this morning. It's pain without words. I try to run from the pain but it chases me. I find momentary escape in activities and people, but always it waits for me in the quiet corners and in the darkness of night. I have no answers. I only have Jesus and the knowledge that He is right here beside me. I cling to Him. □

Gifts from the Sea

☐ December 29, 1993 — God has been doing His healing work in me and I have claimed some new ground in His name. On Christmas Day Paul, Britt and I loaded the car and drove to a tiny beachside community called Bergen-aan-Zee about 40 minutes away from home where we have been staying in a small cottage called "The Free Birds". We have spent the past four days resting and reading, beach combing and playing games. Last night we spent hours telling stories and doing impressions of famous people and of our friends. It was really fun to have this relaxed time together (with no TV or phone calls!). What a tremendous blessing it has been. In the quiet of the morning, the Lord has been molding me and making me new—renewing my heart and mind, showing me clearer vision of myself, my father, my husband and my Lord, Jesus Christ.

This morning, I woke early and went for a walk alone on the beach. I felt my body and my soul come alive. I heard God's voice in the wind and saw His mighty power in the sea. I felt His love and knew I was forever connected to Him—His child and His beloved. I knew His mercy and I began to understand that His love is greater than my weakness or sinfulness. He loves me as I am— not just as I *think* I am—but as I *really* am. He loves the parts of me I hide from others. He even loves the parts of me I hide from myself.

January 1, 1994 — My retreat has begun—a week of solitude. Paul dropped me off here at the cottage in mid-afternoon and as soon as he drove away I was filled with fear and my hands began to shake. I was facing six whole days with no one but me and God and the sea. After spending about half an hour worshipping the Lord with songs of praise, I got up my courage and went down to the beach for a walk. What a glorious time! The air was brisk and the sun was low on the horizon. The sky was a shimmering silver-blue above the grey waters. God's awesome creative power was wonderfully displayed and I was filled with an awareness of His majesty and might. My fears and problems suddenly seemed so small and insignificant. To think that with a word, He created the heavens and the earth, with a mere wave of His hand, He brought forth the rolling seas and the thundering clouds. Could my struggles possibly be too much for a God such as this? I have come home from my walk humbled and full of both confidence and gratitude: confidence that God and I together can handle my struggles for healing and wholeness, and gratitude that the great Creator God of the universe actually cares about my struggles!

January 2, 1994 — I hate myself. I hate every aspect of myself that was hated or rejected by my parents. I hate that I need love and attention. I hate that I am angry. I hate that I am fearful; I hate that I am sexual. I hate that I am vulnerable. I hate that I am boisterous and enthusiastic and full of life force and energy!

My parents could only accept part of me part of the time, so I hated and rejected the parts of me that they rejected and then I constructed the internal bad parents to "protect" me from the annihilation that would surely come if I ever owned or even acknowledged those parts of me. Being only half-alive was better than being dead. I want to live! I want to be whole! I want to be the person God created me to be! I want to surrender my fear of being myself and sacrifice the "glittering image" I created to replace my authentic self.

God, give me courage, I pray, to face myself in the mirror without the mask. Jesus, nothing is hidden from You. You have always known about all these hidden aspects of myself that I have hated and denied and yet, You have loved me. Search my heart, oh God, and show me the truth of all that I am, and the truth shall set me free. Amen. □

That afternoon the sharp lines of demarcation that separated the "good daddy" from the "bad daddy" in my mind began to blur. I had loved the one and hated the other, worshipped the one and denied and internalized the other. Now I began to see that my earthly father had failed me in many painful ways but he had given me some things of value as well—songs he sang and stories he told. The good and the bad began to integrate and I could see Dad as human and imperfect and begin to love and accept him. Seeing him as he really was seemed to be connected in some way to seeing myself as I was. A poem of love and acceptance toward my father sprang from my heart and I sent it to him on E-mail. Even though I had yet to understand the depth of the damage my father had done to me, the Lord was allowing healing and forgiveness to flow.

Later, when I realized there was so much more damage to be assessed and accounted for, this early work of recognition and acceptance formed a firm foundation on which to build.

Lord, You've given me so many insights in recent weeks. At times I have wanted to turn back and run away from this path we have been travelling together. Just at that moment, You'd reach out and say "Hold on... We're almost there!" So I'd hold on, my eyes fixed hopefully on the horizon, my hand holding tightly to Yours. Lord, the more You show me about myself the more I'm beginning to understand about You — the depth and breadth of Your forever love. So I'll keep walking if You'll keep walking with me. Amen.

□ January 4, 1994 — I woke up early this morning and reveled in the luxury of lying in bed at leisure. I hunkered down under my comforter, pulled my pillow under my chin and just experienced the pure, unadulterated joy of being held in God's loving arms. I just leaned into His love with everything that was in me. The reality of His love was overwhelming to me and brought me once again to that place of mingled joy and sorrow because of my unworthiness. Yet as the tears flowed and I poured out the anguish and shame in my soul, I was aware as never before of His tender ministrations. I felt His hand brushing back my hair from my face and I heard His voice gently saying, "There, there, Judy. It's all right." My love for Him welled up within me and I knew afresh that He loves me and nothing else matters.

Lord, in light of what you have shown me about myself, I stand ready and willing to face the giants. As they say 'We have seen the enemy and they are us!' I rejoice in the knowledge that You love me just the way I am, with all my defects of character, but I also rejoice that You won't leave me this way. I want You to remove these sins and defects which You are revealing to me. Especially, Lord, I pray You will remove the resentment which has burned under the surface for so many years. Help me, Lord, to face my anger honestly each day and surrender it to You rather than denying it or projecting it onto Paul or others. Help me to be angry and not sin. Show me how to express my anger in appropriate ways.

Lord, change my heart. I think I really understand now, at last, that I can never earn Your love yet I can never lose Your love. It's because You love me as I am that I want to be all You created me to be. Amen.

January 5, 1994 — I've just returned from the most glorious time on the beach. I sang! I danced! I skipped! I even twirled 'round and 'round until I got dizzy and I nearly fell down. God is so good. At first I was struggling. I knew there was a song in my heart that wanted to be born but I just couldn't pull it out. Then I heard the Lord whisper, "Just let go, Judy, and love me. I'll take care of the rest."

After a while the clouds started looking really dark and I thought I'd better head for home. As I was working my way back in the direction of home an amazing thing happened. Suddenly the sun broke through the clouds and shown brilliantly over the waters, its rays cascading like a great waterfall into the sea. At that moment, I turned around to look back.

The wind was at my back, the sun was shining, casting a long shadow of me in the sand, its warmth in my hair, and directly above me, black clouds were racing away from me at breakneck speed. I turned back toward the sun again and was stunned by its brilliance. The whole experience couldn't have lasted more than ten seconds but I felt He made me a promise: His Son would always break through for me and He would be the wind at my back, chasing the black clouds away and giving me that little extra push along the way. □

The retreat finally came to an end and it was time to go home. I went home but I didn't go back. The Lord had lifted me to higher ground that week and my view had changed somehow on a fundamental level. Now I would begin the hard work: learning to apply in my daily life the insights I had gained about myself, about my earthly father and about my Father in heaven; learning to live each day in the Light of God's love; learning to really trust Him with all of my needs;

learning to hear His voice above the clattering noise of old patterns of response. These few days alone with God at the beginning of a new year were the seeds of a new relationship. I was no longer relating only to Jesus, my Friend and Savior, I was finally beginning to open my heart to a God called Father.

Matthew 7 verse 11 says *"If you, then, though you are evil, know how to give good gifts to your children, how much more will your Father in heaven give good gifts to those who ask Him!"* Thank You, Father, for Your good gifts! Amen.

More Cracks in the Wall

☐ January 25, 1994 — I have spent two nights without sleep. I'm exhausted. I'm concerned about my father who is lying in a hospital bed with a heart condition and highly elevated blood sugar. I'm confronted with his mortality. I have the urge to reach out to him, to care for him.

Mom, too, is heavy on my heart. The terrible Southern California earthquake and aftershocks have left her traumatized and even afraid to sleep in her own bed.

People here need me, too. My good friend Anne has just recovered memories of sexual abuse that took place years ago when she was only a child. She seems to be handling it okay but I don't know. Sometimes it seems I'm having a harder time with it than she is! Paul is struggling trying to understand and adjust to all the changes in me. And I'm not doing so terribly well either.

I have become much more aware of my own feelings of anger, yet I have not really figured out how to express anger in safe ways without sinning. In the past, I would repress, deny and project my anger. Now I see and feel it, but I don't know what to do with it. I think this is progress, but it is creating a lot of tension, which isn't helping me sleep at night either.

So many things are happening right now, Jesus. In my own power, I can't sort them out and I certainly can't control them. So Lord, I give them to You. They are Yours. My Dad's health, my Mom's fears, my anger, Anne's memories, Paul's frustration, and the kids, Lord, David's insecurities and Britt's struggles in school—I give them all to You. I am powerless over them, but You are not and they are within Your rule and reign, King Jesus. Amen.

January 27, 1994 — One thing I have realized. We are always and at every moment either conforming or transforming: conforming to this world or being transformed by the renewing of our minds through Christ Jesus. There is no standing still. We move from conformity to transformation moment by moment with each choice we make.

Lord God, I pray You will keep me on the path of transformation. Make me more like You—conformed not to this world but rather conformed to the image of Your Son, gentle and humble of heart. As I reach in to that innermost part of my soul, as I reach out to the world of hurting people around me, as I reach up to You in prayer—may You transform me with Your everlasting love. Amen. ☐

Anger continued to be a stumbling block in my life. I was beginning to make uncomfortable connections and comparisons of my relationship with Paul to my relationship with my parents when I was a child.

As I gained access to my true feelings and began to express them more with Paul, he would often respond to them with advice and lecturing. That made me mad! Yet I dared not tell him about my anger.

While Paul did indeed have some anger, aggression and control issues to work on in his life, later I would come to understand that much of my response to Paul was based on the projection of my parental conflicts onto him. He had just enough of the negative characteristics and behaviors required to fit the role of the "bad parent" that projections of my parents' coldness, harshness and insensitivity to my feelings stuck to him like glue. My growing self-awareness began to put a lot of pressure on our relationship.

☐ February 7, 1994 — It's seven o'clock. My appointment with Jan was at three and I am still totally wiped out. I hardly talked at all. I started off by admitting I haven't slept well, especially last night in anticipation of today's appointment. Then I started to talk about how frustrated I am that, after the mountaintop experience of my retreat, I'm back in the pits again. I wanted all the pain and struggle to be over. I wanted to be cured, healed, at peace with the world!

Suddenly I feel so small again, small and scared and angry but unable to express myself. It's like all the rules of the game have been changed but I don't know the new rules. So I just sat there with Jan in silence because he wouldn't tell me the rules either! I sat there feeling all bound up, arms crossed in front of me, feeling stupid. I tried running away from the feelings of confusion but Jan kept pushing me back to them. It was like my mind was shut down, I couldn't figure out what I was supposed to do, so there I sat. It seemed like I had only been there for five minutes or so when Jan said it was time to end. I was surprised and felt kind of panicky. As I was getting up to leave, I said, "I feel like I didn't accomplish a thing today."

Jan just said cryptically, "Didn't you?" and smiled, and I said, "Well, I guess I'll just have to think about that, won't I."

Then I went out to my car and cried all the way home. As soon as I got into the car I figured out what I was supposed to be doing for the past hour. I was supposed to be getting angry and letting my anger rip! If I can't get angry in that office, I'll never be able to express my anger anywhere. So I've made a decision. Next week, I'm getting angry. If Jan wants to see me in all my ugliness, he's going to get more than he bargained for! ☐

That was the day that "the Rebel" appeared for the first time in therapy. I was coming dangerously close to revealing the source of my anger and that would have put one of the most vulnerable of the children within me at risk of exposure. The Rebel's intent was to protect the children. He was an angry, rebellious teenage boy. I was somewhat aware of how I appeared to be behaving but seemed unable to regain control until Jan said the session was over. I "lost time" that day, too, meaning I was partially amnesic to the session—I wasn't always "there" consciously, as I dissociated from the angry feelings. The tears afterwards came from exhaustion, confusion and frustration. It was a scary and disorienting experience. The cracks in the wall were widening.

☐ February 10, 1994 — I am an emotional basket case. Since I have become aware that I need to "dump" my anger at my next session with Jan, I have been really on edge and close to tears constantly for four days. I am literally scared out of my mind at the idea of tapping into the reservoir of rage that is within me. In my mind, anger is so ugly and I don't want to be ugly. I don't want to be a "selfish, ungrateful bitch" like my mother said I was when I was in my teens. And I don't want everyone to hate me and reject me! Being angry was never acceptable. How can I violate this powerful childhood injunction? I don't know if I have the guts.

Lord, I know You know all about the anger inside me. You see it so clearly even though I don't and You know where it came from. I believe You are calling me to begin facing it—to stand before my anger with courage—to see the depth and breadth of it. You call it forth from deep within me. I am convinced that I must let myself see and feel and release the rage in order to become whole and free. I believe I have to walk through this next dark valley in order to achieve the liberation you are calling me to. Can You still love me and accept me even if I must yell and scream and cry out and be ugly? God, help me to find that integrity and courage within me to overcome my fear and face the whole truth of my anger. I can't do this alone, Lord. Help me trust You to love me through it all and to see me through the eyes of Christ who died for the "real" me with all my scars and ugliness. Amen.

February 15, 1994 — I went to my appointment with Jan determined to blast through my barrier of fear into my anger. I planned to give a litany of venomous diatribes against Jan, Paul, and my parents. But first, I had to know if there was really any purpose in it. Was it really going to make a difference if I went through the excruciating agony of exposing my anger? I had to know if it would be worth it so I asked Jan. Naturally, he answered my question with a question: "What happens if you don't do it?"

I knew he was going to do that! My answer was that if I cover the anger back up and keep hiding it from myself and from the world, it will keep me apart from others and exacerbate my loneliness. He added that he thinks the anger is connected to my self-hatred and my sense of rejection. If I can see it for what it is, with accurate perception and proportion, and can find a way to accept my anger, I may learn to accept and love myself more. Okay, so I had to agree there was good sound psychology behind the idea, but I was scared and resistant beyond what I could have imagined. It was incredibly hard to violate the internal prohibition against anger.

Finally, Jan made a comment about how he had let me struggle alone with my resistance last week. Suddenly I became a frightened little girl who desperately needed Mommy or Daddy to hold her tight and tell her everything would be all right. I felt absolute terror like I had never known before as I sat cowering in my chair. I did everything but suck my thumb! Things felt out of control. Jan was really with me through this frightening experience. He leaned forward toward me in his chair and talked me back to the present with comforting words about how God knows all about my anger and fear and pain and He wants to be with me and hold me and He's proud of me. It really helped as I closed my eyes and prayed, but even as I write these words, I'm saying to myself "I don't think so. I don't think God is proud of me about my anger..." and the tears come.

February 17, 1994 — My head spins and I have trouble focusing. My prayers are wandering and scattered. What is next? Where did this cowering little girl come from and why? What could have possibly created such fear in me when I was so little? I don't remember being beaten or abused. Yes, from time to time Dad hit us with the belt but I don't remember any pain associated with it. Besides he surely wouldn't have done that to this little girl who feels about two or three years old. □

What had happened in therapy was a flashback, a reliving of a trauma. In this case it was only the aftermath of an early abusive incident. I was experiencing all the feelings of terror, rejection and abandonment without remembering the actual causal event. I had somehow known that when I reached for the anger I would end up cowering in terror on the floor. I couldn't make sense of what I had experienced in the previous session either, but I couldn't ignore it. Another dissociative barrier was breaking down and the cracks in the wall were revealing terror, abandonment and loneliness beyond comprehension.

In Search of a Mother's Love

□ February 21, 1994 — The regression into my childhood anger and fear is creating a lot of tension. I need to understand exactly what took place when I started to feel my anger and why I became so scared. The fear felt more powerful than the anger and chased the anger away. Experiencing the feelings was painful and scary for me even as an adult, but I also know that it was healing in some way. I'm afraid it will happen again but I am also afraid it won't happen again.

I'm feeling unsettled, unstable and sometimes so frightened, it's hard to function. I'm so tired all the time, I just want to stay in bed. But I've got lots of work to do, a marriage class to teach, a trip to Ireland to do some training with our team up there. I don't have time to be tired. Two more weeks and I'll have a few days in my little nest at the beach again! I must survive until then.

February 22, 1994 — Last night I dreamed I was given a chance to ride a beautiful horse. She was wild but she was good. She had no saddle or bridle and I didn't know how to ride, but I needed her to get where I wanted to go. The first time I mounted her I ended up getting on backwards, but then I got on the right way, grabbed her mane and neck and held on for dear life. I was scared when she galloped off up the side of a steep hill, but gradually I became more comfortable, more connected to her and at one with her. Before the dream was over we had become loving friends. I needed her strength and power to keep me moving forward on the path and she needed my gentle but firm control. We were a team.

I risk mounting my anger, taking the reins and riding it out. It's scary and a bit more than I can handle as yet, but I believe in time I will learn how to harness the anger to use it and its power in my life. Anger is a God-given emotion. It's what we do with our anger that can be sinful. I want to learn to see and accept my angry feelings and seek God's wisdom as to appropriate ways of responding to them. Jan says with my creative capacities and verbal skills, I could develop a broad repertoire of ways to express my anger that wouldn't be sinful: write an angry poem; sing an angry song; take an angry walk; have an angry talk. The possibilities are almost limitless. The key is to ride out the anger instead of locking it up in a stall where it will kick and scream and grow wild and mean.

Oh, Lord, You have once again spoken words of encouragement into my restless heart. This dream was Your gift to me to give me hope and a vision of how it could one day be for me and my anger. Teach me how to ride that horse—how to bend her will but not break her spirit. Amen.

March 7, 1994 — A memory: My brother Charles and his friend are playing with me before school on the front porch of the house on North Street. I am six or seven years old. I show them my dolly's underpants and then they want to see mine, too. Just as I lift up my skirt, Mom appears and she is horrified! She sends the boys on to school but makes me sit in a corner of the hallway for ten minutes. I am angry! I am ashamed. I feel dirty. Worst of all, I know I am going to be late for school and I will have to walk into the classroom in front of everyone. I always come to school early and try to sneak into my seat and be invisible so I won't get seen or hurt by anyone. I am furious with my mother but I know that anger is not allowed, so I turn all the negative feelings inward. "I must be really bad—there must be something really wrong with me."

I realized for just a moment that she had a cruel and judgmental side. This concept of the unloving mother, which blasted into my consciousness when I was so small and powerless, was an unacceptable reality. So I constructed a protective barrier so I wouldn't have to see it. I told myself it was me who was unlovable, me who was bad. That way I could keep my good and beautiful idealized mother and at least some hope of protection.

I am deathly afraid. Even as I am writing about this, the tension in my body is unbelievable and I feel like I want to crawl right out of my skin. I need to stop and take a walk on the beach. Maybe I'll be able to face this stuff later during this retreat.

March 8, 1994 — My mother's mother was a saint, or so she says. My mother's a saint, too; that's what I always said. At least, when she hasn't been drinking. So it follows that I, too, am a saint, or at least, I'm supposed to be one. That might explain why it is so hard for me to look at my anger and rage and even my sexuality. After all, saints aren't angry. Who ever heard of a rage-filled saint? Or a sexy saint?

I don't know if my grandmother really was a saint because she died when I was nine years old. As a mother, she must have made a few mistakes because her daughter, my saintly mother, was very repressed — unable to express her own anger or even her more positive emotions very easily. She was good at expressing shock, disgust and sentimental tears, but anger almost always came out in the form of biting sarcasm, if it was expressed at all, except for the few rare occasions when she exploded. Mom was like a porcupine—you'd best not approach her because if you get too close, it could be painful. Yet she was indeed a very loving mother to her babies! Strange. It seems like she loved and accepted us only until we began to develop personalities and independence, but then, maybe that was strictly my own experience with her.

If my mother wasn't a saint, what was she? And what am I? If she no longer plays the role of saint to my role of sinner, where does that leave both of us?

She was the youngest of three daughters and from what I can tell in piecing what little I really know of her together, she was pretty and popular in high school. Her graduation picture is beautiful. She met Dad while still in high school and I think he dropped out of college to marry her when she became pregnant with my brother.

So she married young and had eight children and three miscarriages in thirteen years. I wonder why she kept on having babies? It couldn't have been because she loved children so much. I don't think she loved me. I haven't a single memory of her ever saying that she loved me when I was a child. Maybe she just loved being pregnant and having a tiny baby to take care of so she just kept replacing them as they got "too old." I do remember being angry at her when she admitted to being pregnant for the sixth time. From my ten-year-old perspective it was obvious that she had more children than she could handle already.

The cocktail hour was firmly established by then and Jean and I were supposed to "entertain the troupes" while Mom and Dad had drinks. Then the bathing rituals and bedtime rituals became our duties, too. Of course, resisting and rebelling only led to further rejection. I wonder how many times my mother actually said those words, "Why can't you be more like Jean?" Maybe she only said them once and has regretted them ever since. I don't know. I just know they were engraved as a big, ugly scar on my soul. The words I never heard her say were, "I love you, Judy." And I'm still left wondering if she ever really loved me.

God, how can You love me? I know only too well that I am not a saint! Even I reject me... and who knows me better than I do? Yet, in truth, God knows me better than I do. He is gently revealing to me only what He knows I can handle with Him walking beside me. And when He's not walking beside me, He's carrying me, like a little lamb close to His heart. My tears fall from my eyes and onto His chest and arms. He understands. He knows. He does not turn His face away. He loves me. He loves me! Like a mother He cradles me in His arms so lovingly and he rocks me back and forth so gently. He looks into my eyes and says, "I love you, Judy. You are my precious little lamb. I have searched and searched for you. How I have longed for you—longed to hold you, longed to wipe away your tears, longed to show you all the beauty I see in you. You are My child—I was with you before you were born and I will be with you for eternity, loving you forever."

Your love restores me. In the shelter of Your mother love I can almost see a way to love myself, to forgive myself for the sins I committed against myself— the anger turned inward, the self-hatred and self-rejection. If the King of kings and the Lord of lords can look at me and say, "I love you" then who am I to turn away from myself in disgust? *Lord, I pray that You will help me to see myself as You see me: broken and scarred, but beautiful in Your eyes. And beloved. One in whom You are well-pleased. Thank You for going into the very darkest places of my soul and bringing me back into Your light in due time. You are my comfort, my courage and my joy. Amen.*

Shattering Glass and Broken Masks

March 9, 1994 — God, for 40 years I have wandered in this wilderness. Forty years! I have been wandering lost and alone, with the burdens I have carried—the glittering images of my father, my mother and my own glittering image as well. I have been heavy laden. I have suffered and cried out in pain and it has felt as though You have turned Your face away from me. Yes, it's true You provided water and manna, my basic daily bread, but Lord, I have longed for the promised land. I have longed for rest for my weary soul.

But You have been waiting—patiently waiting. You have always known I couldn't carry all my glittering images into the Promised Land. You have been waiting for me to lay them down—to let the crystalline idols topple at last into shattering glass—to turn away from the images and worship You alone. Well, the journey into Canaan has begun, Lord. One-by-one, I'm painfully extricating myself from my idols' tangled webs. As I remove the sparkling garments piece-by-piece, first the image of my father "the hero", then the image of my mother "the saint", then my own image of the "good little girl", I am discovering underneath are the filthy rags of hatred, bitterness and resentment. These, too, must be removed if I am to cross the Jordan River without drowning.

Lord, as You gently and lovingly help me to lay all these burdens down, I am frightened. I suddenly feel so small. Though all my glittering images weighed me down, they also made me shine in the eyes of all around. And those filthy rags of hatred and resentment — well, at least they kept me covered. Now I stand naked before You, Lord God. Baptize me in Your forgiveness. Baptize me in Your love. Cover me in Your garments of praise and lead me into the promised land. □

After the retreat where I wrote this, I returned home to face conflicts in almost every area of my life. The first week home held major clashes with mission colleagues, including the pastor of our church. Our car broke down. Our new microwave oven exploded. A ceiling light fixture fell crashing to the floor. The cat threw up all over the house. Two of my brothers were angry at me about an E-mail I wrote in which I was open about my disappointment with my childhood. My grandmother wrote me a nasty, critical letter; and the list goes on. It was just the beginning of an extended highly stressful period for Paul and me, both in our family and in our ministry. The retreat gave me the initial sustenance I needed to survive what felt like an avalanche. All I could do was to affirm over and over again, "God is in control. He knows about all of these circumstances. I surrender to His will. I know that He loves me—just the way I am."

Down from the Lap

□ March 21, 1994 — So many things are weighing on my heart. Besides all the unresolved externals of my present life, I am struggling now with questions about forgiveness toward my parents for the hurts and losses of my childhood. I very much want to put all the pain behind me and just get on with my life, but I want it to be real, not just an act, but a reality in my heart. Am I really ready to forgive? I don't know. Right now I'm just feeling really confused about it all. A voice inside my head is saying, "When are you going to just get over it? Grow up! Don't be such a baby!" It seems that every time I look at myself in the mirror, I attack myself with a torrent of judging words. The voices of condemnation within are gaining on me and I feel they're about to devour me. *Lord, please help me to hear Your voice above all the shouting of cruel accusations and name-calling going on in my head right now. Help me hear Your words of love and wisdom. Help me know the truth.*

So many things are running through my mind. This past weekend I found two books at a friend's house on the subject of healing victims of sexual abuse. I read them so I could understand what Anne is going through because of being sexually molested as a child. Now as I am trying to digest what I read, I'm beginning to wonder if something may have happened to me when I was little, too. So many of the behavior patterns described were like me: prolonged bed-wetting and thumb-sucking; rebellion against authority; a loss of identity; promiscuity; overeating and addictive behavior. It was like seeing myself on every page.

Then I started thinking about that day I regressed into that terrified, powerless little girl when I was with Jan. I have still not been able to understand such a severe reaction. Why was I so scared? As I started to try to go back into my memories to look for what might have happened, I became very afraid and stopped myself. Feeling panicky, I mentioned my fears about possible sexual abuse to Jan. He simply said, "If it happened, you will know about it when you're ready to deal with it." Maybe there's nothing at all. I don't know.

March 25, 1994 — I'm having such a hard time unearthing my "real" mother. My "good" mother and my "bad" mother are still very much separate in my mind and my efforts to integrate them fall short. I know now that my mother is not a saint but that critical voice in my head is telling me I am "bad" again. It's hard to shoot down a saint.

March 28, 1994 — I am extremely upset about possibly having to end therapy in the near future. It feels like I am being told once again to "grow up" when I'm not ready to — like I'm being pushed down off the lap, pushed into big responsibilities, pushed out of the nest before I'm ready to fly. The only really safe place I have in this world, where I can let whatever wants to rise to the surface, is with Jan. Even though the feelings I experience are often painful or scary—feelings of being small and vulnerable and weak—I need those feelings! Today I answered almost every question Jan asked with the words "I don't know." Sometimes I really didn't know and sometimes it was just self-defense— I didn't want Jan to know how much I need him. He is so gentle and his gentleness makes room for the frightened girl inside. I need that gentle space so much! But then "the judge" enters the scene and pronounces me guilty of being childish and self-centered. Jan is willing to give me space that I'm often unwilling to give myself...

Paul just came into the room and flopped down on the bed. When he enters I seem to lose touch with myself, at least that vulnerable part of me. Jan says maybe I can find a place of expression for that part of me in my relationship with Paul, but I have my doubts. Paul is strongly parental in style and that's probably part of what attracted me to him 20 years ago. I was looking for someone to lead me, to take care of me. I know he loves me desperately and would never intentionally hurt me, but I can't help being scared. Maybe over time that will change. Right now the only person I feel really safe with is Jan (and I defend myself against him, too). I don't even feel safe with myself!

Lord, in my heart, I know I'm not ready to end therapy. I'm right in the midst of it. I have been resting on my counselor's "lap" and feeling just a little bit safe and secure for the first time in my life, receiving healing for the painful scars of abandonment and neglect. Now I am being forced to get down off the lap and grow up AND I DON'T WANT TO! And I wonder, are You going to push me off Your lap, too? God, how can it be Your will to take me out of therapy now before I am ready? It will take a major miracle to resolve the conflicts we are having with our colleagues and make it possible for us to stay here after our furlough. Are You going to perform a miracle, Lord? God, I am so afraid! Please help me to trust You, Lord. Amen.

March 30, 1994 — *"And we know that in all things God works for the good of those who love him, who have been called according to his purpose."* (Romans 8:28) *"Give thanks to the Lord for he is good; his love endures forever."* (Psalm 118:1) I have been holding back from Him. I haven't been willing to trust Him with my future and this question of where we will live and minister. I've been saying to Him, "I WANT to stay here!" And it's true, I do, but ultimately, I need to be willing to surrender that want to God and go back to the place where I am saying, "Thy will, not mine, be done." If He requires us to leave Holland, He is still loving us and caring for us and His will is still best for us, no matter how it might look to me.

Lord, please help me to surrender to Your will, whatever that will may be. Help me to loosen my tight hold on Holland, on Jan and on the security of my friends here. Help me to release all of that to You and trust myself, my family and my future into Your hands. Amen.

April 2, 1994 — Last night Paul and I had a communion service at home with friends in remembrance of Good Friday. I was reminded once again of Christ's total identification with humanity. Never did anyone have more of a right to be angry. Never was anyone more unjustly accused and unfairly abused. Never did anyone experience pain and sorrow more deeply. Who could be more lonely than the One who had known perfect union with His Father for eternity and then felt His Father turn away while He bore all of our sins at the moment of His death? Jesus not only understands all of our pain and loneliness, He has experienced it Himself and it is for our grief that He died.

I don't have any answers. All the scriptures I've learned, all the knowledge I've gained, don't seem to be enough right now. I don't even know how to pray, but one thing I know—Jesus is there. He has not abandoned me. He is loving me and watching over me and He cares. He has the power to make all things work together for good for me. I'm trying, not always successfully, to hold onto that truth. *Lord, I believe. Help my unbelief! Again!*

April 9, 1994 — I asked Jan if there were any chance I'd actually be done with therapy by the time I leave here in June. He used the term "rapprochement." It's usually applied to that developmental period between eighteen months and three years. The child begins to have enough confidence to wander away from the mother for gradually increasing periods of time, but always returns to the mother and is very concerned that she is still there waiting and readily available when the child needs her.

In this instance, he was using the term in the broader sense. I have taken some very strong steps toward growth and independence, which is good and healthy, but at the same time has intensified my need to know that he (my "mother") is there waiting and I can crawl back up into his "lap" anytime I feel the need. Boy, did he hit the nail on the head! It's complicated by the fact that, one, this was exactly the stage of development when things began to go wrong for me as a child and two, the availability of his "lap" is threatened by my need to go on furlough and perhaps never return. To permanently end therapy in June would indeed be a forced ending. He didn't think it would be too disruptive for me to go as long as I knew I was coming back in two months. But I can't know that!

That scares me. We talked about what you would do for a little girl who had to go away from her mother permanently for some reason. At first, I said I guess you'd just tell her she was going to be okay, you know, pump her up about how she was a "big girl" and she could handle it. That certainly revealed my upbringing! What a dumb idea! Then I said I guess the best thing would be to make sure she was put into other hands that were loving and nurturing who would make a fair substitute for mother.

Of course, this was about what I would do if I had to stop seeing Jan. He was suggesting I could find someone else to fill the role. Out of the depths of my abandoned little girl's heart, I just shook my head and said, "There is no one... There is no one... And I can't do it for myself."

Finally, he offered me some encouragement by talking about my strength. He says I'm stronger than I think I am. It takes a lot of strength to be weak and to allow myself to experience my pain. It takes strength to keep moving ahead in spite of the danger of termination of therapy. It even takes strength to go deep into the feelings and process them and start to recover, all the time perfectly timing everything to the fifty-minute time slot we have agreed upon. He says I do that—he doesn't do it. Like Alice in Wonderland, I shrank and I grew big again all in the course of one hour, and I left feeling stronger, more capable, more real and more fully alive.

April 10, 1994 — The night before last Paul and I made love, often a bittersweet experience for me. Why? When we make love and I am able to surrender to the experience of receiving his love, I feel weak and vulnerable—something I need and fear at the same time. When our lovemaking is truly intimate and powerful, I find myself close to or in tears that are somehow connected to fears of abandonment and feelings of shame. This was again one of those nights. Again I hid the tears because I don't want Paul to be afraid to make love to me, to think he is somehow hurting me. After I thought he was asleep, I quietly wept. Paul pulled me into his arms. I tried, clumsily, to share with him the feelings I have of not being ready to stand on my own. Then I asked him to pray for me. As I wept, he prayed aloud for me and gradually a peace came over me and my tears stopped flowing, my heart settled and I soon was asleep.

A memory: I was around ten years old and I stayed home from school sick. During the night I had wet my bed and I didn't want to tell Mom because I was ashamed, but I didn't want to stay in the cold wetness of my bed either. I changed my pajamas and crawled into another bed. Somehow I managed to wet that bed, too, that day. Later, Mom came upstairs to make the beds and discovered my sin. She was furious. She grabbed me, pulling me out of bed by the arm and into the bathroom, all the way blaming and shaming me through gritted teeth. She tried to push my head into the toilet. I put both my little hands on the toilet seat and managed to hold my face out of the water, screaming, "Mommy, don't!" and crying in terror. Afterwards I was left, curled up on the floor in the bathroom, alone.

Mom loved her little babies but she really was not capable of loving me as I grew. I must have sensed this even as a tiny little girl and I tried hard to conform to her desires by prolonging my babyish behavior of thumb-sucking and bed-wetting. It's no wonder I'm scared again now as I take steps toward growth and independence which will lead ultimately to my separation from Jan. I'm afraid he'll take his nurturing support away from me just like Mom did.

April 11, 1994 — I've suddenly remembered a recurring nightmare I had many times as a child. I dreamed I died. I flew up to heaven and stood before a great and awesome God who sat on a throne wearing a long, flowing white beard and a robe. I trembled as He looked down at me and said, "You can't come into heaven. You suck your thumb. Go straight down to Hell." The next thing I knew I was slipping rapidly down a long and twisting slide ending in a fiery dark place I knew was Hell where the devil was waiting for me with an evil grin. I always woke up terrified.

My image of God was created in the microcosm of my family. I got my understanding of the nature of God from my experience of my parents. My God was distant, merciless, condemning and judging. By the time I was five, I was already convinced I was unlovable and unworthy. I was ashamed, guilty, bad and deserving of only Hell. No wonder I had to shut down and close off from my feelings. It would have been terribly hard to face all of those feelings alone and there was no one. "There is no one..." That's what I said to Jan in my last session. Deep in my heart, sometimes I'm still convinced that I'm all alone.

My Lord Jesus, You showed me these words today from Your Word: "Humble yourself, therefore, under God's mighty hand, that he may lift you up in due time. Cast all your anxiety on him because he cares for you. Be self-controlled and alert. Your enemy the devil prowls around like a roaring lion looking for someone to devour. Resist him, standing firm in the faith, because you know your brothers throughout the world are undergoing the same kind of sufferings. And the God of all grace, who called you, to his eternal glory in Christ, after you have suffered a little while, will himself restore you and make you strong..." (1 Peter 5:6-10)

I believe You, Lord. You are restoring me and making me strong. Help me to stand firm in the faith when I suffer, knowing one day I will rest forever in Your lap of love. Amen.

First Fruits of Forgiveness

April 27, 1994 — I'm very tired and have been tired for days, maybe weeks. I have suddenly become one of those people who frequently has difficulty sleeping. I never used to have any trouble falling asleep or staying asleep but in recent weeks I seem to have lost that gift. □

I was battling exhaustion, both physical and emotional. I was grieving the deaths of the "saint" and the "hero" and resisting the anger that was boiling just beneath the surface, not only the anger toward my parents but toward the circumstances of my present life which were becoming unmanageable. My house began to reflect the chaos and confusion and fatigue in my mind. My control was slipping away. I was angry at God, blaming Him for everything that was pressing down on me and for "making" me leave Jan for at least two months.

As I look back now, I can see the symptoms of depression starting to show themselves—confusion, loss of concentration, sleeplessness, lethargy, reduced capacity to function in daily activities. After a great deal of hard work, I was again running out of steam. Still I kept pushing myself, straining to bring some kind of closure to the process of facing my mother and my anger at her before having to face her in real life in just a few weeks time. In early May, having faced and felt some of the anger about Mom, I said good-bye to the "saint" and buried my fantasy mother, finally really letting go of the glittering image.

☐ May 2, 1994 — All I have left of my mother is the shattered glass where her image once stood and my awareness of the abandonment and neglect. Somewhere there must be moments of light in the darkness. I know she cares about me now, and all the other children, too. That capacity to care must have always been there somewhere. I don't want to construct another fiction but I want to be open to softening the dark picture I now have of her.

The anger has lost its intensity now as Jan has helped me see some of her realities. She was young.—very young and very much alone. She may have been deprived of love in her own childhood. Her strange "baby love" was not normal and was likely tied to a deep need for love which had gone unmet in her life. Dad wasn't very supportive. These are not to excuse what she did to me and thinking this way does not reduce the pain for me. It does make it possible for me to begin to have compassion toward her and to move in the direction of forgiveness.

May 11, 1994 — My head is spinning. It feels like everything is falling apart. Paul is burning out and seems ready to jump ship. Our finances are in disarray. The kids are having problems with us and we are having problems with them. Where's the solid ground? Jesus is my Rock and I can stand on Him, but even that Rock is feeling slippery to me right now.

I'm so afraid I'm going to fall and drown. You can walk on water, Lord, but I can't. I'm scared! I'm really scared! Help me, Lord, to keep my feet on the Rock. I'm holding onto You by a thread, Lord. Don't let me slip away. Don't let me fall. Tomorrow I am going to share Your gospel with three women. Give me the words to say to these dear women whom You love so much. Help me somehow point the way to You even though I am weak and powerless in the extreme right now. Speak through me in my weakness, oh Lord. Empower me with Your Spirit. Draw them into Your Kingdom and me into Your arms, oh Lord. Amen. ☐

I had read about "non-dominant hand" writing as a way of letting the child within express itself in an uncensored way, so I began to dialogue with the part of me I had been calling Judy Marie. Already there had been more than one child surfacing but as yet I had not made the distinctions between them and saw all of their communication as coming from the inner child that I understood everyone had inside of them.

☐ Dear Judy Marie — I'm so glad you were born and I love you very much. I want you to know that I will always be here for you, I know what your needs are, I appreciate your uniqueness and I love you exactly the way you are. I want to give you all the time you need to grow and develop. I'm so glad you are a girl. I want to give you everything you need. I will never leave you or turn my face away from you. I love you. – Judy ☐

☐ Dear Judy — I'm scared. You have not always been nice to me. But I will try to trust you. I am so lonely. — Judy Marie ☐

☐ May 13, 1994 — I had an odd dream last night. It was about people who I felt were my family though I didn't recognize any of them. I was wearing very dark nonprescription sunglasses. I wore them all the time, indoors and outside, and I couldn't see very well at all. That was bugging me but I just wouldn't take the sunglasses off. Strange.

I woke up tired and sad again. I hate this but it seems to be a fact of my life right now. Thank God, Paul understands that I am in mourning in a sense. So many losses—my childhood and my illusions about it, my lost hero and saint, lost fantasies about the nature of my relationship with my kids, etc. How could I not be sad and exhausted? ☐

☐ Dear Judy Marie — I know you are very lonely. It broke your heart when your Mommy turned her face away from you and seemed to take her love away. You are scared to be angry because you were told only bad girls are angry. You are afraid to be angry or sad or just to be yourself because you fear no one will love and care for you if you act like that. I love you and I will never turn my face away or take my love from you. You can be exactly who you are—even when you are angry. I will teach you some balance and let you be mad, sad, afraid or glad. You can laugh or cry or stomp your foot and so on and I will know and understand and accept you just as you are. – Judy ☐

☐ Dear Judy — I am starting to trust you. You really let me be angry and you still love me! It feels good to be known and loved. Please help me know myself so I can stop being invisible. I have been lonely and afraid for so long! Love, Judy Marie ☐

☐ May 26, 1994 — I talked to Dad on the phone the other day. He's been sober through AA for about ten years now. I got the answer to my question, "When did the drinking become a problem?" He told me he and Mom hung out in bars and drank heavily before they ever got married. After they married, they drank a lot, too, and Dad said they were drunk at least two or three times a week. I am validated in my sense of being an adult child of alcoholics. I needed to hear that because there is so much denial in my family about the impact of the alcohol. He also said both he and Mom grew up in dysfunctional families. He felt his own parents were cold and distant and they used to beat him "to within an inch of" his life. He could never live up to the ghost of his oldest brother, whom his parents idolized. That brother died when he was nineteen. Dad and his other brother were never able to reveal their dead brother's repeated sexual assaults on my uncle and his attempts to rape my father.

Dad assessed Mom's family, too. He said they found it almost impossible to express emotions. Her mother and father always had separate bedrooms. Mom said she really believed the only time they had sex were the three times their daughters were conceived.

Dad said Mom controlled the baby-making in the family and she would lie about using birth control. I asked him why they had so many kids. He said Mom got the most attention and strokes when she had a new baby, so she just kept repeating the scenario. Another perception validated.

Mom and Dad—two wounded adult children playing at being grown-up. Playing house. Raising a family of eight needy children when they themselves were nothing but bigger versions of the same needy children. Our hungry mouths needing to be fed, our chirping voices needing to be heard, our feeble attempts to fly. It must have been overwhelming for the little boy inside of Dad and the little girl inside of Mom. No wonder they retreated into the alcohol. Mom is in her sixties now, and the child inside is still wounded, has never been loved and accepted and healed. How terribly sad.

I forgive you, Mom. Now I understand your pain, your fear, your anger. You couldn't love me because you couldn't really love yourself. You deadened the pain with alcohol and sought your identity in the "babies." I am so much more fortunate than you, Mom. I have discovered my wounded child and am facing the truth of my suffering and the deep loneliness of my life. I am only 41 and have so much time to become whole and to learn new and better ways. You have never even begun the journey. I have time to grow up healthy yet. You will probably always be an adult child. You have hurt me deeply, but you have hurt yourself more deeply. You have suffered more than enough. I forgive you, Mom. I accept the reality of my lost childhood as the legacy of your lost childhood and Dad's. I have passed some of that same legacy on to my own beloved children, which I deeply regret, but I still have time! Time to make amends. Time to be honest. Time to release my children from their overdeveloped sense of responsibility toward me. There is hope for me! A chance to break the cycle. I need to let go of my resentments and bitterness about my childhood so I can release the energy that is caught there, freeing myself up to live in today.

I forgive you, Mom. I forgive you, Dad. Finally, I think I can see you both as you are and I can love you—not the saint, not the hero, but flesh and blood, very imperfect, wounded adult children. I love you, Mom. I love you, Dad.

Jesus, thank You for this unexpected gift You have given me today— acceptance and forgiveness. Now I can face my trip to the States with peace about Mom and Dad. I know I will be able to express my love to them. I have owned and experienced my hurt and anger, and I have released them. Thank You, Lord, for helping me see my parents through Your eyes of love. Help me see myself through those same eyes. I have hated and condemned myself, Lord. Help me give myself forgiveness, too.

Help me to see the truth about myself, the mistakes I have made in my life. Show me how my own dysfunction has had negative impact on my loved ones. Lord, may it not be too late to make amends and help bring healing. Let me be able to say "I forgive you" to myself, and to say "Will you forgive me" to my loved ones. Open my eyes, Lord. I love you. Amen.

Dear Judy Marie — I've already shared with you in recent months about Someone special, Someone very powerful, who loves both you and me just the way we are. We can both feel safe and protected because there is Someone greater than us who loves us. This Someone is God. God showed us what He is like by sending His Son Jesus into the world. Jesus loves me and you, too. He tells us that God wants to be both our Mother and our Father. He tells us that God made us the way we are and He wants us to become all we were created to be. He tells us not to judge others, but to forgive. I like Jesus because we can talk to Him and ask for what we need. He gives us what we need without us having to do anything to earn it. Jesus loves us just the way we are. I want you to know God loves us and will always protect us and be with us. He will never leave us. He is the power we can call on who is much greater than both of us! I hope you will grow up to know Him and love Him and trust Him as I do. Love, Judy

I Don't Wanna Go!

June 15, 1994 — Got word today that Dad may have cancer. Pretty scary. I'm glad I'm going to be in California because Dad will be there, too. I've finally reached a place where I can really love him in a healthy way and I want more time! *Watch over him, Lord.*

Every day I become sadder as I realize my time here is coming to a close, even if it's only for two months. Last night I found myself wishing Jan could be transformed into a little teddy bear so I could take him with me. Then when things got to be too much, I could curl up with him and feel safe again. It's so funny how I swing radically back and forth between independence and dependence, between growth and regression. This morning I was thinking that I only have two more hours with Jan and I just doubled over in gut-wrenching pain. I feel like an idiot! At the same time, I guess I'm getting stronger by allowing myself to feel this pain and not run from it.

Father God, I think I can trust You. I think I can hold on to You. I can turn to You for guidance, for wisdom, for direction. I can look up to You whenever I need a smile or a thumbs up or a word of encouragement. Hold me close in Your arms, Father God. You're so much better than a teddy bear... You hold me! Let me rest in You. Amen.

June 17, 1994 — Less than two weeks until we fly to the States. I'm in one of my "porcupine" moods, feeling bristly and wanting Paul and everyone just to stay away from me. A lot of anger is brewing in me. Why am I so on edge and why do I want to push Paul away from me now? Maybe I just feel too uptight about going to the States and I am afraid to show my weakness to Paul, so instead of going to him with my fears and insecurities and asking for the comfort and reassurance I need, I am pushing him away.

June 24, 1994 — I said good-bye to Jan today and cried all the way home. Why do I still feel so desperate? Why does the therapy feel like a matter of life and death? What is there left to do? I won't know now until I get back in September. The Lord gave me this scripture in my quiet time today: *"The Lord himself goes before you and will be with you; he will never leave you nor forsake you. Do not be afraid; do not be discouraged."* (Deuteronomy 31:8)

I reluctantly board a plane tomorrow morning, Father God. I pray for the grace to trust You with each day as it comes. I pray for the wisdom to stay close to You every moment. Thank You for Your promise to go before me and never to forsake me. You are my Shepherd. Lead me beside still waters. Daily restore my soul. Amen. □

The Wall Comes Tumbling Down

I arrived in California and went straight to my father's side. I stood at his bedside in the hospital all day long for several days, caring for him, giving him ice chips and making sure he had the pain medication he needed. I felt more uncomplicated love for him then than I'd ever felt before, but the hunger for his love and attention remained and my tender loving care was still given with the hope of being seen as special in his eyes. Something in me was still playing the "good little girl" and trying to get him to be the "good daddy." Things were not as simple and pure as I had hoped they would be.

□ July 4, 1994 — On Friday, Paul and I had a frustrating meeting with our mission leaders to discuss the conflict which had been going on between a colleague and us over in Europe. They intend to hire this man for a key leadership position. We have had conflict with him for five years and we are convinced he has character and integrity problems. We stated clearly that we would work with this man but we could not work for him. We felt safe saying this because our boss had told us several times that he wouldn't make us work under the man. We left the meeting feeling completely unheard. We know that our roles within the mission agency are precarious. After years of faithful, committed service, we are shaken.

Lord, in spite of all the busyness and all the people we're seeing, family, friends, supporters, colleagues, etc., I'm lonely. I cry as I lay in my bed at night. I long for a place of safety where I can expose the deepest part of me and know that I will find acceptance. Jan has offered me that place of safety in a tangible way but I am far from him now. Yet I know my true place of safety is in You. Find me and take me there, oh Father God. I need You to be my hiding place. Strengthen me, Lord, for the challenges you have set before me this summer. Help me to trust You with each day as it comes. Show me those things within me, the attitudes of my heart, the sinful thoughts, that create barriers between You and me. Cleanse me, oh Lord. Strip away all of my illusions of independence. Strip away my false dependencies—on Jan, on Paul, on my children, on my image as a successful missionary—and cause me to depend solely and wholly on You and You alone. Amen.

July 11, 1994 — Paul and I met with the mission's board members to deal with the issues which were at the core of our conflict. We worked hard and seemed to make good progress. Then, as the meeting was coming to a close, our boss announced to us, out-of-the-blue, that he intended to offer our former enemy a position in direct line authority over us.

It was like a bomb dropping on us. Paul and I worked so hard all day to own our own "garbage" and stay out of our defenses, and we had done everything in our power to facilitate a peer working relationship with him. We had been told he would not be in authority over us. Now our leader was telling us something that we had already explained would require us to resign. We were shocked and deeply wounded. All during those six hours of meetings, even during the meeting earlier in the morning, everyone else knew what we didn't know. They had decided to take a chance that we were bluffing. We feel so betrayed!

July 19, 1994 — For Anne's sake, I have been reading another book about the damage caused by child sexual abuse and the process of healing the wounded heart. Every time I read about it, I recognize and relate so much to the internal and external damage that is described that I begin to question my own history, looking for incidents of abuse. I know that there is so much I have forgotten, so many blank periods and black holes.

One thing I have realized is that my father's teasing me about my developing body and calling me "Bubbles" was a form of sexual abuse. I have a feeling, an intuitive sense within me, that something happened when I was much, much younger. Was I abused or molested as a very young child?

Lord, I am open. Please show me the whole truth of my history. I am willing now to face it and do the hard work of pain and suffering it may require to deal with it with Your help. Unlock the hiding places in my mind, Lord. I'm willing to work and I'm willing to wait. Your will be done.

July 24, 1994 — The meetings go on as we try to come to some understanding of God's will for our future ministry. I still feel so deeply betrayed. I don't ever remember feeling this betrayed before in my entire life.

July 27, 1994 — *Oh my God, help me! I remembered!* Now I remember when it was that I felt this betrayed once before in my life. Just before I woke up this morning I had a dream. I was about two or three years old and a big, angry-looking, barrel-chested man lay on top of me on the floor. His chest covered my face. I was terrified and trying to scream but I couldn't! Only a small, pitiful sound that no one could hear came out of my mouth. He was pushing something between my legs and rocking on me. Then I woke up and immediately forgot his face.

When I woke up from this nightmare I was alone in this basement room where Paul and I are staying for a couple of days. I have spent the last hour sobbing uncontrollably and reliving the trauma, and the sensation of total fear and isolation that I felt when the assault was over and I was left alone back then. As I wept I thought of that session with Jan months ago when I first tapped into my rage and ended up regressing to a very little girl, crumpled up on the floor. Now I understand why I felt like I was on the floor. This dream is connected to that flashback. Then I remembered the constantly recurring nightmare of my childhood about barrels falling in on top of me and crushing me! After I woke up, the word "barrel-chested" came into my mind immediately.

After sobbing alone for far too long, I knew I needed not to repeat the isolation of the event. I went partway up the stairs and called to Paul to come down. He held me and just let me tell him what was going on. That's what I really needed, to be held and to be heard. To finish this, I need to talk to Jan. I just want to go back to Holland! When Paul tried to help me, he was clumsy because he just isn't trained or naturally talented for intervention. I realized I was starting to shut down, to withdraw in a self-punishing way. He did, too, and expressed his concern. I decided to try to pull myself together so I can go on with appointments here, etc. but not to really shut down.

There's a lot more work to be done here and I know I am going to face this pain again. I'm going to have to call Jan or maybe see Britt's counselor Sandy soon. I need some help with this. I think though that I am strong enough now, with God as my partner, to hold the pain and go on without burying it.

Dear Child Within — You are two years old or so and you are scared and angry and helpless. I want to listen to all your feelings about what has happened to you. It's okay to be angry. It's okay to be scared. It's okay to feel helpless. I am going to be there to help you. Jesus and I feel your pain. We will hold you and love you. You are not alone. Thank you for sharing this long-held secret with me. Thank you for trusting me. I love you and Jesus loves you forever. You will never have to face this pain alone again. Love, Judy.

July 29, 1994 — When I really think about the dream, I start to shake. Sometimes I wonder if maybe it was only a dream. It's hard for me to trust myself and my intuitive feeling that what I dreamed is a real memory. My emotional reaction upon waking from the dream was real, and less than a week before, I had prayed asking the Lord to show me the truth of my history. Even so, it's still hard to believe. I want desperately to process this with Jan but I can't imagine doing it over the phone. I don't know what to do. I guess I'll survive until the Lord shows me His will.

10:30 PM — I'm tired but I'm afraid to turn off the light. In the dark I start to feel so small and scared and I start to remember again.

Lord, I need You to see me through this. I need to know You are close beside me. You showed me my truth, now show me Your grace. You can carry me and guide me if I will only let You. Help me to trust You. I am tempted to ask where You were when I was being violated by an evil man, but in my heart, I believe You were beside me even then, grieving to see my pain and my fear. Your heart was broken as I lay crumpled on the floor sobbing afterwards, unable to comprehend what had happened to me and experiencing the desolation of my separateness, my isolation. Your heart cried as You watched my heart shrink and my trust shrivel.

I felt so terribly alone! To my child's eyes there was no one. There is no one! Where is Mommy? Make him stop! I can't breathe! I can't breathe! I'm so scared! He's trying to kill me! Let me go! Let me go... And then he was gone and I was alone—so alone. Never more alone than after he had gone... You were there, Lord. I didn't know it, but even in those most alone moments, You were there. Even as You watched my tender petals close up tight around my heart, You knew one day Your love and grace would open me again—that from the brokenness of my heart would blossom forth one day the woman You created me to be. Your love and grace would call me forth. I don't see the fulfillment of all this yet, Lord. I'm still wearing the ashes of mourning, but I believe Your promises.

I asked for the revelation of my own true history and You have been giving it to me, piece by piece, as You have seen that I was ready to receive it. Show me all that I need to learn from this most recent revelation. Comfort me in my pain. Help me to love You with my whole heart. Amen.

August 5, 1994 — It's almost midnight and again I can't get to sleep. I'm tired all the time now. Exhausted. But the lights go out and I can't sleep. I want desperately to talk to Jan tonight. I hear the still, small voice of Jesus calling me to Himself but I still want to talk to someone with flesh and bones. I want to look Jan in the eyes and bare my soul and be able to see his acceptance and understanding. I want to hear his responses and have his intervention. I just want to talk to Jan! I really need him tonight...

My heart has been riding a roller coaster of hope and despair for days. The whole situation with the mission is driving me crazy. I want desperately for there to be reconciliation and healing yet I'm desperately afraid for Paul and I to be vulnerable to be hurt again. Trust has been broken and it won't be easily restored. I'm so tired and confused now, I can barely think to process all the many meetings and discussions we have had. We still have no idea what the Lord wants us to do.

In the meantime, I'm feeling the aftershocks of my dream. I wonder who the man was and I get scared, thinking it might have been my own father. When Paul approaches me wanting to make love, the dream/memory comes into my head and I tense up. Last night I let Paul make love to me but I couldn't feel anything. Afterwards, he said he was sorry and that made me feel even worse.

August 7, 1994 — I was lying on the bed reading when Paul came in and started to kiss me. I turned my head away and he started kissing my neck. Somehow my hands were held down by his chest. I wanted to push him away, but I felt trapped. Deep feelings of panic washed over me and I blurted out, "Don't trap me like that! Don't trap me!" and pulled away from him. He was hurt and said, "I was only trying to kiss you" and turned and walked away. All the dream/memory stuff flooded over me and I lay on the bed, clasping my teddy bear and sobbing uncontrollably for a very long time. "The Little One" took over and curled up in fear and desolation. What am I going to do?

August 9, 1994 — My concentration is pretty limited. I feel out of touch with things going on around me. I am very much "in my head" and I'm having a hard time staying on top of feelings, thoughts and moods. Something is very wrong with me. I'm asking myself again, "Where was God when the sexual abuse took place?" It's hard for me to pray. I feel so far away from God. I'm agitated and anxious and drained. I'm not sleeping well. I'm keeping Paul at a distance and I'm impatient and angry with him. The only person I want to be close to is Jan, and I can't. Tomorrow I'm going to see Sandy, Britt's counselor, and I'm going to try to deal with some of this with her if I can. I can feel the adrenaline pumping through my system. All my nerves are on edge. I'm feeling really prickly, physically and emotionally. I'm functioning at a very low level now. I just want to go home! *Lord, I'm falling apart... Please help me!*

Dear Little One — I see you sitting there, crumpled and afraid on the floor, tears flowing in a flood from your large, frightened eyes. I hear you crying out, "Where's Mommy?" I feel your total sense of abandonment. You are thinking, "There is no one!" You are feeling so alone. I hear you. I see you. I love you. The Lord goes before you and will be with you. He will never leave you or forsake you. You don't see it now but Jesus was with you when the evil man hurt you. He cried when you cried. His heart broke when your heart broke. You are his little lamb. He has never left your side all these years. Soon you will learn to rest your head on His chest and listen to the comfort of His heartbeat as He holds you tenderly in His arms. You will cry all your unshed tears until there are no more tears to cry. And as your tears pour out, the pain and the anguish will be poured out and Jesus will fill their places with His love and grace. I promise. Love, Judy. ☐

☐ Dear Judy — I hurt. I'm scared. I didn't want it. How come he did it? Little One. ☐

☐ Dear Little One — I know you hurt and you are scared. Of course, you didn't want it to happen. I don't know why it happened. The man was very evil. God can bring something good out of something that was intended for evil. We'll watch together and see what God does. Love, Judy.

August 10, 1994 — I met with Sandy. She believes I have a chemical imbalance as a result of either the childhood trauma or possibly the time I was raped when I was 21. Strange, I hadn't thought about the rape in years. In fact, I immediately pushed it out of my mind right after it happened twenty years ago. Today when Sandy asked me if I had ever been raped, I told her I had been promiscuous and I had been drinking so I felt "I deserved to be raped." She said no one ever deserves to be raped—ever! Anyway, she says I have symptoms of Post-Traumatic Stress Disorder (PTSD) and that I am in the midst of a major depressive episode. I'm going to get a prescription for antidepressants. I have to admit I have a lot of the symptoms of depression: appetite disturbance, sleep disturbance, loss of energy, restlessness, agitation, loss of concentration, muddled thinking, fatigue, crying frequently, irritability. You name it, I've got it. The good news is Sandy says the medication should make a big difference in how I feel. We'll see.

August 15, 1994 — Talked to one of my younger sisters about my dream. She had a very similar experience while under hypnosis in therapy once. She felt someone lying on top of her and she was suffocating. It was unsettling and eerie to sense the possibility that the same man who hurt me may have hurt her, too. If it was the same man, with our age difference and nomadic life-style, it narrows the field of possible perpetrators down significantly. I'm getting more and more scared that it was Dad. I am also afraid I have only seen the tip of the iceberg.

August 18, 1994 — Night before last I went to bed at midnight and dozed from about 2 AM to 3:15 AM. When I woke up, my body was tense and twitching and I was aware of parts of my body which were carrying the tension from the trauma of forty years ago—my legs, my neck and shoulders, my stomach, my chest. Then I had a sudden shuddering startle response in my body and began to sob uncontrollably for about an hour while Paul held me.

The Lord gave me a promise in the end. He said, "You shall abound in my love."

I believe He was telling me that as I walk through this valley of pain, I will become filled with His love and He will pour His love out through me to others. May it be so.

August 22, 1994 — A week from today we're on our way home. I have been living one long nightmare, but I have a sinking feeling it won't be over just because I touch down in Holland. I can't stop thinking about everything that's happened to me, and to our ministry, and, and, and... Paul is terribly depressed and he has no one to talk to but me, and what good am I right now? Not much.

August 30, 1994 — Touch down in two hours! Home at last! I have been desperate to return to the nourishing, green landscape and the calming routine of our life in the Netherlands. Cool air, warm friends, Max the cat, my great big king-sized bed, Jan, my seaside retreat—all have been calling me home. I don't know if I could have stood another day in California. I was beginning to feel like a two-year-old crying over and over again, "I wanna go home! I wanna go home!" I was going downhill fast. I have been having lots of flashback-type experiences, especially physical sensations like I am out of my body or my hands are numb or like adrenaline is pumping through my system and I should be fleeing or fighting something but I can't. It's really weird.

All I know is I want to talk to Jan about everything that happened this summer. I have missed him so much, but I have grown more independent as well, I think. At the beginning of the summer, I thought of him every day and cried over my loss. By the end of the two months, my thoughts of him were less frequent and less painful.

As Dorothy said "There's no place like home... There's no place like home..."

Chapter 2 — Into the Tomb

The Little One

September 1, 1994 — Thoughts of the abuse have been haunting me all morning and I have been slipping in and out of control. The body memories, the rush of adrenaline, the fear—it's all so overpowering. In five days I'll see Jan. I'm tempted to call him to get in sooner but I'm afraid to do it. I already feel foolish for asking for an extra hour with him at our first appointment. I keep thinking I really don't have two hours worth of things to talk about and there's nothing really wrong with me. Even the "sexual abuse" is nothing more than a bad dream. I feel ashamed because I wrote to Jan admitting my neediness and dependency. The "judge" in me is saying "Don't be a baby!"

Lord God, please help me to know what's real and do what's right. Am I just being a baby? I was just a baby when I was abused—if I was abused! Help me! They say, "no pain, no gain" but I'm not sure how much more pain I can survive. I'm having a hard time praying. It's so hard right now to feel You and to hear You but I know You're here beside me. Help me to rest in You, Lord. Help me to walk through this valley in surrender to Your will. I want to surrender the pain and anger to You, Lord, and wait upon You to change my heart, Lord.

September 3, 1994 — Last night Paul wanted to make love. I couldn't relax. Afterwards, we talked for hours. He's feeling abandoned, afraid he is losing me. He really misses the intimacy. So do I. I reassured him of my love for him and that my problem has nothing to do with him. He knows that but it is hard for him to feel it. I feel so guilty! He needs me and I don't seem to be able to be there. I'm angry with myself for this fear of sex. It seems way out of proportion to what happened to me, if anything really happened at all. Maybe it was only a dream and now all of this pain and these reactions are just a creation of mine.

I didn't get to sleep until 3 AM. I didn't want to take a sleeping pill. I woke up feeling awful. I'd rather take the pills. Maybe I should take them all at once.

September 4, 1994 — *God, You gave me a promise: "You shall abound in My love." I believe You. I can't see it now in this tomb, but You have the power to transform this tomb into a womb—a place where new life can spring forth. You are at work with your creative power in the midst of my pain and fear. You are inviting me to join with You in this work, to be a willing vessel. I want to surrender to Your work of making me into a person who is capable of abounding in Your love. Help me.*

Dear Judy Marie — One more sleep and then you can go see Jan. He's a good listener and he loves you. You can tell him all about what's happened and all your feelings and thoughts. He can help you understand and he can help you begin to feel better. You can trust him. He won't hurt you. You can tell him all the ways you have been hurt. You're safe with him. Love, Judy. □

□ Dear Judy — I will tell Jan about the bad man. I want to talk about it now. You seem too tired and sad to listen. We need Jan to help us both. Love, Judy Marie. □

□ He's a man, too. He might be bad too. Are you sure it's okay to tell him. He might not believe us! I'm scared. Little One. □

□ Dear Little One — I know Jan is a man, but he is not a bad man. He is kind and gentle, like Jesus. He cares about us and he will believe us. He wants to help us. It's very important to him. He has even given us an extra hour tomorrow so we have lots of time to explain everything to him. He will help all of us. I promise. Love, Judy. □

By then I realized that there were at least two little children within me. One had accepted the name I had given her, Judy Marie. She was a relatively healthy, though long-neglected, little girl around seven-years-old. She had lots of wisdom and had remained innocent, untouched by the trauma though now, at least, she was aware of as much as I was. The one that identified itself as the Little One was the part who had experienced the trauma that I had seen in the dream. She was around two-and-a-half, still so young that when she was present, I could feel that she had no sense of her own sexual identity. The two girls' handwriting and verbal skills were different and distinguishable.

September 5, 1994 — Met with Jan today at last. It was hard to tell him about the dream. The Little One was scared to start talking about it. Twice I experienced full flashbacks of the event. The body memories are so terrible! My heart pounds and I can't breathe and everything feels like it's electrified. I want to jump out of my skin! I start to tremble and shudder and stutter and I feel so afraid and alone.

Since I got home from the session, I've been trying to sleep. I'm exhausted. I can't turn off my mind and I keep slipping into the memories. Will I ever be able to sleep without pills again?

It was so good to be with Jan, to feel safe. He told me we don't know yet if the dream was a single actual event or if it was a symbol of numerous events, but he said I am definitely having a memory or memories. My body is remembering terrible pain and fear and suffocation. I am remembering terrible loneliness, too. I have been so alone and so afraid all my life. I always loved my mother and father "from afar" and always felt detached from everyone. I'm beginning to understand why. From my experience, the world was a dangerous place where people tried to kill you and then left you alone holding your pain, and no one came to rescue you.

At least Jan believes me. Sometimes I don't believe myself. He warned me that there will be lots of messages in my head trying to make what I am seeing untrue because I don't want it to be true. Part of me wants to shut the door on this awful tomb and make it go away. Part of me is afraid to go forward into the tomb to see what is there. Yet I believe there is a part of me that is strong enough, trustworthy enough, to walk through this reality and survive. The prize waiting on the other side is healing, wholeness and integration of the Little One who has been carrying this trauma alone for such a long time.

Dear Little One — You did really well today. I know it was very hard for you to share your secret with Jan. It took courage for you to tell your story. You are very brave. I want you to know I love you and I am going to help you so you won't have to carry all your pain and fear alone anymore. I can help you and Jan can help you and Someone who is bigger and stronger than all three of us can help you. I'm talking about Jesus. Jesus wants to bring healing in all the places where you are hurting. You and I and Jan will slowly reveal the hurting places to Jesus, in your time, as you feel ready. Jesus is a miraculous healer and He will touch your wounds and restore you. You have carried your wounds for a long time. Let me help you. Let Jan help you. Most of all, let Jesus help you. He loves you very, very much. Love, Judy. □

□ I have so many tears if I get started I may never stop so WATCH OUT! I hurt everywhere. Inside and out. Can Jesus fix the inside too? Little One. □

□ Dear Little One — Jesus is an expert at fixing what's broken on the inside. And don't worry about all those tears. I want to give you all the time you need to cry every single tear. I can't let you cry all the time, day and night, because I am a grown-up and I have work to do, but I promise, over time, you'll get to finish your crying. Okay? Try to trust me and be patient. I love you. Love, Judy.

September 6, 1994 — My eyes are all screwy again. I can't see right. Everything is jumping all over the page. That's been happening a lot lately. Last night I wanted to make love with Paul but I was afraid. I decided to try anyway. Things were going okay until he rolled over on top of me. I panicked. I dissociated and went numb. I have to find a way to control the flashbacks and stay in the here and now. I finally fell asleep at 6 AM and the alarm went off at 7:30. Not a real good night.

☐ I feel like exploding. I feel full of something that wants to come out. It's scary! I'm angry. Help me! Little One. ☐

September 8, 1994 — Who did this to me? I know it's not just a dream. It happened and maybe even more has happened that I don't yet know. When I had the dream, I saw the face of the man, but when I woke up, I lost it. The Little One knows who did it, but she isn't telling right now. I'm thinking of giving her a chance to write what she remembers but I'm a bit afraid. Ambivalence is the word for me today. ☐

☐ He was mad at me. I don't know what I did to make him angry. He grabbed my arm. It hurt me! He pushed me down on the floor. It was dark and I was scared. He was lying on top of me and making a noise. I wanted to get away. I wanted to scream. I couldn't breathe. I opened my mouth to scream but I sounded like a tiny little kitten. He was pushing something between my legs. It felt yucky. He was rocking and rocking and I was going to die soon. Then it stopped. He left me there. I was so cold. I was so scared. I hurt all over. I was all alone in that dark room. I wanted my Mommy. Why did he do that to me? Why didn't someone make him stop. He was trying to kill me. I must be a very bad girl. I must be a very bad girl! Little One. ☐

☐ Dear Little One — You are not a bad girl. You are a precious innocent child. You didn't do anything to cause what happened. The man who hurt you was bad. He shouldn't have done what he did. You have every right to be angry at him. He can't hurt you anymore because you are with me now and I am strong enough to protect you. With God's help, I will never let anyone hurt you like that again. I love you. Always, Judy. ☐

September 9, 1994 — Jan says I shouldn't try to be a detective. I should just let the memories come. We don't have to convince anyone of the truth of my abuse. The feelings are real and proof of the fact that I was traumatized. Jan wants me to be whole. He wants to give me all the time that I need to let all the parts of myself present themselves for healing. He says we need to just allow all the memories to come up, no matter who it was who hurt me. I have to be first now. I can stop protecting the perpetrator now because I have to take care of myself and become one with myself and whole.

Jan says he takes all of this very seriously and I need to do the same. I need to recognize and accept the fact that I was a victim. I did NOT cause the abuse. Nothing I could have done could have justified what was done to me. I was an innocent child who was badly damaged by an evil man. I have a right to be angry. He hurt me and he stole from me. He stole my innocence. He stole my joy.

He stole my freedom to grow and thrive. He made me afraid for my whole life—afraid that someone would see that I was a bad girl and would get angry and hurt me again. He made me die inside. I HATE HIM!

Dear Little One — Once again you were very brave today. You were very honest. It is good for you to tell your story. You are afraid and angry and afraid to be angry. It's okay. Your anger is good because the one you are angry with is a very, very bad man. He had no right to hurt you. You didn't do anything wrong. You can scream and rant and rave and express all of your anger if you want to and Jan and I will be there and we will be proud of you. I love you, Little One. I know it has been hard for you. You've been hidden away in a dark room for forty years. Today you came out into the light. You were even able to look into the eyes of our good friend Jan. The whole world is not a dark and scary room. There are many kind people and there is much beauty in the world. It's time you got the chance to see it for yourself. I'll be with you. When the wind-chimes sing in the garden, we know the wind is blowing even though we can't see the wind. You can't see my love for you but you can feel it and know it's there. Let the song of the wind-chimes in the garden be a reminder to you of my love. Always, Judy.

September 11, 1994 — The singing time in church was a blessing this morning. I felt able to worship for the first time in a long time. I'm beginning to feel some peace about the future in terms of our ministry. God is in control and I know he has a plan more wonderful than we can even imagine. Listen to me! I'm actually sounding positive and optimistic! The antidepressants must finally be kicking in. I can't get too cocky since I woke up crying this morning.

September 12, 1994 — I just arrived at my little place of refuge by the sea. Ahhh! It feels good to be here. I don't know what the Lord has planned for my time. I'm content just to rest in Him right now. I'm in my favorite chair looking out at the dunes through the window, listening to the roar of the wind and the faint pulsing of the waves on the shore just over the hill. The wind blows fiercely as though it is angry at the tall grass on the dunes. Its determination and persistence remind me of that small but vital force within me that is determined to grow up, to conquer my fears and to become whole.

I need to remember to pace myself, to be gentle and compassionate toward the little ones within me who need time to build trust and skills, not to hurry them along. And I need to remember there is a difference now. When the pain was inflicted on that little girl so long ago, she didn't know she had Jesus to help her handle her physical and emotional pain. She didn't know Him when she was a child. She is just beginning to sense His presence and love now and that's going to make all the difference.

Lord, minister Your love to the Little One and all the other broken little girls within me. Draw all of me into Yourself. Cleanse me with Your tears of compassion. Jesus, I give You these days of retreat. Use them to accomplish Your will and purpose. I surrender all. Amen.

7:30 PM — Had a healing time of worship and prayer this past hour. I meditated on the image of Jesus as the Good Shepherd holding His little lost lamb. Little One understood and began to experience His love. She cried out her fears to Jesus, saying, "You be my Daddy now. You be my Mommy. Hold me. Hold me." Jesus cradled us both in His arms. In the strength of His love, I was able to take some of the Little One's sadness onto my adult self. I, as adult, could feel and carry some of that overwhelming sorrow the Little One has carried alone for so long. That, I believe, is progress toward healing and recovery. I wrote this poem called "Heart of Stone" today:

> He gives her a glare, a storm in his eyes.
> She looks up confused with so many why's.
> "What did I do?" her frightened heart cries.
>
> A twist of the arm, a thud of the door.
> The darkness enshrouds, can't see anymore.
> Can't breathe and can't scream, she's pinned to the floor.
>
> He rocks and he rocks, she doesn't know why.
> All that she knows is that she's gonna die.
> She can't fight or flee; she can't even try.
>
> He's suddenly gone; she's left all alone.
> A crumpled-up rag doll with heart now of stone.
> She buries her pain like a dog with a bone.

September 13, 1994 — It was a beautiful day and I got dressed and struck out for a walk on the beach first thing this morning. It was glorious. I reveled in the majesty of God in His creation. As soon as I returned to the cottage, my back went out. I shuffled next door to let Hannah know so she could check on me in case I laid down and couldn't get back up. It's happened before. I got into my nightgown and was preparing to lie down, when Hannah came to look in on me and pray for me. As I sat down on the bed and she sat down with me, rubbing my lower back, the Little One came forth and began to sob inconsolably. I was trying to tell Hannah what was happening but the Little One didn't know how to explain it in a way that made sense, so for a minute, it was me, the adult, trying to talk through the Little One. Somehow Hannah understood. She put her arms around us and held us tight and prayed for us for a very long time as the Little One cried and cried.

I've been in bed all day because when I sit or stand, the pain is excruciating. I think this was God's way of taking control out of my hands so He could be in charge this week. He has met me so deeply today. The Little One has had a major encounter with His love. At first, I felt trapped, thinking I had no choice but to stay in bed when I'd rather be doing something else. The Lord reminded me that I did, too, have a choice. I could get up and hobble around, a crippled person, causing more damage to myself and maybe even others, or I could submit to Him, lie down, rest and heal. Then He and I laughed together as I realized I've been feeling the same way about facing my anger and other feelings connected to the sexual abuse. I was feeling trapped, but the truth is I could always get up and hobble around, an emotionally-crippled person, causing more damage to myself and maybe even others, or... I choose to heal, no matter how bitter the medicine. It can't be worse than the pain I've lived with all my life.

Lord Jesus, stay close tonight. Especially watch over the Little One. She's afraid of the dark, You know. Thank You for all You have shown us today.

The Wicked Woman

September 14, 1994 — It's been a rough day. Though there have been times of joy in communion with the Lord, there have been times of anguish, too, as my own sexual depravity has paraded itself before my eyes. The part of me I call the Wicked Woman has been presenting all of my sexual sins to me from my teen years onward to the point when she disappeared from my life after I met Paul. I have been trying to lay them at the foot of the Cross, but not very successfully.

The Wicked Woman holds a lot of anger and hatred toward men. When she tells the story of my sexual experiences, she seems more angry than ashamed. Yet, she freely admits to being "bad"—the difference is, she's proud of her badness. It makes her feel powerful. She thinks I'm a wimp to feel guilty. Bad is good to her. Yet she also feels dirty and used by all the men she was ever with.

She thinks it's sickening when I make love with Paul and the intimacy makes me cry. She would never let a man affect her that way. She always faked it with men. I think I'm going to have to let her talk to Jan on Friday. That's really scary because I don't trust her at all. But she wants to talk and she isn't afraid to tell him the things I am afraid to say. They need to be said—confessed. After she tells, maybe I will be able to let them go. I hope so.

September 15, 1994 — This morning I was able to draw more emotions from the Little One and begin to carry them to the Cross of Jesus. She was able to speak to me with less fear and has given me a bit more information about the trauma. He was standing in the doorway and telling her to come into the room.

She said, "I don't wanna!" That's when he grabbed her arm and pulled her into the dark room. The door clicked shut. After a while everything went black. The next thing she knew, she was alone, lying on the floor just staring at the carpet.

She is telling me it was her Daddy who did it! I get flashes of the beginning of the memory where she looked at his face. The images resemble my father, but are still unclear. It is so hard for me to conceive that my father could do this to me. I believe that the Little One thinks it is her Daddy but I guess I'm still hoping it isn't true.

I'm also starting to get images of a very large penis above my face as I lay in bed. They flash in my mind and then they are gone. I wonder if I'm losing my mind. The Wicked Woman has been telling her story. She thinks of herself as "Marilyn" — as in Munroe. She is sexy in a superficial way, hard, angry and manipulative, and she doesn't seem to feel any guilt. She is a controller and a flirt. She wants to talk to Jan. I don't know. She is not very easy to control and her language is crude. I don't think Jan will like her very much. Yet I feel I need to let him see her and hear her story because we need to help her. She doesn't know Jesus and she is full of resentment. I have been trying to repent of the things she has done but it doesn't seem to be working. She has described an interesting phenomenon to me. I'll try to let her write about it herself. □

□ You see I'm out in this bar and I'm having a great time. I've got this man all wrapped around my little finger and he's buying me drinks and all and I'm dancing real sexy—just driving him crazy. Everything's just great. I'm in control.

So then we leave and go to his place or wherever and, this is the annoying part—he starts to kiss me and touch me and, all of a sudden the Body takes over. The Body is his slave. The Body will do anything this jerk wants! I hate it! But I get the last laugh in the end. Ha! I control the orgasm. I won't give him that. So when it's almost over, I go into my act—faking it. He doesn't get to see me really do that. Marilyn. □

I wondered if "the Body" was going to turn out to be another part of me like Marilyn, Judy Marie and the Little One. I was getting scared. It was finally dawning on me that I had multiple personalities. It was one thing to have little children inside that could be directly connected to the abuse, but I was now realizing how active Marilyn had been in my life prior to my marriage to Paul and my conversion to Christianity. All those things she had done, I could vaguely remember but never relate to—it was as if someone else had done them, and now I was realizing that was more or less true. I had been present but in the background while Marilyn had gone to bars and picked up men night after night. Thank God she had been basically underground and out-of-commission since I had married Paul.

☐ September 16, 1994 — I woke up at 6 AM and the voices in my head have been going ever since. Marilyn has been carrying on imaginary conversations with Jan all morning in preparation for her "coming out" this afternoon. She always has these talks with Jan in my head and only actually speaks directly to me every once in a while. I feel like my mind is disintegrating. I was terrified to go see Jan because I knew what was coming.

The first thing I did was to question him about our last session. I was only able to remember the first and last few minutes of the session. I know he was talking to me a lot in the middle, lots more than he usually does, but I can't remember anything he said. I seem to have been "gone" somewhere. It scared me to realize I lost time. Then I remembered it had happened before in therapy last spring when I was trying to access my anger. I lost a whole session then, too. When I lose control of the body, when the Little One or anyone else comes out, my sense of the passage of time isn't nearly as good as it normally is either.

Today, after I had shared about my retreat with Jan, I decided to try to let Marilyn read her writing from the journal. She gladly took control, read the stuff she had written, and took up all the rest of the time! At ten minutes before the hour, Jan said it was time to wrap up. That sent a shock through my system because I was totally unaware of time passing and I had to pull Marilyn back in and come back to Judy with no time to process what had happened before leaving! While I had watched, Marilyn had been telling all about her sexual escapades. Her language is coarse and she is hard and angry but she is really not as bad as she thinks she is. She did what she did for "the Lonely Little Girl" who wanted to have a Good Daddy.

She told Jan it was the Lonely Little Girl who wanted to go to the bars looking for a daddy, but once she was there, Marilyn had to take over to try to get the daddy for her. Unfortunately, the men were not good daddies according to Marilyn. They were mostly "jerks". Marilyn had good intentions in drawing me back toward abusive situations in that it was a form of self-therapy—trying to do it again but with different results, i.e. getting a good daddy. Unfortunately, it wasn't very effective because it didn't work out that way, so it was just a reenactment of the abuse.

Jan tried to engage her in dialogue but she wasn't very responsive. She just wanted to do all the talking, to have his attention. She was so different from me. So powerful. Jan must have been a bit surprised and overwhelmed by this turn of events. It must have been hard for him to listen to her language and the things she said, but he was patient, kind and understanding. He tried to explain to her that the body needs her and she needs the body, because she seems to hate the body so much. Jan said the body needs some of her power so it doesn't have to be a "slave" to any man who touches it, and Marilyn could benefit from the body by being able to feel and experience sensual pleasures even when she isn't in control.

I think it's important for Marilyn to develop empathy for the other parts (including me—she thinks I'm a wimp!). I'm going to try to see some things from her point of view. Maybe that will help her soften up. Actually, she was very helpful today. She helped me get ready when my hands were too shaky to put on my makeup and she explained some things to Jan that I didn't have the courage to say. She has an important function in the system and I appreciate her, but she scares me, too.

I was talking to Paul, trying to explain what is going on in my head. It's not easy. He started saying he didn't want to be in ministry alone and maybe if I was in such bad shape, we'd have to make some changes. I immediately panicked at the thought of leaving Holland and a little girl of about 5 years of age came forward in fearful tears to tell him how much he was scaring her and she needed to stay here or she'd never get better! Wow. I guess a picture is worth a thousand words. He saw what I was talking about. It must be a nightmare for him to see me disintegrating.

Lord, please keep me close to You as I work to unravel the knot of yarn in my head and heart. Guide me, guide Jan, and help Paul and Britt when I can't. They need an extra portion of Your tender care. Amen.

Parts of a Family

□ September 17, 1994 — I cannot believe that I have these split-off parts. It's just too crazy and besides, I can't believe that anything that awful happened to me when I was a kid, so how could I be so messed up? I don't know what's gotten into me but I need to straighten up and fly right! This is really ridiculous. So dramatic and, well, it just can't be. That's all. I really don't know why I've been acting this way but it really has to stop. In fact, I think the best thing would be to stop going to therapy since that seems to be the cause of the whole problem. □

By mid-September, I had become so depressed that I was beginning to abdicate control of the body to any part that was willing to take over. I was too tired and depressed to care. Formerly an extreme extravert, I still hadn't made contact with any of my friends in Holland whom I hadn't seen in ten weeks. I couldn't even shop or clean my house. My life was descending into chaos. The above journal entry was written in a handwriting I had never seen before. The diatribe of denial and judgement was interrupted by another journal entry made, I eventually realized, by the Good Mother.

□ Wait a minute, whoever you are! You're being completely unfair to the Little One and to Marilyn and everyone else who needs help from Jan, even if you don't! I know for a fact that the Little One and Marilyn are real and they both need some help. The Little One has so much pain and Marilyn has so much anger. They both deserve a chance to express themselves. Who are you anyway? Since you refuse to talk to me, I'll just call you "the Denyer" since you seem to want to deny that we have a problem here. Anyway, we promised Little One some time today. Little One, how are you feeling? ☐

☐ I am scared. I can't say why because he might hurt me or kill me. Is Jesus still here? ☐

☐ Little One — Of course, Jesus is still here. He's always here! Try to remember that He was there the day, the very moment, you were created. He will never leave and NO ONE will be allowed to kill you. You are precious. I love you. Jesus loves you. It's okay to be afraid, but when you are afraid, you don't need to be alone. Just call on those of us who care about you and we'll be right by your side. The Good Mother. ☐

☐ 7 PM — I feel like a war is going on inside of my mind. I don't seem to know who I am anymore. I don't know how much more of this I can stand. Am I psychotic? It is incredibly hard for me to believe that I am dissociative and that I have parts of myself that are separated from each other. They are even starting to write in my journal without my permission! The idea that a separate part of me who calls herself Marilyn could use up my therapy hour, talking about all the horrible things that I did twenty years ago as if they were yesterday, is incredible and frightening and I don't know what else. I don't want this exhaustion. I don't want to believe that I was abused. I'm experiencing severe self-doubts and there's a voice in my head saying if I just quit therapy, I'll be much better off. Like my father once said, "Why dig up the ashes from the past? ☐

☐ I've been reading a book called <u>Uncovering the Mystery of MPD</u> by Dr. Jim Friesen. The book is written to explain the disorder that used to be called Multiple Personality Disorder but is now being called, more accurately, Dissociative Identity Disorder. Dr. Friesen asks his DID clients to make a list of characters or roles. I'm going to do that here. Here's who we are so far that I know of: the Observer (that's me!); Little One; Judy Marie; Marilyn; the Good Mother; the Denyer (we don't know his real name yet); the Lonely Little Girl; Judy (she's the Host who used to be in the body most, but she is very depressed now); the Body (Marilyn talked about this but, well, I don't know if it's a part or just the physical body).

I'm the Observer and I'm the one who is watching what's happening most of the time so it makes sense for me to do a lot of the writing in the journal. I never identified myself openly like this before though. Mostly when I am "out" I have appeared to be Judy and I let people call me by that name. I try to be aware of things so that everything goes along pretty smoothly without too many glitches, keeping things in an agenda, stuff like that.

Little One carries all the feelings and body memories from the first trauma. He/she is only about two years old. He/she first came out in therapy on February 14th of this year but didn't share much then. Little One doesn't talk much but is getting stronger and braver and has been opening up. Judy Marie is a young child who is pretty healthy and likes to have fun. She was not contaminated by the trauma.

Marilyn says she came to be when Judy's first love abandoned her when she was 15. Marilyn hates men and "the Body" because the body is weak and powerless. She doesn't feel guilty about the sexual sins she has committed. Her age is around 18. She doesn't much care for weaker parts or anyone who feels guilty or is too sensitive, but she claims she did the things she did to try to help the Lonely Little Girl find a good daddy. She is quite willing to cooperate with others at least some of the time.

The Good Mother comes out to nurture and care for the children, especially the Little One. She also takes care of David and Britt, Judy's son and daughter, when they need tender loving care. She is gentle and extremely empathic. The Denyer tries to cast doubt on the reality of our separateness and the sexual abuse. He wants to quit therapy and doesn't want anyone to know what's going on.

The Lonely Little Girl is elementary school age, around ten, and is always looking for a good daddy. She comes out and seeks love and approval from Jan and from Paul. We don't know yet where she came from or when because she doesn't talk to the system. I'm not sure she's aware of us. Judy is the host and she is the one that handles most day-to-day operations, the mission work, being the wife, etc., unless very strong emotions, especially anger, are involved.

Marilyn talked about "the Body" as if it were a personality but I am not clear on that. Maybe she just means the physical body. Marilyn is not connected to body sensations most of the time. She claims to control the body's orgasms, but I'm not sure she's being honest. She is manipulative and would never want Jan to think she is frigid because that would not be "sexy". □

From this point on (as in the past), most journal entries were written either by Judy or the Observer or the two of them together. You may be able to distinguish their voices because the Observer presents mainly factual and rational data while Judy writes more on an emotional level. Since we were co-conscious most of the time I will not identify which is writing unless it is necessary for clarity or unless one or the other of us specifically identifies herself.

□ September 19, 1994 — Today the Lonely Little Girl came out to tell her story of the time she was raped when I was 21. Marilyn had gone out to a bar to look for a good daddy for the Lonely Little Girl. Her friends wanted to go home after a while, but Marilyn was having fun, flirting and dancing, so her friends arranged for someone they knew to give her a ride at closing time. At the end of the night, this "friend" came up to Marilyn and said he'd drive her home. Marilyn was tired and she'd had her fun and figured her job was done, so she shut down, and the Lonely Little Girl got into the car.

The guy said he needed to stop at his house for a minute to pick something up and told her to come in. The Lonely Little Girl, a very compliant child, did what she was told. He took her in the bedroom, pushed her down on the bed, pulled her pants down around her ankles and raped her. She went into shock, so when he was done, she just lay there without moving. He told her to get up, then pulled her to her feet, pulled up her pants and took her to the car. She sat there silently. When they got to her house, he said, "Get out of the car, bitch."

She never knew his name. He never even took off his jacket or hers. He didn't try to kiss her or engage her body. He had planned to rape her from the beginning and he did. I never thought of this incident again until this summer when Sandy asked me if I'd ever been raped and I answered, "Yes, but I was drunk so I deserved it, I guess."

He was very evil and took complete advantage and what he did was very, very wrong! It was *not* my fault. I did not deserve it!

I have felt it was my own fault—that *everything* was my own fault—for so many years. The truth is I did not deserve to be raped! I was a victim and I am becoming a survivor!

Dear Lonely Little Girl — We love you! You are not ever going to be alone again. You have a great family of people who care and want to help you and give you all the love and attention you need. We are proud of the way you have spoken up and told your stories recently, especially when you shared with Jan and later with Paul. You are very brave to tell your stories and it is good for you to tell them. The people who hurt you were bad and had no right to do what they did. It was not your fault. From now on, whenever you want to tell us something, we will listen and we will help you. In time, Jesus will bring healing to all your sadness. He will change your name from the Lonely Little Girl to the Beloved Child. Love, Judy and the family inside.

September 20, 1994 — The Lonely Little Girl just released some of her loneliness to me. Now I really know what it feels like to be lonely... It was so deep and painful, almost unbearable. She's been carrying that deep loneliness for so long and she has survived; I can't imagine how. I could only take such a small portion of it from her, but I will take more with time. Each time I will take it and lay it at the foot of the Cross. Jesus understands loneliness better than anyone.

Children, listen to me now. Jesus has the very best Daddy in the whole universe—Almighty God, the Father of all. Jesus had to leave His wonderful Daddy and come to the earth all alone so He could tell us that His Daddy wanted all of us to be His children! But before we could be His children, Jesus had to take all the bad things that had ever happened and all the bad things that were ever going to happen upon Himself and die for them.

He took the punishment for all the bad things that were done to the Little One and to the Lonely Little Girl and to all of us and he also took the punishment for any bad things ever done by any of us. Why did He do that? He loves us more than we can know. He wanted to make it possible for everyone to be forgiven and adopted into His family. He wanted us to become His brothers and sisters and children of the best Daddy of all. Since God is neither male nor female but incorporates both masculine and feminine traits, God is also the best Mommy of all, so if you need a Mommy and a Daddy, come to Jesus. He will hold you in His arms of love and carry you to His Father's lap. For you see, after Jesus died on the Cross for us, he rose again from the dead and now He lives forever and ever and He wants you to live forever, too, and never, ever be alone again.

September 21, 1994 — Woke up this morning at five. It was still dark out. There's another child in me. She's very afraid of the dark and doesn't like the early morning hours. Something inside is telling me this is a time of day when I was often molested by my father. As I lay in bed this morning "the Fearful One" was shaking and I had the urge to pull the covers up over my head, leaving only a slit for my nose and eyes like I used to when I was little. I was always terrified of the dark and went to sleep scared every night. Today the Fearful One reached over to Paul and curled up next to him saying, "I'm scared. I don't like the dark," in a whisper. She seemed to be afraid someone might hear her and know she was here.

September 22, 1994 — Just returned from a walk with Paul. He is really hurting right now. We got an E-mail from our leader in the mission this afternoon that was written in a very cold, businesslike way. What happened to our love? Our friendship? He was basically putting pressure on us to... ☐

☐ ...fish or cut bait. He is really being a jerk and I'm really angry at him for what he did and I would really like to tell him where to get off. He is such a jerk! I'm glad we are getting away from him because he is really very abusive and I'd like to make him suffer. Judy keeps saying we need to reconcile with him even if we're leaving but I don't see why. We should make him pay for what he's done. Judy says God will take care of justice but I say he kicked us in the teeth and we should kick him back! Judy doesn't feel any anger. She's afraid of anger but I'm not. Some Christian he is. I hate him! The Rebel. ☐

☐ 9:30 PM — That's the first we've heard from the Rebel. He seems to be a teenager and his job is to challenge authority figures. I sat down to record the facts about our ministry situation and he just forced his way out. Judy had just gone for a walk with Paul and was very calm and detached about the E-mail and the whole situation with the mission. I guess the Rebel really found that frustrating and just had to get his opinion out. He just told me he hates it when any of us just roll over and take abuse from people. He doesn't think we should take it and he sees it as his job to fight back and keep people, especially older or more powerful people, from taking advantage of any of us. When someone pushes, he pushes back. ☐

☐ September 23, 1994 — I'm sitting in the parking lot with forty minutes to kill before my appointment with Jan. On the way here a voice in my head was telling me to drive off the road into a tree and die. I don't know if it's an alter or a demon. It feels different somehow, like it's not connected to the body in the same way as the other alters are. I have heard this voice before many times in my life. It sometimes tells me to open my car door and jump out when we are on the freeway going 65 miles an hour. It's scary. At least one part of me thinks it's better for me to die than for the secrets to be revealed.

September 24, 1994 — I think the Rebel was created when I was around twelve. One night I "ran away" with an older girl; she had talked the Lonely Little Girl into the idea of going with her to a motel. When we got discovered a few hours later, my father came to pick me up. He was being very quiet which was scaring me and then we got in a car accident. No one was hurt, it was just a fender-bender, but Dad got out and started yelling at the teenage boys in the other car. We lived in a small town and these boys had already heard about the motel incident. They made some snide remarks about me and he got really mad. They were tough, smart-mouthed older teens around seventeen or eighteen years old. To my amazement, they weren't afraid of Dad. I was terrified of him. When I got home, my mother was screaming and yelling at me about what an ungrateful and selfish child I was. She threw a half-gallon of milk at me. I had walked in the door a very frightened, young girl, but now I have a feeling that somehow, that night, I identified with those older boys. I felt I was being judged, mistreated and unfairly accused. I decided "If they think that's what I'm like, I'll just be that way." And the Rebel was born.

The Rebel spoke with Jan yesterday. The first thing he said was, "I don't have to talk to you, ya know." But he did talk. He thinks most of us are too passive and that we need to listen to him more because he knows when someone is pushing and how to push back. His job was to keep people from hurting the little girls. He has lots of anger especially at authority figures.

September 25, 1994 — The Fearful One came out today and talked about how terrified she is of the dark. She told Jan she was so afraid, she couldn't get out of bed, even to go to the bathroom. She was afraid of monsters and ghosts in the closet and so many bad dreams. She would be awake when she wet her bed and later it would be cold. It's hard for me to take it in how terribly frightened I was. The Fearful One is around five or six years old. To be so terrified as to prefer to sleep in a cold, wet bed over taking a chance of getting up in the dark— that's fear. Soon I'm going to have to face the memories that explain that fear. I know there is much more to remember. The flashbacks and the body memories are telling me that.

Jan is trying to put the brakes on a bit. He doesn't want me to push things or hurry things. He says this is not something that is going to be over when I do some certain thing. It is going to take lots of time and I need to let it happen naturally as it comes.

September 28, 1994 — Had a bad headache this morning, which I now recognize as a warning that memories are coming to the surface. I began having a series of body memories that are telling me I was orally-raped as a little girl. A memory would suddenly wash over my body; I would start to shake; my pulse and heart rate would speed up and I felt like something was in my throat and causing me to gag and choke. The memory would last about a minute and then it would end only to start up again a few minutes later. It happened five or six times in a row until I finally made the connection to oral sex on a mind and emotional level. Once I accepted what I was experiencing and started to cry, the body memories stopped, at least for now.

I think there is a connection between the oral rapes and my endless battle with laryngitis as a young girl. I would go for months not being able to talk above a hoarse whisper. I know there's a connection between my back pain and the abuse. Every time I go to therapy, my back hurts worse. I'm beginning at last to feel some anger and disgust toward my father. I have always worshipped and adored him, always hungered for his love and approval. He never could have loved me and still done what he did to me. He stole my life! Forty years! I don't know if I ever want to see him or speak to him again. An e-mail came from him the other day and, even without reading it, I was filled with fear—as if he could read my mind and knew I was remembering and telling someone!

I need You, Lord. I need You! In a couple of days, I'm going to have to find a way to cope with three weeks of intensive Christian counselor training in England. I'm going to be away from home, Paul and Jan, and surrounded by people I don't know every minute of the day. I have hardly spoken to anyone this whole month, and so much is happening inside me, I can't imagine how I'm going to function in this situation. Please help me. You hold the key to my traumatic memories and You can keep them locked up while I am busy with this course and so far from home. You are the Lord of all.

Dear Little One — I love you and I want to let you have a voice whenever you have something to say. I want to help you carry your sadness. I want to help you let Jesus mend your broken heart. With love, Judy. □

□ I think I was not a very bad little girl. My Daddy was bad. He hurt me very very much! Jesus is my Daddy now. Jesus loves me and he will not hurt me or leave me all alone. Jesus will watch over me. He holds me when I cry. I am like the little lamb he holds in his arms. Little One. □

□ September 29, 1994 — A memory: I go into the bathroom in our house on Riverside Drive, lock the door, turn off the light, take off my clothes and sit naked on the window ledge looking down on the street below from the second floor. I am eleven. I both dread and desire for someone to see me.

September 30, 1994 — Jan says I was like a mermaid, trapped in a stormy sea, trying to find someone to rescue me. The concentrated symbolism of exposing the "naked truth"—telling the secret of my pain, anger and loneliness by sitting vulnerably naked in the window—was ingenious. It was the same kind of concentrated symbolism as the recurring nightmare about barrels falling on me and crushing me to death. The truth that I had so successfully dissociated from had to find expression somewhere, somehow.

You Will Be One

October 1, 1994 — I'm sinking deeper into the depression. I want to deny the oral rapes. To do that, I have to deny all the voices, all the pain, all the loneliness. In shutting out the voices, I am repeating the rejection and abuse, turning the anger inward and punishing myself and all my most vulnerable parts. For the sake of the "children" I must find a way to accept the horror.

October 2, 1994 — Paul has had to deal with different parts of me a lot recently, especially the children. Last night he said that he is "deeply in love with the articulate, intelligent, extraverted 42 -year-old woman" he has always loved. He is trying to understand what is happening with me and to flow with it but he believes the "parts" are a very small aspect of who I am, and that eventually they are going to go away. The sooner, the better, as far as he is concerned.

He is afraid of how I am going to change as I become integrated. So am I. I'm afraid he won't like *me* anymore and he's afraid I won't like *him*.

Today I was doodling in church and I drew a picture of a girl lying on a bed, blankets pulled up over her head (she looked like a mummy) staring into a dark closet that had a ghost coming out of it. Above the bed floated a blood-dripping dagger. There was a pool of blood on the floor under the bed, dripping from a wounded heart. Will I ever be able to see the face beneath the hood? Will I ever know the truth of his identity beyond a shadow of a doubt?

October 4 — The view from my window here at the Waverley Abbey House is truly breathtaking this morning. Brown rabbits scurry across the meadow to the safety of the shadow of giant sheltering trees. Frost covers the lush green lawn for the moment and a white mist rises from the still pond toward the softly rounded hills. The sky is a cool crystal blue yet holds the promise of a glowing warmth to come.

I've told my roommate Sue about the depression and feel I can be myself with her, at least. Last night we had our first class and I found myself in a "good student" mode; raising my hand to answer all the questions, trying to prove myself. I wanted to quit acting that way but I couldn't seem to stop it, a sign of my current discomfort.

9:30 PM — In classes, I'm okay, but between classes, I have the urge to hide. Part of me says I should be acting the "life of the party" and impressing everyone with my wit and cleverness, filling every gap in the conversations around the table, mixing and mingling—shades of the glittering image; but I just can't do it. I look around at the thirty people who are on the course and staying here with me. They all seem so "nice" and I realize there is no one here like me. I am alone.

October 5 — Had a dream. In my father's house were jars and jars of giant sour pickles. I took one and began eating it and I told him "If they were my pickles, I'd eat one every day." This represents my desire as a little girl for him to be mine, for his undivided attention and unconditional love, and my willingness to do anything to attain that — i.e. eat sour pickles. The symbolism is painfully obvious.

"Though my father and mother forsake me, the Lord will receive me." (Psalm 27:10) *Thank You, Jesus, that even when our own parents don't love us, when they turn their eyes away from us, even when they willfully betray us and hurt us, You are willing to receive us, to love us, to be our mother and father. We need only to seek Your face. I seek Your face now, Jesus. Amen.*

2 PM — Here amidst the desolate ruins of the ancient Cistercian Abbey a tree grows. Rising up from a pile of ancient broken stones that once supported a thick wall of protection is a stately and majestic evergreen tree. Her roots are

gnarled and twisted over and around the rocky rubble of the former wall. She had to reach long and hard for the sustenance of the earth beyond the wall, but she has grown strong and she has a certain dignity. She didn't lose hope. She didn't give up. Now those knots and twists support a mighty tree that reaches out with her strong arms to the world, embracing, sheltering, and gracing the world with her beauty. She loves and she is loved.

Father in heaven, the walls are coming crumbling and tumbling down. My fortress of self-protection stands in a rubble. You alone can sustain and nourish me. You alone can give me strong roots that I might grow and stand firm yet flexible, offering Your shelter to others and embracing others with Your love. Father, I pray, keep me reaching deep down into Your sustaining truth and grace that I might eventually reach out to a hurting world, a reflection of Your beauty. Amen.

Dear Little Children in my Soul — I just want to remind you all once again how very much you are loved. Did you know that God loves you just the way you are? He loves you so much that He sent His Son Jesus to die on the Cross so that it would be possible for you to become His children. He values each of you as much as He values Jesus! You are precious and beloved in His sight. You have purpose and significance, too, because you are made in the image of God and are designed to be a reflection of Him to the world.

And just as God is three beings in one, living in perfect harmony as Father, Son and Holy Spirit, one day soon all of us who live together in this one body will be united and living in harmony. When we become integrated, we will know each other and love each other so well, we will be made one as God is One and we will reflect Him.

All the children and Marilyn and the Rebel and everyone will grow and learn to love and understand each other so well that we will be of one mind and one heart, just as we are of one spirit and one body now. When we become united and whole, we will be able to more fully reflect the beauty of the Lord as we were meant to do. We will no longer need to have separate roles and identities to protect ourselves from pain, or from the truth.

God is our healer, the healer of our heart. He is our strong tower, our mighty fortress, our refuge in times of trouble. We can trust in Him.

It is very important that we learn to communicate together. I want each of us to share our stories as we feel ready. I want to hear what you have to tell and I promise to be open and accepting of all that you have to say, as best I can. I won't push you away anymore or deny your feelings. I will instead try to accept them and make them my own. I want to know the whole truth. I'm ready now to face our reality. It is only through telling the truth that each of us will regain our voices so that we can become one voice.

Remember, I love you and I have made a choice to love each and every one of you who are sharing this body with me. I won't love you perfectly and at times I may run from you, but God loves us all perfectly. He will draw me back to Himself and to you if I stray. We are all safe in His hands. Love, Judy.

October 7, 1994 — *"Streams of tears flow from my eyes for your law is not obeyed."* (Psalm 119:136) I've been looking back on my childhood in light of what I'm learning here at the Institute in Christian Counseling. The basic needs that every human being has for security, self-worth and significance can only be ultimately met by God, but our parents are meant to be His "executive council" until we are old enough to establish a personal relationship with Him. In sorrow, I realize my childhood provided none of those basic needs. My sense of betrayal at this realization was expressed as the Little One came forward to cry out Mommy and Daddy. Then together we called upon Jesus to be our Mommy and Daddy now.

Whenever I tap into those deep feelings connected to my early years, my first response is to dissociate by letting the alter who carried the feeling come forward to express it. I am starting to be able to take some of the feeling upon myself and hold it for awhile. One day soon, I hope to be able to feel the feeling without first resorting to dissociation.

"When you pass through the waters, I will be with you, and when you pass through the rivers, they will not sweep over you..." (Isaiah 43:2) *Father God, I do fear sometimes because I sense a raging river within my soul, a river full of dark and wicked things. I fear it will sweep me away. Yet I know that as long as that dark river is held back by the dam of fear and denial, the water in my soul will remain murky and foul. Father, I want to be washed clean with Your pure, living waters. I desire to do whatever it takes to release and purge the river of blackness I sense is just beneath the surface, that I might make room for a new river to flow—a river of love. Wash me in the river of Your love, oh Lord. Amen.*

October 12, 1994 — *"... that they may be one as we are one: I in them and you in me. May they be brought to complete unity to let the world know that you sent me and have loved them even as you have loved me."* (John 17: 22b & 23)

I'm going to get better! What a joyous hope to believe and have confidence in the truth that God is going to bring healing to my brokenness. As I read the scriptures above, I felt the Lord saying to me, "You will be one as I am one." I believe I am going to be integrated, that all my separate parts will be united to the glory of Jesus. May it be so!

October 16, 1994 — Thursday night I fell apart. As we worshipped together in the lounge here, I connected with just how desperately I need Jesus. As I saw the depth of my depravity, in the sense of my unwillingness to depend on God, I began to cry. I realized how terribly hard it is for me to trust anyone, even Jesus. My crying turned to sobbing and I tapped into horrible pain. I dissociated into a little girl and my roommate Sue put her arms around me and held me to her breast. I cried and cried through several songs. Sue asked me if I wanted to go upstairs to our room. I stumbled haltingly from the room and up two flights of stairs. I was barely able to walk the pain inside was so great. I knew I was regressed and I could hardly tell Sue what I was feeling but she just held me and prayed for me.

Eventually, I dropped out of the pain a bit and I was able to regain "executive control" over the body and to feel some of the pain as my adult self alone. I had never felt such deep pain for so long. The sense of betrayal, the grief, was truly agonizing. I could clearly see why, as a child, I had to run away from such pain through dissociation. The dissociation was a gift from God. A child could never have held that pain in conscious awareness. Even as an adult, I almost couldn't bear it.

The Rebel

October 17, 1994 — Talked to Paul on the phone tonight. He's really down. We sent in our letter of resignation to the mission and got an incredibly callous and uncaring letter in return. It is shocking that Christians could be so cold and hard. Paul and I are both having urges to fight back but we know we have to do what is right before God. Lord God, please give us the strength to be obedient and trusting. Give Paul Your comfort so he won't feel so lost and alone. Right now I am so upset I can't even write what I'm feeling. I feel I need to back away and keep the feelings in check... □

□ He did it again, huh? That jerk is pushing you around again! Push back! You can't let him get away with this. He's a jerk like I told you before and somebody ought to put him in his place! Why don't you let me call him. I'll tell him exactly how angry we are. We have every good reason to be angry at him. He doesn't give a sh— about us and he should be made to pay for the way he's treating us. □

□ October 18, 1994 — I'm exhausted after a long and emotionally demanding day. This afternoon I had an interview with Sally, one of the counselors here at the Institute. She herself has been sexually abused so I feel she can really understand my struggles.

I told Sally about the Rebel and how he comes out in my journal with all this anger. She asked me if the Rebel could bring the anger to the Lord, but the Rebel doesn't know the Lord! That's part of the problem. I want to help the Rebel get to know Jesus, but how? I don't feel he listens much to me. I don't feel very connected to him. I don't feel I know him very well. Maybe that's where I need to start, by getting to know him. I realize that I have to give the Rebel a voice. I need to let him express his anger and let off some of the pressure. If I don't, I will never be able to get him to listen to me so I can share Jesus with him. I have made the decision to invite him to come out and speak at my next session with Jan.

After my appointment with Sally, I had a time of peer interaction. I was discussing my anxiety about talking with my father and my inability to face my anger. Everything was going along fine until someone started to talk to me about God and spiritual things. The Rebel started to get angry and was saying (in my head) "Where was God when the little ones were being hurt?" He pushed forward to try to take executive control but I wouldn't let him speak because I knew the others wouldn't understand what was happening and it wasn't safe for me to start tapping into the anger. It was very hard to control. I think the Rebel knows I have decided to let him speak but he doesn't want to wait until we are with Jan. We have to wait. It's not safe here.

October 24, 1994 — The Rebel spent most of the session talking about how angry he is at the way the children were left so vulnerable and unprotected. He is angry with "the father" and "the mother." It's interesting that he refers to them that way, as if there is no connection, no bond at all, between him and them. He came to be, just as I thought, when the Lonely Little Girl was being yelled at and accused after the "motel" incident. He's not afraid of anger, or rejection and abandonment. He is tough enough to handle it.

He wants to make "the mother and the father" pay for their deeds. He sees the mother as spineless and inadequate but pitiable since "she is destroying herself anyway." The Rebel wants to stab the father in the name of justice because, he says, that's what the father did to the children—he stabbed them. I don't know what he means by that.

It is not difficult for me to agree with much of what he thinks and feels. He is not completely a nonbeliever. He talked a lot about God and his doubts about Him. He sees God as not having done His job to protect the children, but he seems open to hearing what Jan has to say about God. That's encouraging.

Dear Rebel — Thank you for coming out in therapy today to talk with Jan. You were honest about your doubts about the goodness of God. Given what you know about what happened to the children, your doubts are understandable and you make sense. It seemed God wasn't "doing His job" of protecting the Little One and other little children. I, too, have wondered where God was when my father was hurting me.

It has only been in recent days that God has shown me that He was always there with me. He was there and loving me on the very day that I was conceived.

He was there when my father first assaulted me, and I have seen Him bending down to touch me with His tenderness as I sat alone on the floor afterwards, when I was less than three years old. He cried with me every time I cried and He died for my pain and the horrible sin that caused it.

He was with me in the quiet, desperately lonely times when I sat in the woods or down by the river. He gave me places of refuge in nature, His creation, and as I look back I know I felt His presence in those places.

He gave me the gift to be able to dissociate, the perfect defense against the horrible pain of my childhood reality. All through those years, He protected and preserved my spirit and a tiny spark of hope, faith and love so that when I heard Him call to me, I had something left within me that could still respond to His call. He is a good God.

Why didn't He intervene and stop my father from hurting me? He could have, but He created men and women with free will so we have the power to choose to do good or evil. My father chose to do evil, but God intends to turn that evil around and draw something good out of it in my life. I believe when I am finished facing the evil, I will be empowered to help others overcome their own grief and pain in a way that would not have been possible otherwise.

Thank you for working hard to protect the children for so many years. Fortunately, the father can't hurt them anymore because he's far away. I am an adult now, too, so I can say "no" to people who try to push us to do things we don't choose to do. You can relax a bit these days. Sometimes people still do things that overstep my boundaries though, and I'm not too good at recognizing when this happens. I'd really like it if you would be my "early warning system" and help me be more aware of stuff like that. Let me know when you think anger would be an appropriate response because you're much better at anger than I am. Okay? Thanks! Judy.

October 29, 1994 — Even as I give the Rebel all my reasons for believing that God is good, I sometimes doubt it. I still wonder where He was. Why didn't He protect me from my father? Where was God when I was a tiny child and could barely reach the doorknob and I had to handle life all on my own? Where was He in my lonely times? In my fearful times? Does He really love me? How could God love someone like me, a girl who has sex with her father? A girl who wanted love so much, she would do *anything* for it?

Love never comes except with strings attached. Love only comes if you do what you're told without complaining, if you perform to a certain standard. In order to get love, you have to give up your self, your identity, your power. Maybe God will require me to give up myself and my identity so He can control me like my father did and even then He will hold back His approval and His love. I could never be good enough to earn God's love. I'm dirty and disgusting in His eyes. Even in my own eyes. God couldn't really love me, so how can I trust Him? I have had to face every abandonment, every betrayal, every trauma on my own up 'til now so why should I expect anything to be different in the future. □

□ God didn't do anything for the Little One or the Lonely Little Girl or the Fearful One. He let that guy rape the Lonely Little Girl. He didn't protect the kids. I had to do that. Why should we trust God? He seems pretty lame and powerless to me or else he just doesn't care. I don't trust him, that's for sure. Marilyn doesn't either. □

□ I think I can speak for myself, Rebel. Judy, I do think you are being a bit overly idealistic if you are relying on some male "God" to take care of you. Men cannot be trusted. They are all into power and all they think about and care about is sex and that's just the way of the world. Isn't it just typical that God would be a "father"—and you know what fathers do—they use and abuse. The only way to win is to get at them in their weakness. Men can be easily manipulated. Just use your feminine wiles. I don't know much about God, but if he's like other males, don't let him get in a position of power over you or you'll be sorry. Just keep the upper hand, stay in control. By the way, I'd like to come out and talk to that cute counselor of yours again. Now that we're all getting our chance to talk, I think it would be fun to flirt with him a bit. Last time I had to hurry and explain so much to him I didn't really get to enjoy his company and besides, I didn't get to say a proper good-bye. □

A Thief in the Night

□ October 31, 1994 — Jan is helping us learn how to go into the memories and come back out, to "take a peek" and retreat. This will help us to get the memories back without being overwhelmed. At first the Fearful One was just aware of being in her bed and being terribly scared. She was afraid of the "monster in the closet" but she couldn't bear to look at it. When Jan asked her to look for the monster's toes, she said she didn't want to, she wanted to "go away." Eventually, she saw the monster's hand, a man's big hand with flat nails, and a bathrobe sleeve. When Jan asked her where the other hand was, she couldn't tell him because it was between her legs, touching her. She didn't want to see this or know it and she definitely didn't want to tell this to Jan.

I feel so ashamed that I was so desperate for my father's love I was willing to do anything for it. I just wanted him to be mine, to love me, so much that I was willing to give up my soul. Jan says there is no shame in a child wanting her Daddy's love. I agree, but it's wrong to want it so much you'll do anything for it. He asked, "Could you forgive another little girl if she had done such a thing?" Yes. I could forgive someone else, but this is different—this is me! □

In spite of my own harshness toward myself, I was able to empathize with most of the other parts inside me. I came to believe it was important to avoid reinforcing negative self-images with negative labels. In the Bible we read that names are very significant and meaningful. God changed Abram to Abraham, Simon to Peter and Saul to Paul at transformational points in their spiritual lives. I wanted to give my family inside names that would recognize the truth of who they were becoming. So with their permission, I started calling the Rebel "the Guardian", I changed the Lonely Little Girl to "the Beloved Child" (never to be left alone again) and the Fearful One to "the Little Lamb" (held safe in the Good Shepherd's arms). Since I was not able to get permission from the Denyer (he refused to engage in dialogue) I changed his name anyway, to "the Gatekeeper", because I perceived him as having some kind of awareness of and control over the memories. This was a misunderstanding, but I was correct that he was very aware of all the memories, and his motivation was to keep them all locked up.

The flashbacks and memories were beginning to be more clear and detailed, especially since the Little Lamb came forward. I began to see my father beside my bed masturbating himself and fondling me. I was appalled and ashamed to realize I responded to this memory with both horror and sexual arousal. Victims of sexual abuse often have to face this kind of confusion in which terrible fear and repulsion become fused with sexual responses. The body is designed to respond to physical stimulation and it doesn't discriminate. I felt sick with guilt for feeling any kind of pleasure at all in what my father had done. I began to sink deeper into depression as an escape from feelings of rage, grief and shame. The pictures had become all too clear. There was no more denying the reality of the incest or who the perpetrator was. I had seen the face of my father.

November 2, 1994 — All I do when I am "out" is feel depressed and cry. What good am I to anyone? I'm the one who's bonded to Paul and the kids and I'm the one whose job it is to be the wife and do the chores, etc. None of the others seem interested in prioritizing the family's needs. I just hope I can find some medication that works. My life has been chaos since July. I need to start functioning better.

Lord Jesus, the only times I really feel any peace are the times when I rest in Your arms. Hold me, Lord, all of me, in the warmth of Your tender embrace. I need You. We all need You. Lord, I especially ask for Your touch for the Little Lamb. Comfort her and help her to know You are with her and have always been with her. When she wakes up afraid in the darkness of the early morning hours, help her to feel Your presence. Penetrate the darkness with Your light. Penetrate her fear with Your love. Penetrate the pain with Your comfort and grace. Be our Abba Father. Amen.

November 4, 1994 — Today I mourned for the loss of innocence, the child pure and wholesome, that was stolen by my father—a thief in the night. I told Jan about the terrible mixture of arousal and terror that was the result of my father's perverted "loving." I confessed the disgusting fantasies I've had all my life about monsters raping me, public degradation and having sex with Satan and how those fantasies made me feel I was crazy, sick, evil, a bad seed. Jan said the fantasies were another attempt to work through the trauma without actually remembering it.

My father perverted my understanding of love. He taught my body to be aroused when my heart felt terror. I am so angry when I think about how he touched me and how he made me want him to touch me. He awakened me sexually when I was only five years old. I wasn't ready. I couldn't understand. I was so mixed up and confused. He made my body betray me until I came to hate my own body.

It is good that I am beginning to get angry—to verbalize some of the anger against my father. After the anger came a terrible sadness, sorrow for the poor little girl and all that was stolen from her. *I want my innocence back! Can I ever get it back! I want to be the innocent, curious, joyful little girl with all the potential You created me to have! I guess it's too late for that, huh, God.*

1:00 AM — After that prayer I sank into the pain and sobbed out my grief. It is so unfair! My childhood innocence was stolen from me by my father, the one who was meant to be protecting me. Finally I crawled under the quilt with my teddy bears and rested for an hour before going to evening worship. During the service the Lord spoke to me, showing me it's not just the little children inside that need to know Him as Father, as Daddy. He wants to father me, too. He wants me to know Him as Father and He wants to give me all the love I longed for and never had. He wants to restore me and redeem me. He was telling me it's not too late for me. He is going to heal me in a way that will restore the lost potential of my stolen childhood. He's going to be with me as I walk through this tomb containing all the dry and broken bones of my life and He is going to breathe new life where once there was only death and decay. My spirit was moved and my heart was open but then we started to sing a song called "Father, Father Me" and I just fell apart. I had to leave the chapel, to get up and walk out in front of everyone, but I couldn't stay.

Chapter 3 — Hands in the Darkness

The Shadow of Death

November 7, 1994 — I dreamed I was looking for a bathroom. I needed to get rid of something awful and disgusting that was inside of me. I went down and down into the bowels of this giant building. At the end of the stairs, I was still high above the floor. I had to climb down a metal contraption like a fire-escape ladder. When I got almost to the floor of this giant boiler room, a man told me there was no bathroom around. I tried to climb back up but I couldn't! In the end, I found what I was looking for, but the place itself was foul and disgusting and there was no place for me to get rid of my own toxic waste. I had come all that way for nothing and there was no way to return to the upper levels. I had come to the sewer and I was stuck in the sewer!

When I woke up, I told Paul, "I wish I could just go and be with Jesus in heaven now!" I told him about the dream and he just held me and said he would always be right by my side so I'd always be able to find my way back.

I couldn't get out of bed. I fell back to sleep and dreamed again. This time, I had a baby with me—my beloved baby. I was in the process of going insane and I was desperately looking for someone to help me. I was travelling the world with this tiny baby. I flew to a place where someone was supposed to help me. My baby was so hungry. We had traveled for hours and hours and I had only brought a small baby bottle of milk for her. She was crying and trying to nurse from me but I didn't have anything in my breast for her. She was starving. I wanted to feed her but I couldn't! Finally I found some grape juice and gave it to her from a cup but she didn't know how to drink from a cup. I tried to feed her solid food but she wasn't old enough to handle it without choking and gagging and getting sick. But anything was better than starving! I was becoming less and less able to meet her needs. Then some men came and took her away from me. They took my baby away from me! I cried and screamed, "I want my baby back! I want my baby back!" But I couldn't get her back. When I woke up, I wanted to die. What happens to Christians who commit suicide? Does God forgive them? Does He let them into heaven? What happens? I want to know.

Midnight — I just remembered that at the beginning of the first dream, I had planned to go somewhere but when I got there I discovered I had the wrong tickets for the wrong day. I was in the wrong place at the wrong time. I made a mistake. I realize now I have always felt if you make a mistake, you're bad and deserve to be punished. Guilt and shame were the two dominant emotions of both dreams and were the stuff I "needed to get rid of" but couldn't. They have ruled my life for forty years as I have believed that what happened to me—what my father did to me—was my fault; that I was somehow to blame.

November 8 — What he did to me was wrong! I did not deserve it! It wasn't my fault! He is the one who is to blame. He is the one who made the choice for evil, not me! I was an innocent child who was hungry for love—starving for it. He took advantage of my hunger to satisfy his own needs. I am not a bad, shameful, naughty, disgusting, dirty little girl! If I accepted his touching, even if I responded to it, I didn't ask for it. I didn't even understand it. I was starving for touch, for affection, for attention. I took what I could get.

I am cleansed by the blood of Jesus—made pure and white as an unblemished lamb. When the Father in heaven looks down at me, at the Little One, the Little Lamb and the Beloved Child, we are holy in His sight because Jesus died for us. Jesus loves the little children and He loves me and Marilyn and the Guardian, the Observer, the Good Mother and even the Gatekeeper. He loves us all.

"[S]he who dwells in the shelter of the Most High will rest in the shadow of the Almighty. I will say of the Lord, 'He is my refuge and my fortress, my God, in whom I trust.' Surely he will save you from the fowler's snare and from the deadly pestilence. He will cover you with his feathers, and under his wings you will find refuge; his faithfulness will be your shield and rampart. You will not fear the terror of night, nor the arrow that flies by day, nor the pestilence that stalks in the darkness, nor the plague that destroys at midday...

'Because you love me,' says the Lord, 'I will rescue you; I will protect you, for you acknowledge my name. You will call upon me, and I will answer you; I will be with you in times of trouble, I will deliver you and honor you. With long life will I satisfy you and show you my salvation.'" (Psalm 91:1-6, 14-16)

November 9, 1994 — Slept very little last night. Fantasizing about taking the sleeping pills, going to sleep and never waking up again.

November 11, 1994 — I told Jan I wanted to kill myself. He helped me to see that I still have a deep-seated wish for my father to be a good daddy. I wish none of the things I'm remembering were true. The anger and shame that belongs to my father I am turning against myself in order to preserve the possibility of having the kind of father I always wanted. That's why I want to kill myself— especially since a voice in my head is telling me I am making up all this awful stuff about Dad. Jan says there's "not a chance" that I'm making everything up. He says the memories may not be entirely accurate and may change or become clearer over time, but there is truth in what I am remembering. He tells me as I am able to let go of my wish for my father to be a good daddy it will make room for others, like Paul and God, to fill that place that I have reserved for my father.

I am in deep, deep mourning for the death of the good daddy. That's why I cry so much and sometimes turn against myself.

Jan says I am much stronger than I think I am. He said it took a lot of strength for me to come into his office in all my weakness and despair and not just shift gears and "switch" into someone stronger or sexier or more objective. He doesn't know how close I came to asking Marilyn to handle things today, but I didn't. I stayed in therapy the whole time. Jan gave me permission to come in with all my pain and tears. He accepts them and doesn't require me to perform up to a certain standard. He seems to believe in my future and my ability to make it through this valley of the shadow of death.

Father God, I pray with all my heart that I will hold onto the work You have already done in me and not look back. Guard my heart and strengthen me to stand firmly in my position in Christ as one of Your children. Help me learn to trust completely in You as I continue to face the issues of my past. Teach me to look to You to be my Abba Father, my Good Daddy. Amen.

November 15, 1994 — This morning the Little Lamb came out to share more of her story with me. She went into a memory of the "monster" coming out of the closet wearing a bathrobe and his hairy hand was holding something. He made her touch "it" and it felt "yucky". She cried and cried saying, "I didn't want to do it! I really, really, really didn't want to do it!" I called her to come out of the memory and reminded her that she was the Little Lamb in the arms of Jesus, saying, "Just lean into His loving arms. You're going to be okay now. You are safe now. You don't have to carry your fear alone anymore." □

□ Dear Little Lamb — I'm so proud of you for telling more of your story. You're a very brave and courageous girl. I know it scares you to remember but don't forget, it is not really happening to you now, it's only a memory. It will never happen to you again. We won't let anyone hurt you, and Jesus will be with you and holding you close in His arms when you're remembering. Each time you tell the story, the fear and pain will grow smaller. Soon it will be all gone and you will be a joyful little girl just like Judy Marie. That's what we want for you, Little Lamb. We love you! The Good Mother for the whole family. □

□ November 16, 1994 — I think the medicine is beginning to work. I've had two nights in a row of good sleep. That's the first time since July! I have begun to laugh again. Thank You, Jesus, for being my Shepherd through the valley of the shadow of death. □

Talking Together

☐ November 20, 1994 — Okay. I want to try to put into writing a strategy which I discussed today with the "system". I am concerned about uncontaminated or decontaminated child alters becoming contaminated by other alters' memories and abreactions. Here's what I'm suggesting we do. Whenever anyone is ready to tell what they remember, I'd like to send the other children to a safe place. They could all go to the meadow of wildflowers where Jesus is always waiting. The Guardian is not so sure Jesus can do His job of protecting the children so he can go, too, and keep an eye on things.

I'd like the Good Mother and Judy to stay co-conscious with whoever is going to share their story. The Good Mother can be ready to give love, empathy and nurture to the one who is sharing as needed. It's important for Judy, as the core personality, to stay conscious so she can know what's happening and can try to take some of the feelings onto herself. She needs the practice of feeling the feelings.

I told the Gatekeeper that while it may have been his job to keep the memories locked up and the voices quiet, now he should let the memories and voices speak at appropriate times. That's the best way he can help the system now. I'm not sure if he agrees because he still won't dialogue with any of us. He just constantly says "Shut up!" and "Grow up!" and other imperatives like that, and tries to insist that the incest is not real and neither are we! I hope he will cooperate just the same.

We talked to Jan about the imagery of Jesus as the Good Shepherd holding the lamb in His arms. We told him we are using this imagery to frame the memories by starting in the arms of Jesus, moving into the memory and back out into the arms of Jesus again. He tried it with us right away and it really helped the Beloved Child handle the memory work with less pain.

Jan asked us about letting Judy comment on things when one of us is in executive control. That made Judy feel anxious because switching is very draining and uses a lot of energy. It also made Judy think of multiples she has seen on TV that are switching every other sentence. We all think that is gross and "creepy" and we don't want to be like that. Judy talked to Jan about it. He said he didn't want her to switch in when someone else was talking. He was suggesting an internal dialogue. We think that could work. Internal dialogue is happening now but all of us need to learn to communicate better. — Observer. ☐

☐ November 21, 1994 — I showed Jan my picture I drew of my family. When he was looking at it I started to cry cuz my family is not a happy family. I told him how I felt so alone and like I wasn't even real, like I was invisible! He noticed that everyone had a special person and everyone had someone to touch them except me. He asked me if there was anyone inside who could hold me and comfort me and I told him about the Good Mother. Except she doesn't have real arms. She can only think-touch me. I told Jan I wish he could touch me! He said he could hold my hand and he did! He held my hand in both of his hands for the longest time. I just cried and cried. — Beloved Child. ☐

☐ The loneliness is so deep. So overwhelming. I don't know how I lived. Even if nothing else had ever happened to me, just the loneliness was unbearable. Thank you, Jan, for taking the risk of reaching out and taking my hand. Thank you for telling me I am not invisible, that I am real and that you care enough to touch me in a safe and loving way.

November 22, 1994 — Twice today I made contact with the loneliness of the Beloved Child. There's an ache in my gut that runs so deep and so wide I can only stand to feel it for a brief minute or two without dissociating and shutting it down. ☐

☐ Dear Beloved Child — You know that I spent a lot of time trying to find a good daddy for you and it's true, a lot of my attempts didn't work out exactly as hoped for. But I think I did pretty good with this Paul guy. He's stuck around for a lot of years and taken pretty good care of all of us. He's not perfect but he's better than any of the others that we brought home back in the old days.

And I've been checkin' out this Jan guy and he's a pretty good guy, too. He could be the good daddy you need. He's really pretty mellow and, well, he even held your hand like a good daddy does. Yeah, he's okay. Cute, too! But I guess I have to pass on flirting with him because it might mess things up and I know it makes you nervous 'cause you think he'll get mad. I don't think he'll get mad. So don't worry. If he does get mad, I know how to sweet talk him so he gets over it. Don't you worry your pretty little head. — Marilyn. ☐

☐ November 23, 1994 — My daddy was a very bad man and he hurt me so much. But I'm better now and I don't feel so alone cuz Jesus is with me always now and he is my daddy and he won't hurt me. — Little One. ☐

☐ That's right, Little One, Jesus will never hurt you and he will love you and take care of you forever. Have you ever met Judy Marie? She is another child inside. She is a few years older than you and she knows you and wants to be your friend. Maybe she will write you a letter in our journal. — The Good Mother. ☐

☐ Dear Little One, You can be my friend. I like you very much. I am 7 years old. I like to play and go for walks and I love to fly a kite. What do you like to do? Love, Judy Marie. ☐

69

☐ November 27, 1994 — All the hurting children came out to cry as we lay down to try to get rid of a headache that doesn't seem to be responding to medication. (It may be because we had to stop taking the Imiprimine two days ago since it gave us high blood pressure. Just when we found an antidepressant that seemed to be working!) The tears first started when the Beloved Child came out remembering about a man she had hoped was going to be her good daddy. Marilyn had found him in a bar and left him with the Beloved Child at his house. He took her into the bedroom, pulled her over in front of his wardrobe mirrors and raped her on the floor while he watched himself. When Marilyn had described this incident to Jan she had used the words "screw the whore" and the Beloved Child heard her say that (nearly two months ago!). Today she started crying about it and asking Marilyn why she said that. She kept saying, "I didn't wanna do it! Really. I didn't wanna do it! I'm not a whore..." But inside, she felt like a whore, full of guilt and shame. As she cried, Marilyn and the Good Mother tried to comfort her. Marilyn said she knew the Beloved Child didn't want what had happened and apologized for saying such a harsh thing.

After a while the Little Lamb came out to say she didn't want to do it either, but she was talking about what the father had done to her. She is carrying a lot of guilt and shame, too. Even the Little One came out and cried and sucked her thumb and remembered how she had said "I don't wanna!" when the father had told her to come into the dark room.

The whole system was flooded with pain, guilt and shame. After close to an hour of sobbing, the worship music, which had been playing throughout, penetrated through the pain and the children gradually settled into the arms of the Good Shepherd. Then we fell asleep for awhile. The headache continues with no relief and so does the pain within, it is almost unbearable for Judy and the children when there is no antidepressant in the system. We've tried four different ones so far. Hope the next one works. We really need the medication. ☐

☐ November 28, 1994 — Just came from Jan. I was talking about how the bad guys seem to win and the good guys lose, and I started feeling angry at God for sitting back and letting bad people get away with hurting and abusing others. As I started to talk about this I got frightened by my anger and dissociated. The Little Lamb came out and said she better not talk about it because if she even talks about it, something bad will happen to her. Then she started to say how she really didn't want to do "it"—she really didn't want to but she wanted him to see her, to hold her, to be her daddy. She feels so guilty and dirty because of what he did to her and what she did to him. She kept looking at her right hand saying, "He made me dirty!" She cried and cried.

Jan said, "It wasn't your fault. I know you didn't want to do it and your daddy knew that, too." But she said she didn't know if her daddy knew it because, though she didn't want to do "it", she wanted him to be her daddy.

Oh, the shame and guilt she/we have carried for so many years! Her words "I really didn't want to do it" reverberate throughout the whole system and my whole history. Each of the hurt little children cries out, "No! I don't wanna!"

God, I need You! I need You so much! Please help me untangle the terrible confusion in my life and in the lives of all my inner children! Amen. □

□ Dear Little Lamb — No one is going to punish you for telling, or talking about what was done to you. We all know that you did not want to do what you were made to do. It was not your fault. Not at all. We all feel so bad and sad about what was done to you. You are not to blame. You survived and we are proud of you. You wanted your daddy to love you. That is not wrong. He was wrong to do what he did. Every little girl wants her daddy's love. Your daddy knew you didn't want him to touch you in sexual ways. He knew that, even if you didn't tell him with words. He was a grown-up man and every grown-up knows that little girls don't want anyone to do what he did. He was a very bad man, but you are not a bad girl. Not at all. Try to hold onto that idea, Little Lamb. You are not dirty. Jesus loves you and He made you white as snow. No dirtiness at all on His Little Lamb! Just rest in His arms, dear heart. Love, The Good Mother. □

□ November 30, 1994 — *"At the time the disciples came to him and asked, 'Who is the greatest in the Kingdom of heaven?'*

He called a little child and had him stand among them. And he said, "I tell you the truth, unless you change and become like little children, you will never enter the Kingdom of heaven.

And whoever welcomes a little child like this in my name welcomes me. But if anyone causes one of these little ones who believe in me to sin, it would be better for him to have a large millstone hung around his neck and to be drowned in the depths of the sea.

Woe to the world because of the things that cause people to sin! Such things must come, but woe to the man through whom they come!... See that you do not look down on one of these little ones. For I tell you that their angels in heaven always see the face of my Father in heaven... In the same way your Father in heaven is not willing that any of these little ones should be lost.'" (Matthew 18:1-7, 10, 11, 14)

"Do not be afraid. You will not suffer shame. Do not fear disgrace; you will not be humiliated. You will forget the shame of your youth." (Isaiah 54:4)

"Instead of their shame, my people will receive a double portion, instead of disgrace, they will rejoice in their inheritance... and everlasting joy will be theirs." (Isaiah 61:7)

"At that time I will deal with all who oppressed you; I will rescue the lame and gather those who have been scattered. I will give them praise and honor in every land where they were put to shame." (Zephaniah 3:19)

God loves the little ones inside of me! He is angry with the ones who hurt them and shamed them. He will turn our shame into praise and then He will inhabit that praise! Praise be to God!

December 2, 1994 — Today in my session with Jan, I found it very difficult to stay "associated" with my deep feelings of loneliness and sorrow. I told Jan how healing it had been for the Beloved Child when he had held her hand. It was the first time in her life that she didn't feel worthless and invisible and is the only really happy memory she has. It was really hard for me to admit to Jan that I wanted him to hold my hand, too. I was sure he would reject me and say no. I pushed through my fear to ask him if I had to be a little girl in order for him to hold my hand. I said I knew I could become a little girl and get to hold his hand but that would be a form of manipulation and not what I really wanted. I didn't want to take something from him, I wanted him to give something to me, not one of the children inside.

Jan wanted to know what holding hands would mean for me. I have so much pain and so many feelings right now and holding his hand would help me to bear the pain. He asked how I would feel about the fact that the handholding would have to end after a limited time. He was very carefully checking out expectations and setting boundaries. I said, "The normal way with feelings is that they come on, they build up, then they either recede or resolve. I'm not asking to hold your hand forever." Then I got discouraged and told him I didn't want to talk about it anymore. Talking about it seemed like a form of answer.

"Does it seem like a no?" he asked. I nodded my head.

"Is that right?"

"I don't know but it feels like it to me," I answered, feeling ashamed.

Then he said he wanted to hold my hand, he just wanted to be sure there were clear boundaries, understandings and expectations. I reached out and he took my hand in both of his hands. That's when I started to cry.

As he held my hand, communicating his acceptance and compassion to me, I drew strength from him—strength to look at the truth of my history in all its devastating pathos. My father abused me. The songs that he sang, the stories he told, the images of love he chose to occasionally project on the empty screen of my lonely childhood were all lies, lies he devised for his own pleasure as he enjoyed basking in my worship of him. He could never have loved me. He loved only himself.

As Jan held my hand tightly between his own hands, I talked of the times my father made me rub him with that same hand, of how the Little Lamb looks at her hand and says "He made me dirty!" I cried out for the first time my feeling that I

72

should have said "No!"—I should have somehow stopped him! Jan said no, that I couldn't have, that I did well just to survive without getting severely hurt or killed under the circumstances. I felt so dirty, so ashamed, so sad, so alone, but Jan was there, holding my hand, understanding, helping me to see things as they really were and go on.

Hold Me Like a Baby, Daddy

December 3, 1994 — "The greatest thing you'll ever learn is just to love — and be loved in return." That's the final line to a song my father used to sing to us at bedtime. "To love — and be loved in return" is something he never learned. He didn't know how to love, only how to use and destroy, and now, four decades later, he is still unable to sustain a relationship. Divorced four times now, a man in his mid-sixties with hair extensions down his back and a red Corvette, I used to feel sorry for him. Now I feel hatred. His selfish lust has cost me so much. □

□ Why did Marilyn say that I was a whore? He seemed like a very nice man. It seemed like he could be my daddy. He was wearing a nice dark suit and a white shirt just like my daddy used to wear. He took me in the bedroom and he took off my clothes. I thought he was going to make me lay down on the bed with him but instead he took me over in front of the big mirrors. He pushed me down on the floor and then he watched himself. Why did Marilyn call me a whore? I didn't want him to do that to me! I didn't like it. I'm not a whore! I'm not a whore! I didn't know what to do. I let him do that but I didn't want him to! Marilyn, please don't say that anymore! — Beloved Child. □

□ December 5, 1994 — I wish I could erase all the ugliness and scars. I long so much to go back, to start all over again, with healthy, loving parents. I want to regain my lost innocence, to live a life without guilt and shame, to grow up being loved. I feel so tainted, so ugly, so dirty, so hopelessly irredeemable. I was used up and tossed away like a filthy rag first by my own father, and then so many others. I sometimes think even my own children think I'm worthless. Jan must be getting tired of my unhappy whining and crying by now and I really don't think even Paul can stand much more of my miserable presence. Paul and the kids would be much better off if I wasn't around anymore and besides, this pain is unbearable. It would be so nice just to fall asleep and never have to wake up. If I took the pills and quickly destroyed the package they were in—I could burn it up—everyone would just think I had a heart attack. That way Paul and the kids wouldn't have to carry any false guilt about my death. Right now, this seems like the best solution. □

☐ I talked to Jan today. I was really scared and nervous. I was waiting in the outside room to go in and I started to think maybe Jan only *seemed* like a nice man, too. Maybe he would hurt me, too. Then when he opened the door, it made me jump because it scared me so much.

Jan said it was probably not a good idea for me to keep hoping that someone would hold me like a baby when I am in a grown-up woman's body. He said men would not understand the kind of holding I'm asking for and they would want to have sex with me.

Jan says the reason I don't say no and stop someone from doing sex is because I still want them to touch me and hold me. I want them to stop and I don't want them to stop so I just don't do anything. I freeze. Jan says Marilyn was trying to do something good by acting sexy with men. She was trying to gain control over something we don't have a lot of control over by overpowering the men and trying to use them before they could use her. Something like that. Marilyn likes to play a certain kind of game but it can be very dangerous. I think that is what happened. Marilyn was playing a certain kind of game, but I was the one who got hurt. This wasn't the only time this happened either.

Marilyn, I know you were trying to find me a good daddy. But please don't play those dangerous games anymore ever again, okay? Remember the bad men who raped me? I think they thought I was you. But now I understand that you didn't say I was a whore. So I am not mad at you anymore. I hope you're not mad at me, are you? Love, Beloved Child. ☐

☐ No. I'm not mad at you. You're only a kid and I don't expect you to be able to see things clearly. I know you're just an innocent kid. I can see how my sexy games have sometimes ended up hurting you and I'm really sorry 'bout that. That was not my intention, but I will be more careful. I haven't played those games in years anyway (not since Judy married Paul) and I don't think they're very effective because even I ended up being frustrated by them. So don't worry. It won't happen again. — Marilyn. ☐

☐ December 6, 1994 — I am thinking of trying to fuse the Little One and Judy Marie. I am concerned that both Judy Marie and the Little One are being somewhat neglected as therapy progresses. The focus is very much on the Beloved Child and the Little Lamb right now. My thinking is that if the Little One and Judy Marie were joined together in fusion into "Little Judy Marie", that would be a good blend. Both are pretty healthy and both have a relationship with Jesus. They would just be stronger together. I am not exactly sure how to facilitate a fusion but these are the steps I am proposing: Ask the Little One and Judy Marie if they want to be joined together as one. Schedule a day and time and ask all the alters to be cooperative and supportive. Ask the Christians inside to pray for a good fusion. Have a time of worship and meditation on Jesus as the Good Shepherd before fusion.

Here's how I envision the fusion ceremony itself: the Good Mother would stand beside Judy Marie (to give prayer support and encouragement) and both would stand in front of Jesus in the meadow which is the spiritual core of our being. Jesus would lift up and hand the Little One to Judy Marie who would pull her into herself as fusion takes place. Then the Good Mother and those of us who are Christians inside can gather around the newly formed Little Judy Marie and pray for her while she is lifted up into the arms of Jesus to rest and, perhaps, sleep for awhile.

This is my proposal. I am open to suggestions if anyone wants to add any ideas. Let's spend some time thinking and praying about this and talk more about it later. — Observer. □

□ December 7, 1994 — I feel so happy! Today we all gathered around to witness the joining together of the Little One and Judy Marie into a new union— Little Judy Marie. They were both excited to become one. Judy Marie reached out as Jesus handed her the Little One and pulled her into herself and they melted together. Afterwards everyone was full of peace and joy. We are all praying for an easy time of integration for Little Judy Marie as she adjusts to the blending of memories, experiences and sensations, etc. We are all hoping the fusion is successful because we know that we ourselves will one day be joining together in the same way. — The Good Mother. □

□ Well, it's going to be interesting to see how Little Judy Marie feels after she wakes up. I expect there will be some confusion and a bit of disorientation as the two parts come together. After all, one was less than three years old and the other was about seven. And while Judy Marie was completely free of trauma, the Little One carried the first remembered trauma of the father's assault. So Little Judy Marie should be a healthy, happy, secure little girl who also happens to have one particularly unhappy memory. I hope everything goes well. It's the first time we've done something like this but it was a good plan, and with the Lord's help, it should be a positive step forward for the whole system. One of the positive effects it has already had is today was a cooperative effort and we all worked together for a common goal. That is excellent! — Observer. □

□ December 8, 1994 — Another bad dream night, only this time it feels like a memory again. I dreamed I was a little girl, maybe five or six. I wanted to stop the incest, wanted to tell someone. Daddy came to me in the night. He said I couldn't tell anyone because no one would believe me because it isn't true. Then he started to touch me with his hands and his mouth, first on my neck, then my chest, then down my belly and beyond. He was saying, "Look what you made me do. You made me do this. You are such a naughty girl to make me do this to you. You like it, don't you. Only naughty girls like this. You better not tell anyone! Everyone will know how naughty you are if you tell. You made me do this."

All the time he was saying this, he was touching me and putting his mouth on me. I was trying to cry out to make him stop. Finally in the dream I managed to bark out the words, "Help me!" I don't know if I actually shouted them out loud or just in my head but it woke me from the dream. When I awoke, I was sexually aroused. How can the idea of being abused by my father elicit such a response! Gross. The man has really screwed up my mind and my body. Rage is stirring within me.

December 9, 1994 — I feel a deep sense of longing when I go more than a few days without seeing Jan. I don't know if this dependency is normal under the circumstances or not. It seems pretty appropriate in some ways because the "kids" are like orphans. They need to be re-parented and, thanks to my depression, I'm not capable of doing that right now, not to mention that I myself need re-parenting! I never had a role model for how to parent. Jan seems to be the only person who can fill the substitute daddy role for now.

December 12, 1994 — I told Jan about the dream. The guilt I feel connected to my need for my father is sometimes more than I can bear. Little Lamb and I both feel somehow to blame and my father obviously fed that guilt. Jan says it's good that I'm having these dreams and talking about them because they will help us untangle all the confusion of feelings I have carried for so long. The compact compression of feelings like guilt, fear, anger, shame, longing and sexual desire is a result of my experiences as a child. Addressing how this entanglement took place and unpacking the feelings, from a bit of a distance, will bring healing, but it is hard for me to get distance from the feelings without dissociating. I worked really hard today to stay with them but I slipped back and forth, in and out of touch, and switched a couple of times. Still I am aware of having felt deep guilt and shame and violent anger. I stayed with the anger, which was focused on my desire to kill my father, but I felt dizzy and extremely frightened at the same time that I felt strong and powerful. It seems I never have one, simple, straightforward feeling anymore. All is much more complicated now. I'm so tired.

December 13, 1994 — Last night I wrote a letter to my father. I haven't sent it yet because I want to share it with Jan and see what he thinks. I really want to end the "No-Talk" rule, to break out of the stranglehold of secrecy. I want to confront my father and let him know that I know what he did. I want him to admit his wrongdoing so I can stop doubting myself, but what if he denies everything (like the vast majority of perpetrators do)? How will I feel then? What if he tells all my brothers and sisters that I falsely accused him? How will I feel then? Am I prepared to risk losing him completely? Yes. Am I prepared to risk losing the whole family? I don't know.

December 15, 1994 — What is my motivation? My hope? I don't want to go on pretending nothing has happened, relating to Dad as I have in the past, as if I have no memories of incest. That's a relationship built on lies and I can no longer live with that. I feel I must break the silence and bring the secret out in the open between us. That is the only hope for us.

What I want, of course, is for him to admit what he did, be truly sorry and repentant, and offer to make amends. It seems like a pipe dream and it probably is, but miracles do happen! I must be crazy! He's a sociopath. What he wants is for his kids to worship him. I won't worship him anymore. No, never again. Good-bye, Dad.

December 16, 1994 — The Little Lamb came out and she was really scared. She was afraid she would be in trouble if she talked about the abuse. She told Jan she was afraid maybe he only looked like a nice man but maybe he was really a bad man. She said everyone said she should talk about things but she was afraid because "somebody" could get real mad at her. She said when that happened, sometimes she would get punished.

Jan asked her what she would do to make herself feel better after she was punished. She told him she would hide under the covers with all her stuffed animals., and she very guiltily admitted she would suck her thumb, "but that wasn't allowed." She's not supposed to do that. Then she said that God would be mad at her.

Jan said God was not very concerned about whether she sucked her thumb or not. He told her God sent His Son not only to solve the problem of whatever she did wrong, but also whatever wrong was done to her. He wants her to be His child if that's what she wants. She said, "You mean, God could be my Daddy?"

Jan said, "He is your Daddy and you are His child, if you want that. You just need to tell Him that you want that."

"I want that," she said, nodding her head. Jan then told her she could rest in the arms of Jesus and He would hold her. She closed her eyes and went back inside.

☐ Dear Little Lamb — We are all very proud of you. You are very brave. You will slowly learn to recognize that then was then and now is now, like today, when Jan asked you if your daddy was coming now with the belt to punish you. You were feeling very scared and for a moment, you thought he was coming, but when you really thought about it, you knew he wasn't coming. He can't come to the office where we go to see Jan, can he? That was then and this is now. You did really well today. Love, The Good Mother, Judy and the rest of the gang. ☐

77

□ It is very scary to talk even if Jan is a nice man. He seems so nice. I like it when he looks in my eyes. One time he held my hand. I want to talk more to him because I like him very much. But I get scared cuz I think he might get mad at me. If he gets mad at me I am in big trouble. It is hard to tell him about all the bad things what happened in the night. They are very bad and my Daddy told me I made him do them. He said I am a very bad girl. He said if I tell I am in BIG TROUBLE! I'm scared. But today I knew that my Daddy doesn't know I am with Jan. He can't find me there so he can't hit me with his belt! I think I am safe with Jan. I like his smile. He is very gentle. He says God isn't mad at me cuz I suck my thumb. He says God can be my Daddy but I rather have Jan. I want Jan to hold my hand cuz he is a real person. I hope God isn't mad with me cuz I want Jan to be my Daddy. Good night, Little Lamb.

December 18, 1994 — I remembered my daddy doing that bad thing to me. I didn't want him to do it! I didn't like it. It hurt me and made me so I couldn't talk. The yucky stuff was in my mouth. I wanted to spit it out but you're not allowed to spit. I think Paul was very sad that I was scared and crying. He is a very good man. He told me Jan is also a very good man. I hope I can talk to Jan tomorrow cuz I want to tell him some things but he FORGOT to save a time for me to come see him tomorrow! How could he forget? What if he FORGETS us again! Maybe he really doesn't love us. I feel scared when I think about that. Love, Little Lamb.

December 19, 1994 — I told Jan how I remembered my Daddy would make it so I couldn't breathe and I was choking cuz I was too little and it was too big and something would break in my throat and I couldn't talk for a long time. Jan said my Daddy was a very, very bad man and he did those things to me but it's not my fault. Even if I didn't want my daddy to hold me and look into my eyes, Jan says my daddy would have hurt me anyway. I was scared to talk about things cuz the feelings are so awful. I don't want them. I was scared to be in big trouble by my daddy, too, but Jan says my daddy can't hurt me anymore. I hope he is right. I told him I don't want God to be my daddy cuz God is invisible. I want a real daddy, but not a bad daddy, not one that does bad things to me. I was scared to tell him I want him to be my daddy. I think he is trying to tell me that I can never have a good daddy. That is so unfair. Love, Little Lamb. □

□ *Jesus, You gave up all of Your infinite power and came to earth as the child of a poor teenage girl. You identified with human helplessness in a fallen world. You know how it feels to be powerless before an abuser. You endured the crown of thorns, the nakedness, the nails and the Cross — forsaken even by Your Father in heaven — as the weight of all the world's sin rested on Your shoulders.*

You understand my sense of powerlessness, my helplessness, when as a little girl my father chose evil. His choice to do evil took away my choice. I was powerless to stop his abuse. You didn't use Your supernatural power to stop my father, but You gave me the gift of dissociation. You found a way to preserve the spark of Your life in me until I was strong enough and deep enough in love with You to be able to face these truths that had been hidden. Thank You, Father God, perfect in power and love, for understanding so completely my pain and my powerlessness, for knowing how it feels to be a victim of the most unfair treatment. You are the God of all comfort because you do understand. Help me to always remember Your suffering when I'm tempted to say I suffered alone.

Vengeance and Forgiveness

December 22, 1994 — After all that I have realized and all this time, still the Guardian is the only part of me that is really in touch with anger and able to express it. He came into being when I was twelve. Where is all the anger I must have felt when I was younger? Are there angry child alters still in hiding It is strange that, with all the emotions I have been discovering—betrayal, abandonment, rejection, guilt, shame, loneliness and grief—anger still has such a low profile. Where is the anger? I hope if there are child alters inside who are full of rage, they will see that it is safe to come out and share their feelings with Jan and with the rest of us.

December 23, 1994 — I told Jan I feel like I have opened a door for the anger to come out. I'm standing in front of the door saying "C'mon!" but at the same time, I'm terrified and ready to run away. Then I said, "You can't possibly know what it was like, how awful it was, how lost I felt. He was so big and strong and I was so small and helpless. Where was my mother? Busy. Always so busy taking care of the babies, while life just became noisier, more chaotic, more out of control!

I want my father to feel what I felt. I want him to be powerless, to know how it feels to have no control, no way out, to be terrified, hurt and abandoned. No horrible thing that I could do to him would ever be enough to make him feel what I felt—to make him pay the same price I paid. The letter seems like such an impotent response. I want him to pay for what he did to me... what he stole from me... I hate him! I hate him!"

December 30, 1994 — Mom called. She is getting a bit nervous now that the word is spreading and quite a few of my siblings know about the incest. She said my older brother Charles knows now and his attitude is "that was 40 years ago" and he needs his relationship with Dad. That's fine. I don't expect anyone to choose between me and Dad, but I am angry because Mom said my brother

79

hopes I can handle things by forgiving and just avoid any kind of confrontation. He doesn't know what he's talking about. He doesn't know the meaning of forgiveness. Only one who has been deeply betrayed and hurt can really understand what it means to forgive. Yes, I'm willing to forgive! That is my choice and is not contingent on anything Dad does or doesn't do, but forgiveness is not the same as reconciliation and relationship. No! I'm not going to pretend it never happened! Dad needs to be confronted as much as I need to confront him. If we are going to have any relationship, it is going to be based on truth, not lies. I am not called to forgive and pretend! I am not called to forgive and forget! I am only called to forgive.

December 31, 1994 — It's New Year's Eve. Paul left for California this morning to be by his father's hospital bedside. He is dying of cancer. I'm back up at my little seaside nest for a week of retreat. The first thing I did today was take a walk on the beach. Big, fluffy clouds sailed in the blue sky and the wind played with the scattered kites and the scarves of children, all bundled up against the cold sea air. As for me, I started to remember just how big my God really is. I am amazed at how people can walk along the shore, watch the seabirds dance with the wind, hear the crashing surf against the sand and view the endless expanse of rolling silver and white and not realize how incredibly awesome is our God. I'm blown completely away every time I experience it all again.

Later the Beloved Child expressed her deepest longing for a good daddy and the terrible loneliness she carries. It is almost too much for us to bear. We double over, curl up in a ball, clutching our stomach where the pain seems to be physically located. Only Jesus could possibly heal this kind of wound. □

□ *Dear Jesus — I want you to be my daddy. You are the only really good daddy who can really make me better. I have a very big hole in my heart because my daddy didn't love me. He didn't need me anymore so he threw me away. When he did that I hurt so bad I had to go away in my mind. I wasn't big enough to feel such awful pain. It was too big and I was too little. So I just kept on pretending that there really was a good daddy and if I tried hard enough, I would find him and he would love me and hold me and never, ever leave me alone again. Now I see that there will never be a good daddy like that. Is it okay if I still need to sometimes get a hug from Paul or if Jan can hold my hand? Sometimes I just really need real arms and real hands to hold. I hope it is okay with you. I love you, Jesus. Love, The Beloved Child.* □

□ What is Forgiving?

> Forgive us our trespasses as we forgive
> those who trespass against us.

He commands forgiveness because He forgave,
And because I love Him,
I desire to obey.
But what is forgiving?

Forgiving is not forgetting.
Forgiving is not pretending.
Pushing the pain under a rug
like some small residue of dust —
a mere inconvenience,
forgiving is not.

Forgiving is not relationship.
Forgiving is not restoration.
Forgiving is not living a lie —
acting as if it never happened,
forgiving is not.

What is forgiving?
Forgiving is a choice I make.
It doesn't depend on you
or what you choose to do.
I choose to forgive for me —
not for you.
Forgiving is letting go.
Forgiving is letting God!
An easy way out?
Forgiving is not.

Cries from the Pit

☐ January 1, 1995 — This morning I was thinking that I want to tell Jan that I want him to be my daddy. I was thinking that he will tell me he already has children. I got really mad cuz I don want to hear about other children, especially babies! He has a new baby girl. I know about that but I don like it! I would tell him not to say that cuz I want him to be my daddy only!

But then the Good Mother told me to look at myself, my body. She said even though I am a little girl I am inside a grown-up body. Little girls in grown-up bodies can't really get new daddies. It is terribly sad. I cried and cried cuz I really really need a daddy but now I saw I can't get one.

So then I cried to Jesus cuz I want him to be my daddy but I was afraid. I am so dirty and bad and naughty. He knows about all the terrible things I did what were even worse than sucking my thumb and wetting my bed. He knows about all the naughty things I did with my daddy. I thought he wouldn't want such a dirty, bad child like me. But he did. He washed away all the dirt. He took me and held me. I need him so much! He is the only one who can really be my daddy even tho I am in a grown-up body. He doesn't care about that. He knows about all the bad things but he still loves me and he can see that I am just a little girl even tho I don look like one. Jesus is my daddy now. I think he is going to make me all better. The awful feeling in my tummy I think he can fix it.

Dear Jesus — Thank you for being my new daddy. Please help me to be good. And please help me with the awful feeling in my tummy. I need you very very much. Love, Little Lamb. □

□ *Both the Little Lamb and the Beloved Child have professed their faith in You, Jesus, and asked You to be their daddy. As we worship You today, it is as if we are a full choir of voices inside. What deep joy to be able to sense our unity in You! I look forward to the day when all the parts are united under Your Lordship. We shall be one—that is the promise You have given to us. May it be soon, Father God. Amen.* □

That evening a fusion ceremony took place and the Little Lamb and the Beloved Child were joined together to become "the Beloved Lamb".

□ 8 PM — The fusion appears to have gone well. At the moment of blending I got a little nervous because the Beloved Lamb burst into tears and doubled over in pain, but the Good Mother soothed and comforted her and Jesus held her in His arms. He spoke to her, telling her she was His little lamb, His child, beloved in His sight. He said He had made her white as snow. She said, "I'm not dirty anymore?" and cried happy tears. At last she fell asleep.

The Guardian said he hadn't been too sure the kids could handle it, but he felt it went pretty well. He said maybe he'd like to fuse with someone one of these days. He admitted to getting pretty lonely at times and he figured fusion was kind of like getting married.

I asked him what he was thinking about God these days because he used to be pretty mad at Him. He now thinks God is probably a pretty good guy because he sees how much happier the children are since they got to know Jesus. I think he also understands that God has always been there protecting the children in His own way—just like the Guardian has.

When I asked him if he would like to have a relationship with God, to be friends with Him, he said he might but he'd have to think about it. He was afraid God might tell him he couldn't be angry anymore, but I told him that God understands anger. He even feels anger when something sinful is done. I said the anger that the Guardian has is very important to the whole system and I don't think God would make him get rid of it.

Then I asked Marilyn how she felt about the fusion. She felt it was going to be good but she was wondering what her role is going to be now that the children are all looking to Jesus to be their daddy. Marilyn is going through an identity crisis. I think it would be good for her to talk to Jan at our next session.

I talked to her a little about Jesus, too. She thinks it looks like He will be a good daddy for the kids. She is open to having a relationship with Him but she is afraid it will cramp her style. I think we all need to get to know Marilyn better— to understand what her strengths are and how she can function now that the system is changing so much.

The Good Mother was very happy over the fusion. She is a tremendous optimist and a woman of faith. She is confident that we did the right thing. She is really anticipating and praying for complete unity and oneness for the whole system.

Little Judy Marie was glad about the fusion, too, because she wants all the children to be one and she knows this is a step in that direction. We have gone from eleven alters down to nine and there's now a lot of overlap of experience, awareness and memories between me, Judy and the Good Mother. I think things are progressing quite well. □

□ January 3, 1995 — I'm sad because now I know even more bad things that happened than I did before but Jesus is my daddy now. He is the best daddy cuz he owns everything in the whole world. He even made everything like the sun and the ocean. I'm glad he is my daddy now. He is going to help me get better so I can laugh and sing just like Little Judy Marie. — Beloved Lamb. □

□ *Lord, You have been showing me that I have been looking many places for my identity. I have looked to Paul, to Jan, to my mother, to my father and to my children to tell me who I am when I need to be looking to You. I have been bent over toward all these idols when I need to be standing straight and reaching upward with open arms to receive Your affirmation and healing. I can find my true identity in You and You alone. Lord, help me to break free of the lie that anyone other than You can fill that great pit of emptiness in me.*

January 5, 1995 — A deep sadness has descended over me like a low cloud for most of this week of retreat. A fog has enshrouded me, making it difficult for me to see what direction to turn. I know the Lord is with me and is doing His work in me, but most of the time it's hard for me to feel His presence or see His face. *Lord, may Your light pierce this darkness in my soul. I need You, Lord. Right now I feel so lost and alone. Penetrate my cold heart with Your love. Let me worship You.*

January 6, 1995 — Once again, God shows me His faithfulness and love. He listens. He knows. He cares. This morning I have been meditating on His goodness and all the things I can praise Him for — a loving husband, my children and grandchild, kittens, snow, a quiet place of retreat, a comfortable home, being able to sing, to write poetry and lyrics, to know His love and share it with others! He is worthy of our praise!

The Lord inhabits the praises of His people. We want Him to inhabit us more, so we are going to praise Him more. ☐

☐ *Dear Jesus — Thank you for dying on the cross so that I don't have to be punished for the bad things I did. I know now that you are not angry with me for the things my daddy made me do. You don't want to punish me. You just want to love me and hold me and let me cry when it hurts so bad inside. Please help me, Jesus. I love you so much. I want to do what you say. I want to trust you. But sometimes I get scared and I forget that you love me. Help me remember, okay? — Beloved Lamb.* ☐

☐ January 8, 1995 — Somehow in the midst of deep pain, the Lord continues to sustain me. Paul called from California this morning. He's really worried about me and I can't give him much of an argument against the worry. When I allow the pain to come to the surface, I feel suicidal again. I promised Paul I wouldn't try to kill myself while he is gone.

God, I need. I need. I need! The hole in my gut is like a giant Pit of Longing in the floor of this tomb I'm living in. Will there ever be enough time, enough faith, enough love, enough anything to fill this aching hole?

January 9, 1995 — My plan to let someone else do the talking today failed. Nobody on the inside would bail me out. Someone even convinced Little Judy Marie to stay in and I know she was dying to talk to Jan, to show him the shells she collected for him. As hard as I tried to back away and let anyone else have executive control, there were no takers. Eventually, I had no choice.

I talked. Ever so fearfully, I cracked the door on my feelings of loss, grief, loneliness and insignificance. I even allowed some anger to surface, directed at Jan because he was trying to help me gain perspective, to step outside of the feelings just enough to see that things really are better now than they were a year ago. I argued with him and challenged him to make me see things in a better light because I feel my life is in a shambles.

Behind the anger came the next big surprise—horrible, overpowering feelings of unworthiness. That's when I tapped into the part of me that wants desperately to die. The despair of absolute insignificance and invisibility, that sinking feeling that scares me so much, showed itself in all its humiliating force.

I was curled up on the couch in the fetal position saying, "If I close my eyes, nobody can see me," and "I want to die... I want to die..."

These feelings do not come from the external circumstances of my present experience. They are memories. They rise from the very depth of my shattered soul. They have been silent but deadly for four decades. Now at last they are coming out into the light of day. There is hope, at least. Jesus can heal their ugly scars now in His time, if only I have the faith to stay alive until His work is done.

January 10, 1995 — In the middle of a night of nightmares, one stood out as especially repugnant. I dreamed I was lying beside my father and he started trying to fondle my breasts and body. I was disgusted and repulsed and kept pushing him away but in the end he raped me. This has to be just a dream—it can't be a memory! *Help me, Lord.* □

□ January 13, 1995 — I got to talk to Jan for a very long time cuz I had lots of important things to talk about today! I really like to talk to him. I told him I wanted to talk to him last time but everybody said Judy needed to talk to him so none of us was allowed to say one word. But I wasn't mad. I was only sad but it's okay now. He still had the jar full of shells and I showed them to him. I poured them all out on the floor and he looked at every one. I especially liked the shiny brown one with the funny shape and that was his favorite, too! I told him to keep it safe just for him and he could share the rest with his children. Then I told him that the Little Lamb was very angry about those other children and she don want to hear about them. But I told Jan finally Little Lamb let Jesus be her daddy and so did the Beloved Child. And now they are together and her name is Beloved Lamb. I liked to tell him that story cuz it has a happy ending and it made both of us feel happy. I showed Jan the other pictures some of us made, too. Some are not very happy and I didn't like to look at them but I told Jan when I can look at them and know what the sad pictures mean, then I am growing up so I can join with the Beloved Lamb. I want that! So I am trying to understand about what the Beloved Lamb remembers. I know it now but I don't know the feelings. I'm so happy I could talk to Jan today. He is so nice! — Love, Little Judy Marie. □

□ After Little Judy Marie went inside, I came out and found myself sitting on the floor. I got up where I belonged and talked to Jan about idolatry. Now that all the "kids" have accepted Christ as their daddy, I have had to come face-to-face with the truth that I still want Jan to be my, I don't know, special forever friend, a friend who would always be there, not some temporary arrangement for a fee. I feel so bereft, so empty. I have had to let go of so many things. I can't stand the thought of one day letting go of Jan. Yet I know it is only going to be possible for the Lord to fill my emptiness inside when I stop looking elsewhere for the filling.

God help me to obey Your call to allegiance. Help me once-and-for-all to declare my dependence on You and You alone. Right now it is so hard to imagine my life without Jan. Lord, I need You. I need You!

January 15, 1995 — For me, to be needy is to be afraid. I seem to hate myself for needing anyone. I blame my own neediness for what happened to me as a child. It seems I think it's my fault Dad abused me because if I had been stronger and less needy, he couldn't have done what he did. In my life today, this is all replayed in relationships. When I feel my deep need for Paul I get scared. I think if I need him too much, he will hurt me or desert me. When I feel my deep need for Jan, I have the same fears and I also feel ashamed.

It is painful to feel and acknowledge the terrible longing I have to balance the relationship with Jan; I want him to be so much more than my therapist or, as he so rationally pointed out, my "employee". I want to know him beyond his therapist role, to be a real part of his life, for him to want the relationship to go beyond the hard, professional boundaries it exists within now. Yet, I know it's the very distance in the relationship that creates the safety I need in order to open myself as I have. An expectation of permanence would create a lot of danger and get in the way of the process, of my journey to healing.

When I look into the blackness of the pit, that hole in my heart where the longing lives, I feel so hopeless. It seems impossible that the hole, the need for love and self-worth and significance, could ever be filled up. Can it, Lord? Can You fill it up with Your love if I can learn to trust You? I don't know.

Growls from the Cave

11 PM — I think Dad knows that I know what he did to me. He is highly intuitive. He has noticed that I have stopped addressing him directly in my family E-mail letters. He knows that I am severely depressed. We have had no contact since I left the States six months ago. I think he may be feeling scared or even a little guilty. Anyway, I don't think my letter of confrontation is going to come as a big surprise to him.

I need to get past my anger. It's festering beneath the surface and blocking me from being able to move on toward emotional forgiveness. I need to bring the rage out of the darkness into the light so Jesus can bring healing. I think at least some of this work needs to be done before I can send the letter confronting Dad with the incest.

January 17, 1995 — I called Paul in California to tell him I'm not doing so well, how crazy I'm feeling, how reckless. I'm planning to send the letter to Dad soon and I am finding myself wanting to push all my brothers and sisters away before they can reject me first. I'm suddenly so angry. I really don't want to send this calm reasonable letter to my Dad. I want to scream and yell and pound him with my fists and tell him I hate him and I want to kill him! My equilibrium is shot. My sanity, even my spirituality, is slipping away. While I was talking to Paul, the Beloved Lamb started to cry and tell him she needed him to come home. I need him but his Mom and Dad need him more right now. But I am falling apart. We are out of control. We are in danger! Things aren't working very well. We want him to come home to hold us and protect us from ourselves. ☐

☐ What's the matter? Scared of a little anger? What's the big deal. I'm glad we sent those nasty E-mails, especially the one to the father. He deserves it. He's the #1 jerk in the world and someone should stand up to him. It's about time! What can he do to us anyway? He's 3000 miles away. He's a wimp anyway. He's only tough when he's up against five-year-old little girls. Why don't you let me talk to him. I've wanted to tell him off for a long time. I could think of a few choice words... Guardian. ☐

☐ I wish we wouldn't have sent those bad E-mails to everybody in the whole family, even to the Daddy! We told them we think they are stupid and selfish and stuff! Now I'm really scared! We could be in big trouble and Paul is not here and its three more days before we can talk to Jan! I feel very nervous now. I feel we are in danger and there is no one to protect us! Why did anyone do something like that? I'm scared. Don't send any more bad letters, okay? It's probably already too late. I wish Paul could come home or we could go see Jan. I think we are in big trouble now.
Dear Jesus — Please don't let anyone get mad at us. It wasn't my idea to send the bad letters or say the bad words either! Are you mad at me? I'm sorry. I should have made them stop! But I couldn't! I'm sorry. I really didn't want to do it. Really. Will you forgive me? — Beloved Lamb. ☐

☐ January 19, 1995 — Paul's Dad died and Paul needs me in California. I'll be on a plane tomorrow. I felt I needed to write an apology to my family for my bad behavior so I sent this E-mail:

"Dear family — I feel I owe all of you a debt of repentance for the really ugly E-mails I have sent out recently. There is absolutely no excuse for the childish temper-tantrums I threw and I want to ask all of you to forgive me. For anyone who took the messages personally, I especially ask you for forgiveness for the pain that must have caused you. I was rude and hurtful. I can offer no excuses. It was just wrong. I'm sorry. Love, Judy."

But it wasn't really from Judy, it was from me. — The Good Mother. ☐

☐ January 20 — My father called me to tell me he "forgives" me. He said he had a feeling I was mad at him because I didn't send him a Christmas card and I didn't thank him for the Christmas check he sent me. I was all over myself trying to make him feel better! It's hopeless. I'll never have the guts to send the letter to him. I'm just as powerless as I was when I was five.

When I realize that I start to get angry, angry with myself for being so weak and needy of his approval and angry at him for everything he did that created this helplessness in me. Tomorrow I want Jan to help me send the children who are frightened by anger to a safe place in my mind. Then I want him to help me access the Cave of Anger within me and somehow really go into it and express it in some safe way. I just need to get rid of some of the pressure so the anger won't surge out in uncontrollable and irresponsible ways. Oh, but it's such a big, dark, scary cave where the anger lives!

January 21, 1995 — Today I asked Jan to consider giving me one-and-a-half-hour sessions instead of one-hour sessions. I always feel I don't have enough time. He pointed out that this feeling is rooted in my childhood deprivation. He's right, but I also know I have held back from addressing certain issues, like anger, because I'm terrified that, like Humpty-Dumpty, I'll fall to pieces and I won't have time to collect all the pieces back before our time is up. I gave him all my good logical reasons for the change. He said he would consider it and we'd talk next time about it.

Jan said I'm not there yet in terms of being able to integrate anger. He said I should try to pinpoint the anger and make it more clear and exact rather than visualizing bloody revenge scenes and homicidal fantasies. I need to try to clarify exactly where the anger is coming from, who it is against, and specifically why, what, etc. But it's dark in that cave! I don't want to go in there alone!

In the end, I talked about my father's phone call—the one where he said I'm forgiven! I got so mad, I threw my journal with a slam onto the floor! I was angry with Dad, but I was more angry at me, disgusted really. Again Jan just said I'm not there yet. I need to give myself the time I need and not rush into confrontation. It's the same old story—pacing, pacing, pacing. I'm not good at that. I've always felt like I was being chased. I'm beginning to be aware of the tremendous pressure I put on myself and how that can backfire on me.

Lord, help me to trust You and Your timing for the journey. Help me not to either rush things, leaving unresolved gaps, or to drag things out unnecessarily. Help me to simply trust You with the pacing and follow Your lead. Amen.

January 25, 1995 — I'm in California. It's been so good to see Paul again at last! To be held in his arms and under his protection and love, but I've had several headaches in recent days and my eyes are acting up again. I wonder if new memories or another alter will be surfacing soon. I'm recognizing the headaches and the vision problems as warning signals now. Something is going wrong inside of me and has been going wrong for a couple of weeks. I had disturbing dreams all night long. I woke up tense, anxious and depressed. When Paul tried to hold and kiss me, the Beloved Lamb came out scared and sad and started to cry.

January 28, 1995 — Paul began talking to me today about his fear of a total loss of intimacy in our relationship. On the first day I arrived in California we had a passionate reunion, but since then I have not been able to handle any kind of physical intimacy with him. When we start to make love, I always end up flashing back to childhood images of incest. I know it is not good to go on with what we are doing when that happens, so I need to stop. When I do, Paul feels rejected and fears that the problem will never end. He also feels that since I have connected with my different selves I have moved away from him emotionally.

As he was sharing all of these deep feelings and frustrations, I tried hard to stay associated and really hear him, but several times, others came forward to respond. The Beloved Child kept saying in my head, "He's going to leave us! He's going to leave us!" She shook with fear and bowed her head in shame.

January 31, 1995 — I dreamed about a giant blue snake being pushed up into my vagina. I also dreamed about being raped by my father again. Could it be possible? Did he actually rape me?

Father God, this whole process of remembering began with an answered prayer. I cried out to You for a revelation of truth regarding my history and You began unfolding the memories one-by-one. Lord Jesus, please finish what You have begun. Give me the courage to face it all and stand with confidence in Your peace and strength. Don't withhold any evidence from me, but rather let me see all there is to see that I may be healed. Amen.

February 2, 1995 — Spent the night with friends last night. Something about the room made me fearful. It was dark. I got up to go to the bathroom and couldn't find the doorknob. I started to panic and saw a dark moving shadow above my head and to the right of me. It seemed like more of a presence than a shadow and it reminded me of the "monster in the closet." I cried out to Paul in my fear and he got up, turned on the light and I opened the door to "escape." When I came back to bed I couldn't get to sleep for a long, long time.

Still later, I needed to get up to go to the bathroom again. As I sat up, a shadow appeared on the wall. I was too scared to get out of bed so I laid back down. When I was desperate, I sat up again. Again the shadow scared me. Paul woke up, sensed my fear and asked if I was all right. I told him I didn't know so he turned on the light so I could get up. What a night.

I'm beginning to fear I was raped by my father. It's not a body memory or a flashback. It's an intuitive sense of knowing. I am afraid new memories are about to come to the surface. Of the memories I have so far, the only one I feel is fully resolved is the earliest memory. The other memories have no beginning and no end. Did the sound of the door opening wake me? I have a pretty severe startle response followed by anxiety when doors are opened unexpectedly.

Afterwards did he just walk away in silence as if nothing had happened? Did he say something punishing or rationalizing? Did he comfort or hold me and say he loved me? Did he threaten me?

I need to know these things! I need closure. I need to see the whole story from start to finish. I know it is all there, somewhere. How can I access it? I don't want to wait and just hope that it surfaces. That makes me feel like a victim again. I want to actively work to retrieve the memories. I want to be pro-active in my recovery!

God, there's something inside me which drives me toward recovery, toward more than just surviving! I know You want me to be whole, too, Lord, just as You created me to be. Show me what I need to do. Continue to guide me on the journey. Thank You, Daddy God, for all that You have already done toward my healing. Amen. □

Puppet on a String

□ February 6, 1995 — I had a talk with Jan which I called my "State of the Union" address. First though, I gave him a list of all the many books Judy and I have read on the subject of DID and childhood sexual abuse. I did this mainly so he would know my ideas and suggestions aren't created in a vacuum.

Then I went through our "family" inside and shared with him about where I feel each one is in the process right now. I talked about the Guardian's openness to a future fusion and to friendship with God. I told him about Marilyn's identity crisis. I mentioned my concern that the children are being neglected. My main concern is about the Beloved Lamb. She seems to be having a difficult time ever since the fusion. She has a lot of pain and still needs lots of time and loving attention in and out of therapy. After I finished I said, "Okay, now you can tell us what you decided about our request for one-and-a-half-hour sessions."

I had a feeling his answer was going to cause a major emotional response so I would be going in to let others handle it (I don't really "do" emotions). He explained to me that he would let us come in for 1 1/2 hours twice this week, but starting next week we could come only once per week. The net result was, of course, less time in therapy instead of more. I was somewhat okay with this in that the outcome would probably be more effective sessions and less dependency, but while I was calmly acceding to his conditions a roar went up all over the system of "No! Not again!" My voice of reason was silenced by the internal scream of betrayal! — Observer. ☐

☐ Why did Jan do that? I was afraid. Doesn't he want to talk to us? I thought he was our friend. I was so scared to talk to him then. I really wanted to talk to him, too. I never, hardly ever get to talk to him cuz I never get a turn. I told him that it is hard for me to ask for a turn cuz when I ask for things, when I want things, I get hurt. He promised me he would make sure I would get lots of turns cuz he wants to give me the help I need. He said he would call for me. I asked him to promise me and he did. I hope he doesn't forget his promise!

I'm glad I told him about the scary room and how I had to go to the bathroom so bad it was hurting me real bad but I was scared to get out of bed. He said it was like all the times when I was alone and I needed to go to the bathroom but I was afraid of the monster so I wet my bed. Only this time Paul helped me so I didn't wet my bed. Paul is a very good man. I still want to go see Jan two times every week because he is the only real person out there that I can tell the truth to. I hope he will change his mind and let us. He said he will see in a few weeks but maybe then he will take away even more! *Please Jesus — tell him not to do that! Tell him we need him! Please*! — Beloved Lamb. ☐

☐ Jesus knows all about your needs, honey. You can trust Him, as your Good Daddy, to make sure that your needs are met in every way. He loves you more than you can even imagine. Now you need to cuddle up with Him and just go to sleep. It's been a long day. — The Good Mother. ☐

☐ Jan noticed that I scratch and pinch myself on my arms when it seems to him I have some anger to express. He says it seems like maybe scratching or pinching myself makes it easier to hold the anger in check or to repress it. ☐

☐ February 7, 1995 — The whole system is still reeling from yesterday's session and the decision Jan made. Couldn't sleep last night because everyone was talking about what we should do now. Some want to cancel the appointments we have and never go back. One idea is to go Friday and let everyone say good-bye and then quit. It seems even the Beloved Lamb is angry. She is upset because he is making her come only once a week when she wants to come twice. She colored a very sad picture and a very mad picture today. It's good that she is getting in touch with her anger. Yet as she colored the angry picture she felt very fearful and she shudders now when she looks at it. I think the best idea so far is to write to Jan expressing why we don't want to cut back and try to get him to renegotiate. The general consensus is it's worth a try. ☐

☐ February 10, 1995 — Jan knew I wanted to talk to him but I was afraid. He talked to me and he asked me if I would let him hold my hand. I was scared but he promised he wouldn't hurt me so then he held my hand and talked to me for a very long time. He promised me he wouldn't make me go away cuz I was mad with him. I told him I didn't want to be a bad girl, but he said it wasn't bad to be mad sometimes. He promised me he is going to help me. When he holds my hand, I feel like a real live person. I showed him the pictures I colored and he told how good I did on them. He said when I am mad I can color mad pictures or I can write down my mad feelings and bring it all to show him. I can tell him about it and he can help me learn how to be mad without being bad. I want to do that. I still hope I can come two times. Maybe he will tell me on Monday. *Dear Jesus, thank you that Jan wasn't mad with me. Amen.* — Beloved Lamb.

February 13, 1995 — The door opened so loud it made me jump! It was only a nice lady who had come to see Jan. I was resting quietly inside but the door scared me and then I came out and I was shaking. Jan said I could go in and I told him about the door. He asked if it made me think of other doors. I don't remember my daddy coming into my room. I think I was asleep. Maybe it was the sound of the door that woke me up.

My mommy was bad cuz she didn't notice that anything was wrong with me! She did mean and scary things to me and she didn't see me or hear me or know my name. My mommy and daddy didn't love me. I felt so scared because I was too little to be all alone with no one to help me. I'm not all alone now. Jan will help me and he will hold my hand when I am very scared. Judy hears me when I cry or when I need to say something. She helped me go to rest in the arms of Jesus when I was all tired after I talked to Jan today.

I want to have a real name, like real people do. I don't like being called Beloved Lamb. I want to be called Mary! Mary had a little lamb whose fleece was white as snow and everywhere that Mary went, the Lamb was sure to go. Jan called me Judy today. My name is not Judy but I think it is hard for him to call me Beloved Lamb when he talks to me. I'm going to ask him to call me Mary. Judy, do you think it would be all right for me to be called Mary? I want a real name. Mary is like your middle name and like Marilyn, too. With love from Mary. ☐

☐ Mary stayed out with Jan for almost an hour today and worked really hard getting in touch with many deep feelings of fear, shame, hopelessness and even anger. After she went inside, Judy came out to take on some of Mary's pain. She was so broken by the weight of the guilt, shame and loneliness it was hard for her to stay present with the pain, but she told Jan she had to stay there and feel it because Mary deserved that. She is getting stronger and more able to stay with the feelings. Her heart was full of compassion for the little girl she once was. Judy, we are all proud of you and the progress you are making, too.

As the session was coming to a close, Judy wondered what Jan had decided about the sessions schedule, but she was afraid to ask. Jan brought it up. He expressed concern over the impact therapy was having on Judy's ability to manage things at home with the family.

Judy said, "I've got to get out of this tomb! I have put the needs of everyone else ahead of my own for more than twenty years. Now I have some needs and I have to take care of them. My family is just going to have to adjust. Jan, please..."

He smiled saying, "You don't have to beg. I'd like to plan for a one-and-a half-hour session every Monday and a one-hour session on Friday."

Giant corporate sigh of relief! Aaaah...! We needed that. — Observer. ☐

☐ February 14, 1995 — Last night Paul asked me if I had a good time in therapy. I decided to really try to tell him something about what it is like and why it's not a "good time" but it is a vital time. I began to tell him about how Mary had talked to Jan about how alone and helpless she was, and how guilty she felt for her failure to get her parents to love her. I told him when she was done, she went back inside, and I came out and cried as I took on the burden of her pain and grieved over her/my childhood.

He wanted to know why I couldn't just put the past in the past. I know he wished I would just "get well soon." I can only hurry the process so much. I want it to be over, too, but I can't just wave a magic wand.

Dear Lord, please watch over my family. I am so weak and distracted. I feel I am failing miserably as a wife and mother. Fill in the gaps, Lord. Nurture my husband and my children. Be a father to us all. Amen. ☐

☐ My daddy made me do things I didn't want to do and they were bad things, too. I was just resting quietly and then he would come to me in my bed. I wanted him to love me and touch me but not in a bad way! He touched me in a bad way and he made me touch him. He made me dirty and sometimes I would nearly die because I couldn't breathe anymore. He was a very bad man. HE HURT ME! I HATE HIM! I WISH HE WOULD DIE! I WISH HE WOULD DIE! KILL HIM! KILL HIM! KILL HIM! — Mary.

If I Should Die Before I Wake

Coming to my room at night. Shaking, hiding from his sight.
Cover up my face in fear. Too late now, the monster's near.

Tender touch is turned to pain. All my love is now in vain.
He is big and I am small. In the darkest hole I fall.

I don't fight or scream or shout. No one comes to GET ME OUT!
I am trapped within his power. Feelings fold up like a flower.

Anger makes a girl so bad. Madness must be turned to sad.
Inside is an awful rage. Outside I must act my age.

Cannot hold the anger in. Now I see my daddy's sin.
Don't let me die before I wake. I WANT MY DADDY'S LIFE TO TAKE. □

□ Dear Mary, our thoughts and feelings can't kill Daddy so it is safe to give them expression. Later, when we are ready, we will confront him with his bad behavior and tell him how much he hurt us. If he is not really sorry for what he has done, we will never speak to him again. We have the power now to push him away and protect ourselves. Love, Judy.

Rest for the Weary

February 20, 1995 — The past year-and-a-half has been the most painful time in my adult life. Pebble by pebble, stone by stone, my fortress-like defenses have been dismantled, sometimes gently and painstakingly as if with a delicate chisel. Other times great holes have been blasted away. The whole operation has been under the supervision of a holy and loving God who I thought I had known but I hadn't. I'm getting to know Him now in a way I could never have imagined two years ago. I am slowly but inevitably moving from being a painfully frightened and ashamed "daddy's girl" into a joyful, trusting and strong child of God.

I always related to Jesus as my savior and my friend, but I could never go near the idea of God as Father, much less Daddy. Now the little children within me have the daddy they always wanted. Their simple faith in God the Father has shown me that even the grown woman in me needs that kind of father.

Father God, how can I ever express the depth of my gratitude? I am not worthy of the love You have poured out for me. Yet I drink it in with deep satisfaction. I am alive now only because You live within me and nourish me with Yourself. When I'm hungry, when I'm thirsty, help me to remember to reach for You to fill the aching need. You are my Source. You are my mother and my father. You are all I need. You love me as I am—no strings, no demands, no conditions. I depend on You. I trust in You. I love You. I need You forever and ever. Amen. □

□ February 21, 1995 — We got a lot accomplished today. That's something I haven't been able to say in a long time. It feels good today to look at a clear desk which yesterday was covered with piles of papers, bills, files, books, mail, etc. Aaaah... the simple joy of a task completed. Another sign that we're getting stronger.

Marilyn is following Jan's counsel to interact more with Judy. She is cooperating much more actively in Judy's activities, lending her strength, power, enthusiasm and a sense of humor. This is having a very positive effect on Judy as she has been able to accomplish more, and even more important, to laugh more. Marilyn, you're doing a great job and a really valuable service to the whole system! Thanks! Good Mother, I'd really like to hear from you. You've been awfully quiet lately. – Observer. □

□ I'm doing fine, really! Of course, I'm very concerned about Mary and all the pain she has been experiencing lately. I just wish I had been better able to protect her from the horrible experiences she went through. I'm also concerned that Little Judy Marie is being exposed to so much that is negative. She was on the verge of tears on Monday because she loves Mary so much and wants her to be happy. Little Judy Marie needs more time in the body to play and have fun to counterbalance the sad realities she is learning about now.

I don't feel quite so optimistic as I used to. I am seeing the world for the evil place filled with evil people that it is. I realize now that I probably can't protect the little ones from pain just by saying nice words to them. The words of encouragement help. They do make some difference. I just wish I could do more. That's all. Well, my goodness, I almost sound as if I am depressed. Don't worry. I'll be okay and I'll keep doing my best to care for the children. We'll all be fine. Really. — The Good Mother. □

□ Thank you for sharing from your heart like that. You have done a lot for the children. Your nurture has kept them alive and given them the spark of hope they needed to risk coming out for help now. Now that Judy is learning to love and care for the children, it is okay for you to relax your vigilance a bit and take some much-needed rest. You may even decide you want to fuse with Judy soon. That's fine, too. The choice is yours. Just keep in mind that all of us are grateful to you for the role you have played in our survival. We love you! — Observer. □

□ I agree with the Observer that Marilyn is moving closer to me. I also feel the Observer and the Good Mother and I are all beginning the process of integration. The Observer and I are so close now that I myself am sometimes surprised when the journal writing talks about me in the third person. I am so in tune with the Observer's thoughts, I feel like it is me writing when it's not. We do almost everything together now except the emotional stuff. The Observer still sits back and observes when I am in the process of taking on Mary's pain or the

Guardian's anger, etc. I am open to fusing with any or all of the adults. I want to talk to Jan about it first though. — Judy.

February 23, 1995 — *"...There is nothing covered that will not be revealed, and hidden that will not be known."* (Matthew 10:26) *Father God, You know that I have been frustrated about not being able to remember certain specifics about my childhood. You were there. There are no secrets from You. Father, help me to trust that You will reveal the truth to me in Your perfect timing. You will complete the work You have begun. I praise Your name. "But when he, the Spirit of truth, comes, he will guide you into all truth..."* (John 16:13a) *"Then you will know the truth, and the truth will make you free."* (John 8:32) *I claim these promises from Your Word today, Lord Jesus. I desire with all my heart to know the whole truth — to move beyond flashes, images and disconnected emotions to see the full picture of the damage that was done. I believe You can reveal all that I need and desire to know. I ask You now, Father, to open the lock on the door of my memories. In Jesus name. Amen.*

February 24, 1995 — The Good Mother talked to Jan for the first time today. She shared her feelings of failure and her sense that she is quickly fading away. Jan pointed out that she had been giving herself to Judy so she wasn't really disappearing and he affirmed her significant role in the system. It's time for a fusion to take place if she is willing. We need to begin talking and praying

February 25, 1995 — Dear Good Mother, when I think of you fading away, I am filled with grief and sorrow and my eyes release their tears. You have been so important to my survival, to our survival! Every word of comfort you ever spoke to the children, inside or out, every act of love, has held great value and made a world of difference. I never had a model of a warm, nurturing mother in my childhood. Without your presence within me, the inner children would long ago have given up all hope and David and Britt would have inherited the same empty legacy I received.

You have not failed in your mission. Not at all! No one could have prevented the terrible things which happened—the incest, the rapes. None of us could have stopped the evil perpetrated against us. Your gentleness, your tenderness, your selfless love provided a balm to soothe the wounded heart.

I will miss having you as separate part. I will be sad to see you "go" in that sense. All of us will. In truth though, you won't really be gone because, rather than walking beside me, you will be within me. All your love, faith and wisdom, your strength and hope, will not fade away. They, and you, will live on as an integrated aspect of who I am. I need you, Good Mother. Don't leave me—join me! Love, Judy.

Father God, thank You for bringing the Good Mother into my life. Her presence helped to preserve hope and faith. Now it seems it may be time for she and I to be more fully united. If this is Your will, Father, I ask for Your peace and assurance for myself, the Good Mother and everyone within me. I ask for Your presence and power in the fusion ceremony itself. May Your Spirit unite us and make us one. Amen. ☐

☐ 1:40 PM — After Judy wrote that prayer, we sensed that God was leading us to go forward with fusion right away. We all gathered to pray for awhile and worship the Lord. Then Judy and the Good Mother stood before Jesus in the meadow. They stated their desire to be united. Jesus placed His hands on their heads as they stood side-by-side holding hands. He blessed them and their union. They turned to face each other and hug each other. As they hugged, the Good Mother melted into Judy and they became one. Now Judy has all of the Good Mother within herself. This is the first fusion of a personality into the core personality. It is a milestone on our journey! — Observer. ☐

☐ The moment we hugged each other we began to blend and our hearts became as one heart. The emotions were intense and it took perhaps 30-60 seconds for the fusion to become complete. During that time I was flooded with feelings and sensations. I felt grief and joy, tingling sensations, dizziness, pain... I cried and rejoiced. The others gathered around and I moved into the arms of Jesus. He held me and everyone prayed.

I felt fuller, as if I was somehow more substantial than before. I was exhausted. I knew the Good Mother was now within me, that I had all of her; nothing of her beauty or her faith, her love or her wisdom had been lost. She will be with me, in me, always now.

I had to rest for awhile as is always the case when fusion takes place. Integration of our differing experiences, viewpoints, etc. will come gradually over time, but I know already that I am not the same. I feel empowered with love and compassion greater than I have ever known. I feel optimistic. I feel a deeper level of abiding faith and peace.

Thank you, Father, for restoring this beautiful part of myself to me today. The Good Mother stood as a reflection of Your love and mercy and now we are one and I can be a better reflection of Your image. There was a hole inside of me only she could fill, as if I am a jigsaw puzzle and she one of the missing pieces. Thank You, Lord, for preserving and protecting her until You could give her back to me.

Chapter 4 — The Pit of Longing

The Silence is Broken

February 27, 1995 — A child came out of hiding today. I started to try to tell Jan about the memory that had been surfacing this weekend about oral rape. I thought the memory was coming from Mary but it wasn't. This little girl is about five years old. As she relived the memory of his penis choking her throat and his hand blocking her nose while he masturbated, her terror was overwhelming. She couldn't breathe. She believed he was going to kill her. She covered her face with her hands to try to make the memory go away, but she didn't cry.

Jan drew her out of the memory when she was in danger of hyperventilating. He asked her to let the images fade and to look at him. He spoke soothing words to her, assuring her it was only a memory. She was afraid it would happen again, but he told her the memory and the images remain but the event can and will never happen to her again. She is safe now.

She didn't know who Jan was or where she was. She asked in a whisper and he told her and asked her who she was. She didn't seem to have a name. She was terribly frightened and sucked her thumb for comfort. She sat very quietly and listened while Jan spoke to her, then she started to speak ever so softly.

She told Jan she was very quiet and when the bad things happened she had to come out because she wouldn't cry or make a sound so no one would get in worse trouble. Inside her head she was screaming and crying out, "Stop! Stop! I don't want you to do this!" Outside she didn't cry or scream or shout. She had to endure some of the most horrifying abuse because she was strong enough to take it in silence.

As I watched her going through the memory from a distance, I was thinking to myself, "Cry! Why don't you cry?" Now I see it was her job not to cry! She stayed out with Jan for a long time, mostly listening, occasionally whispering a few words. She wondered why, when she was so little, she had to be the one who was pushed out to cope with the worst stuff. Jan told her she was very strong to be able to be so quiet and that was what was needed to survive. He told her he was very glad she had survived. After awhile she said she needed to go and she went back inside.

I came out sobbing and Jan said, "You didn't know, did you."

He was right. I hadn't been aware of this one, hadn't been expecting her. My heart was breaking for this little girl who silently endured so much without even the comfort of tears. I wondered aloud, "How many more?"

Seeing this little girl's pain and terror, I am angry. I want her to have a voice, to scream and cry out all that was locked up inside her during the abuse. I want her to be free to cry. She will get her voice, she will be allowed to scream and cry.

Dear Angel — We want to thank you so much for coming out today, for daring to tell a part of your story. We are so glad you came. Jan has been our friend for a very long time. He will be your friend now, too. We all want to help you so you won't have to be afraid anymore of the bad things that were done to you. The man who hurt you, the daddy, is old now and he lives many miles away across a big ocean. He can't hurt you anymore. Never again. The silence has been broken at last! Welcome, Angel! We love you!

March 1, 1995 — Maybe I should have known better than to tell my brothers about the incest. Though I asked them not to say anything to Dad, to allow me to be the one to confront him in my own time, one of them broke his commitment. I imagine he was in desperate need of hearing his dad say, "I'm innocent!" Dad didn't disappoint him. Last night I got an E-mail from him denying everything and aggressively attacking me while claiming to be a loving father. He sent copies of the E-mail to all my siblings.

When Paul said there was an e-mail from him, I knew what it would be about. As I read it, I realized it was pretty much what I had expected—denial and judgement, self-righteous indignation and a good dose of deflected guilt and shame. Then, of course, his piéce de resistance, "None of your brothers and sisters believe you and they are all concerned about your mental health."

His parting words were, "I will have nothing more to do with you until you come to your senses and admit to everybody that you created this out of whole cloth. Tell the truth, stop being a victim and take responsibility for your life."

All this and I had never even sent him the letter! I knew my only recourse was to send him the letter I had originally planned (with some minor alterations) so I went to the computer and typed it out and sent it. Only afterwards did I take the time to check in with my feelings. I was disappointed but not surprised that one of my brothers stole my right to be the one to confront Dad. Yet I had been praying for God to show me when to send the letter, so this may have been His way of opening the door. Here is the letter I sent to him:

"Dear Dad — This letter has been very difficult for me to write and will be very difficult for you to read. It relates to your abuse of me as a child.

As you know, this past summer Paul and I went through some traumatic events. Things occurred which caused me to feel a deeper sense of betrayal than I could ever remember feeling in my entire life. The operative words in the preceding sentence are "could ever remember". When I reached the lowest point in the emotional valley of despair, I suddenly remembered when I had felt that feeling before. It was a very long time ago, when I was a very little girl.

At the end of July, the dam began to break that had so relentlessly held back the storm of emotions which were far too much for any little girl to carry— emotions buried so deep, along with the memories, because the sense of betrayal that was associated with them was so great, my only means of survival was to separate myself from them by complete dissociation.

These last few months have been a nightmare as memory after memory has flooded into my conscious awareness. Each one more vivid, more detailed and more devastating than the last. I know now, Dad. The secret that I hid so well from myself is out.

Now I understand all the blank pages of my childhood. Now I understand why I can remember all the names of my friends on North Street, but can't see anything past the threshold of the front door into our house. Now I understand why I have had no memories of you prior to the age of twelve, no memories of you before Riverside Drive at all. Now I understand why I was so afraid to get out of bed at night. Because of the "monster" in the closet, I would lie awake in terror in the middle of the night and wet my bed, knowing that soon the warmth would turn cold and in the morning I would have to endure the shame of another failure. Now I understand the recurring nightmares of barrels falling on me, of drowning, of being sent to hell by God. It all makes sense now.

I understand, too, why I went from being the compliant "good little girl" always trying to please, to the rebellious teenager who didn't care about you, myself or anyone else. I understand the self-destructive drug and alcohol abuse. I understand the promiscuous behavior that constantly drew me back into abusive situations where I could try to reenact my childhood, hoping for a different result. The happy ending I was longing for never came. I was looking for the "good daddy"—the one who would hold me like a baby and tell me how much he loved me and how special I was to him. I never found the "good daddy"—and it's been a desperate longing and a moving force in my life for so many years, it's a hard dream to give up.

Last June, before all of the memories came, I had grown enough to have accepted the reality that you were never the good daddy I had so longed for as a child, and yet I loved you all the same. You are my father, and I had come to terms with my disappointment at your neglect and I decided I still loved you. I was so happy to have the chance to express that love for you by being at your bedside before and after your surgery for cancer.

It was a month later, just a few days after my 42nd birthday, that I began to realize that you had been at my bedside many years before, but without such loving motives. It's important to me that you understand something of the cost that your "bedside manner" has exacted from me. Aside from the obvious consequences in my youth, such as self-destructiveness and sexual promiscuity, there have been many less obvious but none the less devastating effects of the abuse.

All of my life I have viewed the world as a dangerous place and I have believed that love and intimacy were hurtful and to be avoided at all costs. I desperately needed someone to love and care for me, but I could never let anyone get close enough to really know me. I couldn't allow myself to become that vulnerable. You taught me that love hurts, Dad. I learned my lesson well, and in spite of many people who would call me their friend, I have been painfully lonely and self-protecting my entire life.

I have carried a burden of guilt and shame so heavy that I couldn't even let myself be conscious of it and instead dissociated from it. Yet, deep in my heart, I always knew there was something terribly wrong with me, I was a "bad seed" and if anyone ever got close enough to really see me, they could never possibly love me. That guilt and shame has driven me to perform, to work myself into burnout over and over again, just to prove I'm worthy. That burden of guilt and shame belongs to you, Dad. I'm choosing one day at a time not to carry it anymore. I wonder if you, too, have dissociated from your own guilt and shame. It must have been a heavy load for you to carry all of these years—the knowledge that you abused your own daughter.

It has taken me four years of therapy to build enough trust in my therapist to even begin facing the deepest truths of my life. Now I am remembering not only what you did to me, but also things which others did to me and which I myself have done when in a dissociated state (some things of which I am not proud). Perhaps, you, too, may have forgotten about the things you did to me—perhaps drowning the memories in alcoholic blackouts. Then indeed, this is a difficult revelation of truth for you to hear. Please try to have the courage to remember. If you are the "loving father" which you claim to be, if you care about me at all, if there is any genuine love for me in your heart, if any desire for the possibility of a loving father-daughter relationship—then I need you to at least be willing to face and acknowledge what you did to me.

For it is restored relationship which I truly desire, but a relationship based on truth, not on lies. I still love you though I confess I sometimes hate you. To say that this has been difficult for me would be to minimize it almost unbearably. I did not choose to be a victim, and I would prefer not to believe what I have come to know about the abuse. It is my intention to become a survivor and this letter is part of that process. You have hurt me deeply, Dad, yet I am willing to forgive you. But true restoration of our relationship will depend on your willingness to admit the exact nature of your wrongs, to become willing to make amends to all whom you have harmed and to make amends to those that you can, namely me (and anyone else you may have hurt in this same way).

Whether you ever admit anything to me or anyone else, you will one day stand before a Holy God and face the truth, Dad. I hope you will make your peace with Him at the very least. He alone has the power to forgive you and release you from the penalty for what you have done to me. He is willing and able to forgive, if you will but come to Him and confess. I hope you are strong enough to do it.

Please do not make any further contact with me until you are ready to deal with these issues in an honest and thorough way. If I don't hear from you, I will call you to invite further discussion. It is my hope that full restoration of relationship between us will be possible. Know, however, that denial or cheap apologies with excuses will not bring reconciliation. True repentance is the only door to our continuing relationship. With love and sorrow, Judy."

It all seems so final. The chances that Dad will ever admit the truth are zero to none without direct, miraculous intervention by God. I am praying for Dad to be broken and contrite, for him to repent and confess before God. It is possible through Christ. Yet I know I must accept the strong likelihood that I will never see my father again, will never have any kind of real relationship with him. I need to release him without bitterness so that I may be released from him. So I let him go. He is in God's hands now.

Last night the children were afraid as they realized the daddy was angry. I told them they are safe now and no one can hurt them or punish them anymore. I will never turn my back on them or deny their existence or their pain! Never! They are going to receive the love and healing they need even if I have to lose my father, my mother and all my brothers and sisters in the process! Someone has to love them and bring the light and life of Jesus into their lives. I refuse to abandon them. They have suffered enough!

March 3, 1995 — Angel saw herself in a mirror for the first time today while we were waiting to go in to see Jan. She was really frightened and confused. I had to struggle to regain executive control and had just gotten my body back when Jan came out to invite us in.

I talked about Dad's letter to me and my letter to him. I had been feeling so strong at first, but since then my confidence has eroded. I asked Jan, "What if none of the trauma that I remember ever really happened? What would be your diagnosis of me then?"

He said he would view it as a reaction to severe neglect and emotional abuse and said it could be that I need a "theatrical" stage in order to express the pain and other emotions that were denied to me. I wrestled with that idea for awhile. Then I began to think about Marilyn and the life she had lived, and the Lonely Little Girl, the things that had happened to her, and I said, "No!" I know they were real, are real, and I know what happened to them is true! Jan agreed that there is no question about the dissociation. He wouldn't tell me that what I believe is true in his opinion because he says that's not what's important. What's important is for me to trust myself. All this doubting is connected to my continuing, hopeless wish for my father to be the good daddy after all.

Dear Angel — Again today you were strong and brave and honest. You were very angry at the bad man for what he did to you. Angels can get angry, too, and when they see evil, they take a strong angry stand against it. A long time ago, when all the awful things happened, you were too little to fight back. The only revenge you could take then was not to allow the father to see your pain or hear your cries. You did well with that. Now the father is far away and, as you saw today, we are in a grown-up body. We are stronger now to be able to stand against anyone who would try to hurt us.

You don't have to be quiet and keep still anymore. Today you showed all of us the power of your anger. You are very powerful, very strong. You did really well today, Angel. We all love you! — Judy.

Swinging on the Pendulum

March 4, 1995 — Doubts are plaguing me again this morning. As I contemplated the idea that all of this hideous pain might be based on some fantasies I created in my head, I wept. As I wept, I remembered how many times I have prayed, asking God to reveal truth to me, to show me my true history. Could I be such a poor, phony Christian that I could even use God to justify my fantasies and illusions? Could God, in His mercy, allow that? Is it possible that I could sincerely pray for Him to reveal truth and in response my head could be filled with ugly lies? I don't want to believe that. This whole thing started with a prayer in this journal in which I begged God to show me the truth! Just one week later, the original dream came and when I woke up I was dead sure that it wasn't a dream, but an answer to prayer.

So many times since that day, I have prayed for further truth and God has answered by giving further revelation. He has never turned His face away from me even when I have turned away from Him in anger or in shame. He has not accused me or called me liar. He has held me. He has poured out His love over me. *Father God, forgive me for sometimes wanting my fantasy of a good daddy more than I want the reality of You. Forgive me for bowing down before this idol I created with my own hands instead of bowing down before You. You alone are worthy. You alone are real love, tenderness and compassion. You alone are true justice and mercy. I will trust in You and You alone, so help me, God!* □

□ Dear Judy — I am afraid because of the letter we sent and the one he sent to us. I am afraid of Angel and her memories and how she is so angry. I want to hide when she is around. I know she had a awful job to do and I am glad she did it but it scares me to feel her terror and rage. I don't think I am strong enough so I have been hiding. I want to talk to Jan. Maybe if he holds my hand and asks me I can tell him how come I am so scared. He was calling to me yesterday but I felt afraid but I will try next time. I'm sorry to worry you. Love, Mary. □

☐ Dear Mary — I love you so much. I understand your fear. I'm afraid, too. Just remember, the father can't hurt us anymore. And Angel desperately needs and deeply deserves the chance to give voice to her terror and rage. I think it is okay for you to keep some distance from that right now. Just promise me you won't go into deep hiding where I can't reach you anymore, okay? Come close to me as much as you can so I can hold you and listen to your fears and wants and help you find your way into the arms of Jesus. You are still the beloved lamb, even if you did change your name! With love, Judy.

March 5, 1995 — I've been awake all night and when I finally fell asleep at seven this morning I had horrible dreams. A power struggle is taking place within me and the battle was in full swing. All night I was struggling "to believe or not to believe" that I am a victim of incest. After all these months and all this pain, I still struggle with doubt! The battle has escalated since Dad's angry denial—as if I ever thought he'd admit it!

4:40 PM — Just got off the phone from calling my father. I told him in my letter if he didn't contact me I would call him to invite further discussion. He continues to deny that he abused me. He told me the antidepressant drug I'm taking is creating "false memories" but I told him the memories started long before the medication.

I asked him to honestly examine the possibility that he could have abused me while in a dissociated state, i.e. drunk, high or whatever, and therefore, not remembered doing it. I was really giving him the benefit of the doubt. I told him he has a choice. He can flat deny that he abused me and close the door on our relationship, or he can concede to himself the chance that he might have done it and search for the memories.

He said right now the wound is too raw and he thinks it best if we just leave things as they are. He said when my brother told him, he burst into tears and he felt like someone had stuck a knife in his heart and twisted it. The truth is, there was a tiny flare of satisfaction in my own heart when he said that. Just a very quiet "Now you know how it feels" floated up from a dark place within.

10 PM — Good-bye, Daddy. I can't be Daddy's girl anymore. It hurts to say good-bye. No matter how bad a daddy may be, a little girl never wants to lose her daddy. You see, Dad, the problem is, I'm not a little girl anymore. I'm a "woman fully growed" as they say, and I can't pretend anymore.

March 6, 1995 — I continue to wrestle with doubt and I have been feeling suicidal again. I wish I could know the truth with a capital 'T'—and that stands for trust. It all boils down to the question, "Who can I trust?" When I begin to doubt my own reality, when I start to wonder if I've created all this pain in my imagination, my trust in myself and in my Lord are both eroded.

I started out my session with Jan today by saying, sarcastically, that I've learned, since starting therapy, that I'm a woman of many talents! I've discovered that I'm a writer, a poet, a songwriter and now, I might even be an actress and a playwright! This was a cynical referral to his comment last session that I might need a theatrical stage in order to express repressed feelings, even if the memories aren't true.

When Jan asked me if I was angry with him for letting me wrestle with my doubt, I took a giant step back in retreat and an angry adult part came forward. I think it was the Gatekeeper who proceeded to talk as me and allowed Jan to think it was me. He ignored the question about anger and instead told Jan some things about me and my past that I had never confessed to him before—ugly things communicated in an ugly, punishing tone. When Jan tried to talk again about the anger that he was perceiving in "me," the alter became silent for a few moments, again refusing to talk about it, then started telling Jan in detail about perverse sexual fantasies I used to have. When Jan asked if these disclosures were a form of self-punishment, the angry alter said, "Well, isn't that what I deserve?"

When Jan asked why, he answered, "Because I'm a sick, evil person who makes up horrible lies about her father."

Jan and I made a deal to get me through this week. I'm taking a position in my mind that the children matter most of all right now. They need to be heard and nurtured without judgement. It's their turn now.

March 8, 1995 — I received an e-mail from Dad which shook me to my very foundations. He wrote: "Dear Judy, I guess I just want you to know that I still love you in spite of the current circumstances. I did not say that to you this morning on the phone because of the pain. I felt your desperation and your complete belief that what you have said about me is true. There is nothing in my experience that could even remotely indicate it as having happened. So for now we will have to hew to our separate beliefs. I don't know how this will play out but since I am powerless over people, places and things, I am satisfied to leave it in God's hands. I have been praying daily for you and will continue to do so. I am deeply sorry that you have been going through all these struggles and pray that all will be well with you soon. Love, Dad."

In one short poignant paragraph, he is offering me all the love and tenderness I have always wanted. All I have to do is bury the last year of my life, and all the painful feelings and memories, and what I have hungered for can be mine.

By faith, I hope my father will eventually face his own dark side and depravity and own his need for a Savior. By faith, I hope I will find the grace to eventually truly see my father through the eyes of Christ, with all of his potential for goodness revealed as clearly as his potential for evil. By faith, I hope for my father's healing. By faith, I hope for my own.

Father God, I love You. Thank You for loving me and standing patiently by as I swing on my pendulum, going backward and forward, backward and forward, propelled sometimes by fear and sometimes by faith. You wait on the side for me to settle down, to come to a stop, put my feet back on the ground and run, exhausted, into Your arms. Then You carry me home to the meadow, my head resting on Your shoulder as You quietly whisper words of comfort and encouragement in my ear. You know me by heart. You know my love language. You know just what this tired and confused child needs and You give it freely. I love You, Lord. ☐

Angel of the Night

☐ March 13, 1995 — I told Jan I am sad because I ran away when the bad things happened and left Mary and Angel. I told him I was so sorry that I did that and I think Mary and Angel won't be my friends now. Jan said it wasn't my fault that Mary and Angel got hurt. It was the bad man who hurt them and I couldn't stop him no matter what! He said it is good that I ran away cuz then I could still be happy when happy was the right thing to be. But I cried cuz I really love Mary and Angel and I want them to be my friends! Jan says maybe I can learn to play the kind of play that they might like more. More stronger play like running around and fighting bad guys and things like that. I like soft things like teddy bears and pretty things like leaves and shells but I'm scared of guns and swords and things. But I will try. Our talk today was not very happy but Jan says sometimes talks can still be good even when they are not happy. He said it made him happy when we had a good talk. He is like a teacher. I was happy that he said he was happy about our talk. I love him very, very much. He is my friend. When he smiles at me I feel happy even when I am sad. — Love, Little Judy Marie. ☐

☐ I talked to Jan about the angry adult voice within me, the one who came out and said, "I don't feel anything" and told Jan to "shut-up" a couple of weeks ago. I think it's the Gatekeeper (or Denyer). When that voice takes control, I tend to "exit - stage left" so I'm not really in touch or co-conscious with it. That's why I'm so unsure about it. All I know is he (I think it's male) seems to be all about keeping secrets, quitting therapy and criticizing the rest of us. There's still no cooperating at all with that part. Then as I began to tell Jan how afraid Mary is of Angel's anger, Mary came out to speak for herself. ☐

☐ I told him I was scared by Angel cuz she's so mad and I think we will all get in big trouble if she tells about how mad she is. She wants to kill the daddy and I am afraid that she will want to kill me cuz I ran away.

Angel is mad cuz the daddy hurt her very much and he almost killed her cuz she couldn't breathe. It is right that she is mad. I am mad, too. He shouldn't have done that to us! Angel is very strong. Her anger made her strong enough not to scream or cry. She is very brave. I'm glad that she is mad! ☐

☐ I talked about my fear of giving Angel a voice. I was afraid to invite her to come forward because, first of all, the memories are so painful, and secondly, because I am afraid of her anger. Thirdly, I am terribly afraid of what she remembers that I don't know yet. Like Mary, I want to run from the awful truth. Yet I know that Angel needs to tell her stories and I need to hear them. Jan probed for her and she came forward to talk and share some more.

She began to go into an abreaction and Jan reminded her that it was a memory. That helped her to take just a tiny step away from the images she was seeing, but it was all still terribly real to her. She described the "bad man" beside her bed (Angel denies he is her father):

"He takes out his thing."

Jan says, "He took his penis out."

"Yeah... He's rubbing it with his hand and it's getting bigger and bigger!" she says with rising fear.

"Where's his other hand?" Jan asks.

"It's on my head. He's holding my head so I can't turn away and he's pulling my hair and he wants to do something I don't want him to do!" She begins to panic.

"What does he want to do?"

"He wants to put it in my mouth and I can't breathe cuz it's too big and I'm too little and it hurts me and his hand is rubbing on it and it covers my nose and I can't breathe at all! I'm going to die! I'm going to die...! I'm choking and I want to spit it out but he won't let me! I have to swallow it now. And then it's over. He lets go of my hair and stands up and walks out of my room. I hate him! I wish he would just die!"

"Does everything still hurt?" She nods her head.

"Where does it hurt?"

"My throat hurts very bad. I'm thirsty," she responds.

"Does your hair still hurt?"

She nods, "Yes, and my arms, too."

"Did you try to push him away?"

"No, I couldn't do that. I had to stay very stiff and still cuz I was screaming and crying inside but I couldn't scream and cry outside so I had to hold everything very tightly."

"You did your job very well. He was a very bad man. You were able to survive because your anger gave you strength. You did very well," Jan wrapped words of encouragement around her and she began to relax.

"I'm very tired. I need to go to sleep now," Angel said softly.

"Yes, you worked very hard today. You can rest now," he answered her.

She went to sleep sucking her thumb. She never shed a tear and when I came forward again, I couldn't either. I couldn't let myself feel the reality of all that she had just revealed to me. The face of my father, the awareness that Angel knows—she knows all the ugly details that have been hidden until now. She watched him walk out of the room without a word after he orally-raped her so brutally. He just let go when he was done and walked away! No cuddle, no comfort, no compensation... He just walked away. She lay there in the dark, relieved it was over and terrified for the future and the next night visitation.

I couldn't cry for her. I was numb. Jan said she was a brave little girl. I said, "Braver than I am," to which he responded, "That's a paradox." I guess he's right.

March 15, 1995 — The memory of the oral rape has been haunting me all day. I am trying to own it and accept it as having happened not just to Angel, but to me. These horrendous things which happened didn't happen in the third person—to some child "out there"—they happened to me! It was my body that was shattered, my mind that was scattered, my heart that was tattered and torn to pieces. 'First person singular' became 'first person plural' in order to survive but every horrible act of abuse and betrayal was done to me. My father, young, strong (a former football player), tall and powerful, violated my trust, took advantage of my neediness and stole my innocence when I was five years old.

March 17, 1995 — Jan told me today that he believes the things I have been remembering are substantially true, even if they are not completely undistorted. He has said all along that the dissociation is real, but today he said he also believes that I was sexually abused. I needed to hear that. I was really struggling with how to go on with the healing process, how to even talk about my feelings about what Angel is showing me, if I had strong reason to doubt my memories.

We talked about the origin of the perverse sexual fantasies that started in my late teens. The severe abuse caused a lot of very strong emotions that could not be expressed and at the same time became sexualized and that could have created the fantasies. Their self-contemptuous nature reflects the "need leads to punishment" dynamic of the abuse. They are just further confirmation of the incest.

I was realizing that everything that "we" remember happened to me, and Jan asked if I had talked to Jesus about this painful recognition. I feel so far away from Jesus right now. I feel like I'm losing my grip on Him. Jan reminded me that I might lose my grip on Jesus but He wouldn't lose His grip on me. As he talked to me about the love Jesus has for me I felt my body start to relax and I sensed the loving arms of the Good Shepherd holding me in a warm, solid embrace. *Jesus, hold me and don't let go, no matter how I struggle to run away and hide from Your love.*

March 20, 1995 — I am numb and shocked still, one hour after my session with Jan. Angel began to share a memory too horrible for me to take in. She had been talking about her anger and how she wanted to kill the bad man when suddenly she became very frightened. She didn't want to talk about what she was feeling or seeing and she kept shaking her head no and fending off the memory. Then Jan asked what her hands were telling us and we looked down and saw that they were crossed at the wrists, held together as if bound, and shaking uncontrollably. Jan asked, "Is something holding your wrists together?" Angel nodded her head and said, "He's holding them with his hand and they're over my head."

Slowly, and with a great deal of hesitation, she began to reveal more of what had happened. She was on her back on the bed and he was above her, his one hand holding her hands in a painful grip. With his other hand he was pulling her legs apart. She saw his face and he looked angry. She didn't know why.

He was trying to push himself into her. The pain was sharp like the tearing of a knife. Her hands hurt. Her tummy hurt. Her legs hurt. She didn't want to or couldn't handle knowing anymore and she made the memory go away before it was done. I was left unsure whether it was an attempted rape or a successful rape. There's not much reason to believe he left the job undone.

Dear God, I don't want to believe this memory could be real. I don't want to believe he could have actually raped me! But what would cause Angel's fear, or her hands to do what they did, or the memories? There is no other explanation for these things other than that they really happened. She was raped. I was raped! By my father. My God, help me to take it in. Help me have the strength to accept and own this terrifying reality. Right now I am shaking like a leaf, breathing shallow, all my muscles are constricted and my head is killing me. I feel so afraid. All that is in me is resisting this information, yet Angel needs to be believed. Lord, help me to be strong now, strong enough to take this burden from her so that she can begin to realize that life is not just fear and anger. Life can mean love and acceptance, comfort and consolation. If I turn away from what she is telling me, I will be repeating the abuse. Help me stay. Hold me. Give me courage and faith. Amen.

Dear Angel — I believe you. It's difficult for me to accept the truth you are telling me now but I do. You were very brave to keep going back and looking at the memory even though it scared you very much. Angel, you are very strong and even though the memories make you feel weak, you are getting stronger every time you face another one. You are gaining power over the memories. Already you are not as afraid of your anger. Soon the memories will lose their power over you as you examine them now from a distance. You did well today. I love you, Angel. □

□ It was like a knife! He hurt my hands, too, cuz he squeezed them so hard. He was mad at me I think but I was mad at him too cuz he hurt me very bad. I was scared almost to death and it hurt everywhere inside and out. My hands and my arms and my tummy and my legs. I hate him. When he hurt me I was so scared cuz he was so big and I was little but when he left me alone after then I was very mad and I want to kill him. I want to stab him with a knife so he can see what it feels like. I want to kill him and now I could cuz I am in a grown-up body now and Judy says he is old now. I could kill him except Jan says I would have to go to jail. It's not fair cuz he is the one who should go to jail, not me! How come it's unfair always and the bad people never have to pay for when they hurt people? That makes me really mad. — Angel. □

□ Dear Angel — It doesn't seem very fair when someone hurts you and doesn't get punished. I believe that the father who hurt you is being punished in a way now because he has to live with the guilt of what he did. He will be punished by God for his sinfulness because God is just and fair. The one who hurt you will not get away with it in the long run. I have watched God over many years and He has never failed to execute both His justice and His mercy. You can trust Him to do exactly the right thing.

He loves you, Angel, and He knows you feel you don't have a daddy and you're not sure you want one because the only daddy you ever knew was a bad, mean and cruel daddy. God wants to show you a different kind of daddy. He wants to be your daddy and for you to be His child. He wants to love you and hold you gently in His arms, just like the picture of Jesus holding the little lamb that I have shown to you. When you remember the terrible fear and the anger you felt when the father hurt you, He wants to be with you, to comfort you, to love you. Whenever you are afraid or lonely or full of anger, Jesus is there to give you courage and comfort just like a good daddy should. I hope you will let yourself trust Him soon. He loves you and so do I. — Judy.

Sisters in the Lord

March 22, 1995 — *"'For I know the plans I have for you,' declares the LORD, 'plans to prosper you and not to harm you, plans to give you hope and a future.'"* (Jeremiah 29:11)

"'I am with you and will save you,' declares the LORD. 'I will restore you to health and heal your wounds.'" (Jeremiah 30:11, 17)

In spite of the fact that the memories I'm now facing are worse than any I've ever faced, God is showing me that He is indeed healing me. I feel stronger and more integrated than I have ever felt. I am walking on with optimism about our future ministry since we have changed mission agencies. I am trusting Jesus more. I have more peace and more hope.

Father God, You haven't forsaken me or abandoned me even when I have lost my grip on You. I will trust in Your plans for me and in Your restoration. Amen.

Dear Marilyn — I want you to know I appreciate your efforts to meet the children's need for a good daddy. Even though some of your methods weren't very effective or healthy, I know you tried your best. I respect you deeply. I am grateful, too, for your energy, your enthusiasm, your extraversion and your humor. For many years, you have not been able to be in control of our body and I know that has frustrated you. I think fusing with me might be a good idea because, by joining with me, you will have much more opportunity to connect with the body and with others on the outside where your many strengths would be very useful.

Marilyn, I need all the wonderful characteristics you have. I don't want you just to fade away. I want all of you to remain with me. You won't die but both of us will be changed by each other. We will be a new creation—a person with all your assets and mine rolled into one. What do you say? Love, Judy. ☐

☐ Well, I don't know exactly what to say. I mean, yeah, I think it would be a good idea for us to fuse—I've said that before. But I wonder what will happen? I know theoretically that I won't die but what if I end up joining you and then you/we end up doing things that hurt the kids or mess up the family situation? Do you think it's safe? I'm willing but I just hope it doesn't mess things up for everyone. I mean, I know some of my choices were pretty bad for the kids, especially the Lonely Little Girl. Maybe I should talk to Jan tomorrow about some of this stuff, ya know? Besides I hate to "leave" without saying good-bye. I really kinda like the guy. He's one of the few guys that's never tried to use me. I'm gonna miss being able to talk to him as "me" and flirt with him, ya know? Marilyn. ☐

☐ March 23, 1995 — Marilyn became a Christian today! She came to our session with Jan to say good-bye and she and Jan had a long talk. She told him we were going to fuse but she was concerned about what might happen as a result. She talked about how she felt when she first came into contact with him, how her goal was to gain control over him. She used to think he had too much power over me, that I was too vulnerable and trusting toward him. She thought I was a wimp.

Yet as she watched the progress of therapy, she realized that by trusting Jan I was getting stronger, not weaker. She had always thought it was foolish to trust anyone. The choice was either to control someone or be controlled by them. She began to see another alternative—the concept of being in control of your own life and letting others be in control of theirs.

It was amazing to hear her telling Jan she knew she had done a lot of wrong things and she wanted some kind of absolution. She wanted to have a relationship with Jesus and be forgiven. She told Jan she was hoping maybe he could help her with that and asked if he would pray for her. That took so much courage and vulnerability!

When Jan said he would pray for her, she said there was one more thing she wanted to mention first. Then she told him that no one had ever touched her in a nonsexual way. She wondered what that would feel like. She wondered if maybe he would hold her hands when he prayed for her. Marilyn, you blew my mind! It must have been so scary to risk the chance that he might say no. You're brave.

After she asked, she looked away for a moment, fearing his rejection, but when she turned back to him he said yes, he'd like to hold her hands while they prayed. When he took her hands, her tears began to fall as he prayed for her. Then she prayed, too, asking God to forgive her and saying she wanted to be a Christian now, and finally asking him to help her not to do the wrong things she used to do. After she prayed, she asked Jan if she was a Christian now and he said yes. Then she simply said good-bye and thank you and went back inside.

It was so beautiful. I came out crying and praising Jesus. I prayed a silent prayer of thanksgiving and joy. Marilyn and I will fuse soon. I know it will be good for both of us.

Lord, I praise You! You have called Marilyn to Yourself so she can know first hand Your peace and comfort. Guide and direct us now in the days ahead as we get ready for fusion. May Marilyn sense Your presence and Your love during this time of sad farewells to the others inside. You are fulfilling Your promise to make us one!

March 24, 1995 — Marilyn, tomorrow is the big day! I am really looking forward to our fusing, but I have a feeling you still have mixed feelings about it. Perhaps you would like to write out your good-byes. I know saying a proper good-bye is something important to you. — Judy. ☐

☐ Well it's not as if I'm dying but it is true I won't be able to speak as a totally separate individual anymore after our fusion. I'm ready for it and I don't really have any fear or regrets. I am glad I waited this long because it took me a long time to understand how much I really wanted to be forgiven for all the things I did in the past. Now I'm forgiven and I feel so much more calm and relaxed about everything. Can you believe it? Me? A Christian? Hard to imagine, but it's true!

I do have just a few parting words. First of all, Guardian, I just want to say, "Go for it!" I know you've been checking out Jesus and I know you've wondered if it would be possible for you to be a Christian. No, you are not too bad or angry. I think Jesus can help you learn to deal with your anger in more mature and manly ways. Also, think about fusion. You can't marry someone on the outside 'cause you're a male in a female body. It won't work! But you could join with me and Judy internally and then you won't be so lonely. Give it some thought. In the meantime, take care of yourself and the kids and keep watching and growing.

Judy, thanks for listening, for trying to understand. You're a lot different than I used to think you were but so am I, and you helped me see I could be that way. Love to all! — Marilyn. □

□ March 25, 1995 — We are one! The fusion of Judy and Marilyn is done! I'm a new creation. Thank You, Jesus, for blessing our union and joining us together. I feel wiser and stronger. When fusion took place, I laughed and cried at the same time. It was like a joyful reunion, another perfect fit, just like the Good Mother. The tears were tears of gratitude and joy. After fusion, I was dizzy and I'm still seeing double but that will fade away in a day or two as integration progresses. Fusing just after Marilyn made a commitment to Christ is great. I feel I have a heightened awareness of renewed "first love"—a sense of wonder and awe and joy in my salvation! I'm so happy. Two days ago we became sisters in the Lord and now we are united as one. *Amen! Thank You, Jesus! I will never be the same. You are renewing my mind and restoring my soul.*

Counting the Cost

March 27, 1995 — I have spent forty-two years with this awful "Who am I?" feeling and finally, piece by piece, the puzzle is coming together and I am beginning to feel that I am. *Thank You, Father, for this work of reconciliation and restoration You are doing within me.*

I called my Mom. It was so healing to have her tell me she absolutely believes me about the incest. She knows I would never make something like this up or even imagine it. She understands that I love Dad and I didn't want anything to come between him and me. She totally and unreservedly affirmed my reality. Her affirmation touched me in a deep place in my heart...

Sometimes I wonder if I'll ever be done counting the cost of the incest, the cost to myself, to my husband, to my children. Jan said, "It's hard to stop running when you're being chased," meaning the damage that I did in running from my past was somewhat inevitable. There are so many things I wish could have been different. So many of the things I did were acting on compulsion. I was driven by the demons of guilt, shame, fear, loneliness and anger. Indeed, I was being chased. Counting the cost, though painful, is good. It causes me to be more determined than ever to quit paying the price today. It strengthens me to fight the good fight for recovery to the very end. I will be free! In the name of Jesus and for the sake of His glory, I will be free!

"My purpose is that they may be encouraged in heart and united in love, so that they may have the full riches of complete understanding." (Col. 2:2)

March 30, 1995 — After dinner last night, Paul and I went for our usual walk. When we were on our way home I suddenly realized my legs were in severe pain. By the time I got home, my whole body was aching and I was shaking with chills. I laid down on the couch with a blanket and stayed there for three hours with severe pain in my arms, my legs and my abdomen. I finally crawled off to bed, and as I lay there in the dark, the emotional pain that belonged with this body memory began to be expressed. Angel came forward to remember the rape as it had occurred nearly four decades ago. Only this time, unlike when it happened originally, she was able to cry over the pain.

Again, at a certain point just after penetration when the pain became unbearable, the memory skipped to the end like a scratch in a record makes the needle jump to the next song. Then she rolled onto her side, knees curled up into herself, and sobbed, "Mommy... Mommy... I want my Mommy..." But Mommy never came. She eventually settled herself by sucking her thumb, but the physical pain lingered. I cried, too, as I thought about the impact my father's abuse had on me, on my marriage, on my whole life; the impact it is still having today.

March 31, 1995 — Jan wasn't there when I arrived at his office today. As I sat in the waiting room I thought about the fact that he'd be coming through the front door. I told myself not to have my usual Post Traumatic Stress startle response of fear when he opened the door. It didn't work. The door handle turned and I jumped and my whole system went into chaos upon seeing Jan.

The "kids" wanted to talk and so did the Guardian. He's struggling with a sense of uselessness, loneliness and frustration these days. Jan was talking to me and I was trying to talk to him, but it was tough because of all the noise and confusion in my head. He asked if it was because of the door opening and I realized that was only part of the problem. The other part was that we had all been thinking about having to go the next ten days without seeing him while he was on vacation. This thought of separation was upsetting in itself but it brought up an even more upsetting one: two months in America this summer. That is a really scary thought. We talked about it for awhile. I have a feeling we'll be talking about it a lot as the time draws nearer.

I told Jan Angel had come out and started to remember... Then Angel did indeed come out to tell the rest of the story. She started by saying, "He hurt me. He hurt me so much everywhere."

As she talked about the memory of being raped, she felt the sharp abdominal pain and the pain where his legs had pinned her legs down. She cried this time. Crying helps. Again she skipped past most of the rape to the end when she was left alone in the darkness. She cried out again, "Mommy... Mommy... I want my Mommy."

She talked for a long time until some of the pain in her body subsided, while Jan comforted her with reassuring words. Once she settled down I came to take her place and I was working on staying numb but Jan said, "Go for it. Just let it come."

For the first time I was able to cry for Angel and all that she had experienced. Up until that moment, whenever Angel spoke in therapy, I would back away and shut down because I don't want to feel what she feels and know what she knows. Today I gathered all my courage and let the feelings wash over me. I grieved for all the things that should have been so different. I grieved for the little girl lying alone and frightened with a broken body, curled up in agony, waiting for a "rescuer" who never came.

"He reached down from on high and took hold of me; he drew me out of deep waters. He rescued me from my powerful enemy, from my foes, who were too strong for me. They confronted me in the day of my disaster, but the LORD was my support. He brought me out into a spacious place; he rescued me because he delighted in me." (Psalm 18:16-19) *I pray one day soon Angel will come to know that You, Jesus, are her Rescuer and You always were, always are and always will be with her. Amen.*

10 PM — When I got home from my time with Jan, Paul was waiting eagerly to talk to me about a difficult letter we received. One of our supporting churches wanted more information about our conflict with our former mission agency and we had the distinct impression our position as their missionaries was in question.

I knew it would be my job to compose a response and I really wasn't up to having a long discussion about it right away. First I needed time to process the work I had done in therapy today. I snapped at Paul and he felt unimportant to me so he got up and walked away. His reaction made me feel unimportant to him and so on and so on, ad infinitum. We made a couple of attempts to use our better communication skills but we kept bogging down in our defenses. Our argument continued on and off all day, flowing out of both of our reservoirs of pain and frustration. Just when I thought our battle was over, Paul pessimistically predicted that the church would stop supporting us.

All of a sudden, I just lost it! I mean I literally lost control. I went wild! I was so angry at all the injustice in the world, but I couldn't stay with the anger because of my fear, so I ran away and Guardian and Angel took over. — Judy. ☐

☐ "All the good people get screwed and all the bad people get rewarded!" We screamed and ranted and raved and defended our right to be angry when Paul tried to make us shut up! We are all furious at how the bad one could hurt us over and over again and nobody stopped him. We had to just lay there and let him hurt us and we couldn't stop him! We tried to be good as we could but we get punished but the bad one gets to have anything he wants! It's not fair! Why didn't God stop him? Somebody should have made him stop! We are very mad. Paul did not understand but we are mad at the bad people! After we screamed and yelled for a long, long time, we sat on the bed and cried and Judy told God that we don't understand. Even she doesn't understand why!

Paul came and we told him we don't understand and he put his arms around us and tried to help us understand. We still don't understand much but we felt better when he came and held us. We are tired now. Good night. — by Guardian for Angel. ☐

More Gifts from the Sea

April 3, 1995 — Home at last! As I entered my "little nest" by the sea, my heart and soul were lifted up in anticipation of my time here with Jesus. I spent most of today in worship and prayer, inviting Angel and Guardian to listen in and from time-to-time talking with them about Jesus, His love, His power and His presence.

Dear Father God, I commit this week into Your hands. My desire is to hear Your voice and be obedient to You with every moment of my time here on my retreat. Give me the grace, Lord, to surrender all to You, that I may know You more completely and love You more deeply, and especially that I may reflect Your beauty more accurately in my innermost being. I can hide my sin and hypocrisy from the people "out there" but the people on the inside, Angel, Guardian and even the Gatekeeper (or whatever his name is) see me as I really am. They hear all the things I would never say out loud, all those selfish or careless or negative comments that, if spoken aloud, would damage my glittering image as a "mature" Christian. I've never been able to hide my sin from You, Lord. Cleanse my heart and purify my soul that I may please You and be a witness for You both within and without. Thank You, Daddy God, for giving me these special days just to be with You. Guide me and do Your will in and through me.

Dear Guardian and Angel — A few nights ago you were railing at the seeming injustice in a world where evil people get whatever they want and those who are good or innocent or righteous seem to get punished. It certainly seems to be true sometimes that the bad guys win and the good guys lose. It doesn't seem fair and it's enough to make a person think about choosing "badness" over "goodness." The Lord has just shown me a few verses in the Bible that explain things from another point of view:

"... the One you are looking for will come suddenly... Yes, he is surely coming... Like a refiner of silver He will sit and closely watch as the dross is burned away. He will purify the ... ministers of God, refining them like gold or silver, so that they will do their work for God with pure hearts... At that time my punishments will be quick and certain; I will move swiftly against wicked men who trick the innocent, against adulterers and liars, against all those who cheat... and do not fear me, says the Lord Almighty.

Listen, you have said, 'It is foolish to worship God and obey Him. What good does it do to obey His laws? And to sorrow and mourn for our sins? From now on, as far as we're concerned, "Blessed are the arrogant." For those who do evil shall prosper, and those who dare God to punish them shall get off scot free.'

Then those who feared and loved the Lord spoke of Him to each other... 'They shall be mine,' says the Lord Almighty, 'in that day... I will spare them as a man spares an obedient and dutiful son. Then you will see the difference between God's treatment of good men and bad, between those who serve Him and those who don't.'" (Malachi 3:1,3,5,14-18 TLB)

God is just and His justice is righteous. Those who have hurt you will receive their punishment. At the same time, if you commit your ways to the Lord and trust in Him, you will be rewarded! Angel, your anger at the man who hurt you so terribly is a righteous response to something evil. Guardian, your anger at everyone who hurt the children is perfectly appropriate and, in fact, it provided some protection to the children. Yet anger and arrogance that is directed at God is unrighteous, unjust anger against a Holy God whose justice is perfect and perfectly tempered with His mercy.

Be angry at the abuser, angry at the perpetrator, angry at the unrighteous behavior of an evil man, but when you are angry at God, you need to go to Him and confess your anger and repent, asking him to forgive you.

God is just but He is also merciful and because He loves you, He desires to forgive you. That's why He sent His Son Jesus Christ to earth. Jesus was both man and God. He was the only man who ever lived without ever sinning against God or man. Because He was without sin, He took on the burden of the sins of the whole world. His punishment, taken in our place, was death on the Cross. He loved us so much, He gave His life for us just so we could be forgiven and spared the righteous punishment we deserve from a Holy God.

When Jesus died He provided the way for us to come back to God. When Jesus rose from death to life, He provided a way for us to have eternal life. Jesus died to atone for every sin ever committed by us and every sin ever committed against us. He wants to remove all your sins from you and wash you as white as snow. He loves you, Guardian, just the way you are and He wants to help you become everything you are meant to be. He loves you, too, Angel. He wants to reach out and heal you in all your broken and wounded places, to take away your pain and fear and give you instead peace and comfort and joy. This week we will be spending lots of time talking and listening to Jesus. You will both have a chance to get to know Him better. Do not be afraid. Jesus is gentle and loving and the truest of friends. Seek Him and He will reward you with treasures you've never known. He loves you and so do I. With love, Judy.

April 4, 1995 — Spent the morning walking on the beach. Little Judy Marie collected shells to bring back as gifts for Hellen and Jan. It's a sparkling spring day today with a warm sun, a cool, gentle breeze, a soft blue sky with clouds like strands of cotton candy. We went to the animal farm with a loaf of bread to lure the baby goats to the fence. Angel's whole life experience once consisted of enduring the ravages of an evil man in the dark of a bedroom tomb. She never saw the sun, never experienced God's glorious creation. Today she is seeing beauty and goodness she never knew existed in the world. Her eyes are finally opening up to a world of sights and sounds and other sensations that bring pleasure rather than pain.

Angel, listen to the rooster crow, to the caw of the raven and the cry of the sea gull. Hear the lilting children's laughter and the braying of the baby goat as he kicks up his heels in the pure joy of being alive. Feel the warmth of the sun as it pours its golden glow down upon your head and the touch of breeze in your hair. See the bright blues and greens of the peacock on the roof. Smell the salt-air of the sea. The body and its senses were created by God for pleasure, but you, Angel, have known only pain. Set the pain aside now for just awhile, Angel. You can pick it back up, examine it and resolve it when the time is right and with help from others, but today is a day for pleasure. Feel and enjoy the goodness of life, the glory of creation, the gifts of God. Just let us love you, Angel.

April 5, 1995 — I haven't left my "little nest" all day. I've worshipped with songs of praise and I've prayed and I've sorted seashells—Little Judy Marie had to choose which ones to give to Jan. Angel held her teddy bear and looked at the picture of Jesus, the Good Shepherd, and cried out her confusion. She wants to trust Jesus but she is so afraid.

Dear Angel — Take your time and get to know Jesus. He is more than just a man. He is the Son of God. One day you will know that He is always with you.

He was even with you when the bad man was hurting you. He was the One who gave you the strength to survive so that one day you would meet Him face-to-face. He wants you to know you are His child and He will wipe away your tears.

He longs to hold you tenderly and whisper, "You are my beloved child." He waits patiently for you, Angel. He will not touch you without your permission or against your will. He waits instead with open arms for you to run to Him.

9:30 PM — Mary colored a picture expressing her growing sense of isolation and loneliness. The sun was setting, so I put on my coat and hat and took a short walk while Mary and I had a talk. She told me that Angel is the important one now and she's not important anymore so no one wants to talk to her at all. I explained that she is very important. When she wants to share her thoughts and feelings she will be given the time but now Angel has a lot to share and really needs to talk. It's her turn, but that doesn't mean Mary is unimportant or unloved.

I asked Mary what I could do to help her feel better and she said she wanted to fuse with Little Judy Marie. She thinks she won't be lonely then because Little Judy Marie is always talking to everyone. She thinks she can learn to laugh and play by fusing, too. Little Judy Marie practically jumped for joy within me when she heard all of this. I was not quite so sure about it.

I told Mary I think it's a good idea but not until all of her memories are decontaminated and healed. Mary needed to search her heart and open all the doors to see if there were any hidden things in the dark that needed to be brought to the light for healing.

When we returned to the cottage, we prayed, asking God to search Mary's innermost places and reveal any broken or wounded place. We began to walk together through Mary's memories. The scenes that once belonged to the Lonely Little Girl seemed to be pretty well healed. Mary felt pain as she remembered various scenes of seduction all the way back to when she was eleven and her music teacher gave her private voice lessons in an attempt to seduce her. She expressed her feeling that every contact with men had involved an attempt on their part to seduce her in her innocence.

As we traveled back farther into the past, we crossed over into the Fearful One's memory banks. There we found a memory that still held a very strong charge. Mary was remembering the early molestation, before things became truly violent. Her daddy had come to her room to caress and fondle her. She was scared and confused and she knew it was bad. Yet she was so hungry for touch, she let him do it and as she got used to it, the sexual touch became pleasurable. Her body responded to what her mind rejected. She was desperate for any kind of affection. She came to believe she wanted him to touch her.

As Mary viewed this memory projected on the video screen of our mind, she became overwhelmed with shame and guilt. No matter how much I told her it wasn't her fault and she never wanted what he did to her, she just couldn't let go.

Finally, I managed to get her to release the feelings to me. I had never felt such shame. It was so deep I nearly vomited. I carried it to Jesus and laid it at the foot of the Cross, crying out for Him to wash me, wash Mary, as white as snow.

Jesus reminded us that He had died long ago for every sin and that He had already forgiven us for trying to meet our needs and satisfy our hunger outside of Him. He assured Mary and I of His love which is freely given to us because we are His children. Praise God, tonight He broke the power of that shameful sense of compliance and complicity that was holding Mary in bondage.

I love You, Lord. Thank You for calling me chosen, for saying I am Your beloved child. Let me dwell in the presence of that reality. Help me communicate it to my own children and the people inside of me. I give You glory for the healing You brought to us today. Amen.

☐ I am so excited cuz we might get to join me and Mary together! I want that and so does Mary! Please, please, please let us! — Little Judy Marie. ☐

☐ April 6, 1995 — I've been thinking a lot about Mary's request to join with Little Judy Marie. I feel a sense of peace that Mary has been healed after last night's encounter with the root and depth of her shame. I think she is well enough now that it would be safe to do the fusion. I spoke with both girls and together we came up with a new name for the new creation they will become. Both are delighted with the idea of being called Merry. I love it, too. It retains Mary's name but adds to it the essence of Little Judy Marie's character. When they fuse, they will become Merry.

I want each of the girls to have a chance to talk it over with Jan before we take this step though, and I want to ask his opinion about whether it's appropriate to do the fusion now.

Abba Father, how can I express my gratitude? Words are hopelessly inadequate to the task of describing the sense of joy and freedom I am tasting now. With each passing day, as I surrender more and more of my long-hoarded memories and feelings to You, and receive Your grace and healing in return, I am set free! You are reaching down deep into my yesterdays and erasing the pain. You are redeeming my life, even the past. You are the Lord of my past. Thank You!

2 PM — Angel just had an incredible encounter with Jesus. As we have worshipped and prayed and talked about Jesus these past few days, Angel has been watching with uncertainty. Awhile ago, she was looking at the picture of Jesus the Good Shepherd and she began to talk to Him. In tears she told Him she wanted Him to be her daddy but she was afraid. She knew she wasn't really an angel because an angel wouldn't want to kill the man who had hurt her. She thought she must be very bad to want to kill him and so Jesus wouldn't want her.

He assured her that He wanted her to be His beloved child and He offered her forgiveness. She told Him the bad man had made her do awful things and had done awful things to her and the dirtiness was still sticking to her and she couldn't make it go away. Jesus said He would cleanse her from the dirtiness. Then she asked Him to be her daddy and to forgive her. After Angel asked Jesus to be her daddy, she started to release some of her pain to me—deep, wailing pain out of the darkest caverns in the tomb. Together we carried it to the Cross of Jesus to be washed away by His blood.

Dear Lord Jesus, You know how much Angel must yet face in order to reclaim her life, all the memories and anguish and grief. You will be with her and Your presence will be her comfort and strength. She has always been Your beloved child yet she always felt like an orphan, unaware as she was of Your presence. It's a new day with a dawn of new hope for Angel. Thank You for drawing her to Yourself.

10 PM — *"I will not leave you as orphans; I will come to you."* (John 14:18) Angel is an orphan no more. A child consumed by the fire of an evil man's desire, she will rise from the ashes in beauty. By her profession of faith in Jesus Christ, she will mount up with wings like the promise of her name. She will be free!

In these days of retreat I have been able to move much closer to Angel than I had been up to now. Her intense anger and the terrible reality of her memories have kept me at a distance and prevented me from being able to truly empathize and feel her pain. I have been a coward. Now I feel things are different somehow. I have begun to allow Angel to transfer some of her feelings to me so I can help her with them. Perhaps soon I will be able to move in close during her memory work, too. I know it will help us both that she can retreat into the arms of Jesus when things get too difficult.

Don't Look Down

April 9, 1995 — Last night I watched a movie about father/daughter incest. Doing that sort of thing helps me break out of the isolation of feeling I'm the only one this ever happened to. The film involved the repeated rape of two daughters and, twenty years later, a granddaughter. Based on a true story, it reminded me that it really is possible for a small child to be raped and no one to suspect it at the time. Sometimes when I try to come to grips with Angel's memories of rape, I wonder. Couldn't anyone see the physical manifestations of a little girl being raped by a six-foot-two, two-hundred-pound man? I so often doubt my own reality.

On the other hand, the movie also showed the father in absolute and outraged denial about what he had done, using almost the exact words that my father used against me, yet it was clear he knew exactly what he had done. It made me wonder about my own fragile concept that Dad doesn't remember what he did to me. The fantasy that he doesn't remember becomes harder to swallow. How could a man rape his own daughter repeatedly and not remember?

April 11, 1995 — Little Judy Marie was the first to arrive and she gave Jan the shells she collected for him at the beach. She told him how excited she is about the idea of fusing with Mary. Jan encouraged her that it was good that she and Mary were becoming closer even if they didn't fuse right away.

Then it was Mary's turn. She talked about wanting fusion because she felt so lonely and sad all the time and she wants to be happier. She began thinking about having to say good-bye to Jan and she couldn't do it. She asked, "Will you still care for me if I'm not sad all the time?"

He said, "Sometimes it's easier to show that you care when someone is sad but that doesn't mean you don't care when they're not sad."

She asked him if he would miss her when she was gone and he said yes, he would. She was holding his hand and looking into his eyes with so much love and vulnerability and need and she told him she didn't know what she wanted. Saying good-bye was too hard for her. She wanted to fuse, but she was scared. As long as she wasn't sure what she wanted, he thought it might be better to wait, so she said good-bye but she promised she would talk to him again before any fusion. □

□ Angel came out and Jan asked her how many times she had been raped. She answered, "Lots of times. Every time the door would open."

"Did you ever go away somewhere in your mind to escape it?"

"I just kept saying over and over 'I want to kill you! I want to kill you!' but not out loud."

Then she said she had been afraid Jesus wouldn't want her because she wanted to kill the man who hurt her and because of her dirtiness. She said He said He'd forgive her and wash her clean "but I don't think Jesus understands. I still want to kill him!"

All her muscles were tensed and her legs were shaking. I wanted to stop the legs from shaking and get the body to relax so I pulled Angel in and pushed Judy out. She was numb and said, "I can't feel anything. I feel so guilty for not being able to respond to Angel as I have to the other children. I want to help her but I can't."

Jan said, "She's helping you right now by showing you truth you need to know. You'll be able to help her later." □

□ How many times will I knock down this fantasy of the good daddy only to see it resurrected again and again? I don't want to accept it that I became an abandoned orphan. I still had a father of sorts when he was molesting me, but when Angel came into being, when the violence was initiated, the daddy of my girlhood dreams was destroyed. I was abandoned. I was alone. I was beyond help and hope. Only Jesus cared then, but I had no one to lead me to Him, no one to show me the way into His arms.

April 12, 1995 — All day I have felt a restless sense that something was troubling the children. I finally drew away to my office to write and Mary came right to the surface in tears, crying, "I don't wanna go!"

"Go where?" I asked. She doesn't want to go to America and she doesn't want to "go away" inside by fusing with Little Judy Marie. She is afraid she won't see Jan anymore. She is deeply attached to him and she is terribly afraid that if she changes by fusing he won't love her anymore.

Dear Mary — I understand how you feel about not wanting to go to America. I will miss our talks with Jan very much, too! But Jan isn't going to forget you just because you don't see him for a few weeks. He cares about you and all of us very much and he won't abandon us. He'll keep right on caring even when we're gone, and Jan is not your only friend. Paul is your friend, too, and you have me and the rest of the inside family and you have Jesus! You will never be all alone ever again, I promise!

I'm so glad you are a part of me and I look forward to the day we are so close we become one, but I will not force you to fuse. You will fuse when you decide you are ready, in your own time. So try to relax, Mary. Stay close to Little Judy Marie so you will become the closest of friends. That's a good place to begin. I love you, sweetheart. Love, Judy. □

□ April 14, 1995 — It's difficult to face, even in these private pages of my journal, the level of dependency and need I feel related to Jan right now. Mary spent the majority of our session today relating to Jan her anguish about going to America. She kept saying, "I don't wanna go!" over and over again. For Mary, the time between appointments, between Monday and Friday, is an eternity. Two months apart feels like dying to her.

"Do you think I'm bad cuz I need you so much?" Jan shook his head. "It scares me cuz if I get used to talking to you all the time, I will forget how to be alone and then I won't be able to handle it anymore."

Jan just kept on loving and accepting her even in her neediness. When he said it was time to start winding down, Mary left and I came out. That's when I realized just how closely aligned my own feelings about Jan are with Mary's. I was sobbing in shame and grief as I said, "It's one thing for a ten-year-old girl to have these overwhelming feelings of dependency, but it's another thing... her feelings are so close to mine!"

"It's good to look at these feelings and just let them flow," he said, "to face them and to let them develop and yourself to develop beyond them."

He didn't run away from my neediness. He didn't abandon me in the face of my terrible longing for fusion with him. He understood. He accepted it. He didn't push me away. He didn't think I was a bad client. He loved and accepted me just as he had loved and accepted Mary.

April 17, 1995 — I haven't been able to bring myself to write in my journal these past few days because I don't want to see my thoughts and feelings made real and concrete. All I can think about is how desperately I don't want to go to America, how desperately lonely and vulnerable I think I will be without access to Jan. My dependency on him, this awful neediness and longing I feel, scares me and repulses me.

April 19, 1995 — I've been making myself numb using dissociation ever since I made deep contact with my dependency feelings. Jan says the hunger goes back to my abandonment by my mother when I was an infant child.

I don't want to talk about my mother! It just seems so cliche and infantile. He even made the most repulsive analogy of himself as the breast and me as the baby who is so hungry, I will pull and claw and bite the breast to get what I need. Ugh! Yuck! I'm grossed out... What good does it do to want or need? The desire is left unfulfilled and you're left hungrier than ever, with the added pain of rejection.

All during the session, Guardian was making negative comments in my head like, "Why do we need to talk about that witch anyway?" He wanted to talk with Jan and was trying to push his way forward but I stopped him. I didn't know I was strong enough to do that but I am getting stronger. Guardian seems to be weaker since I integrated Marilyn.

I managed to look at the transference involved in my feelings about Jan. I was able to hear, and for a short while really listen to, a small voice from deep within me crying out in sorrow and loneliness, "I want my Mommy..." It's true, I'm wanting Jan to be my mommy now.

I was able to feel the sense I had as a child that my mother was beautiful, like a queen, and that I was admiring her from a long distance away. I was aware of how nurturing and tender she was with the babies. How I wished she would do that to me, to look into my eyes with love, to hold me gently in her arms. Somehow I "knew" that she didn't love me because I was bad and dirty. Seeing it this way made me feel more in control then, because it was "my fault". I was rejected, but I could always hope that, one day if I cleaned things up and got things right, she could love me.

Deeper into the Pit

April 24, 1995 — I finally gave in and let the Guardian come out and talk to Jan today. I was really scared but Jan helped me to relax and let go of control. □

□ Finally! I really don't know what your big problem was. Did I do anything so terrible? Did I? No. All I wanted to do was have a little time in the body, a little time to hang out with Jan. Granted you did piss me off royally by trying to keep me clammed up. What are you, paranoid or something?

Then I got stuck the whole time I was with Jan talking about that witch of a mother of yours! What a waste of time. I don't know why you're so determined to preserve her pristine image. All I know is she did a lousy job of protecting the little girls. I wouldn't have needed to come around at all if she had been doing her job. — Guardian. □

□ After awhile Guardian was distracted by someone wanting to come out and say something. He didn't want to give up "the floor" because he had waited so long for a voice. Jan helped him tune in enough to hear that it was Angel who was trying to interrupt. He cares about her so he backed away and she was out. She was very upset and said, "I only wanted Guardian to tell that I want my Mommy." Then she curled up in a ball crying, "I want my Mommy... I want my Mommy."

Jan spoke soothing words to her. He helped her remember where and why she had those big feelings of being helpless, powerless and alone, crying out in the dark for a Mommy who never came. She said she didn't want to hold herself, she wanted her mommy to hold her. Jan said there are others who can hold her and want to hold her but they are not her mommy. She looked at him with sadness, saying, "She's not going to come, is she?" He had to tell her the truth. "No," he said, "She's not going to come."

She turned her face to the wall and sobbed inconsolably. Gradually her breathing became more regular as she found ways of soothing herself. I called Angel inside and I came out. I knew we had gone well over our time slot so I numbed myself and got up and out of there. Just outside the office door, the sobbing overtook me and soon it was Angel behind the steering wheel crying, "I want my Mommy!" Fifteen minutes later I was finally able to start the car and drive home.

9 PM — Angel couldn't really cry out for her mommy after the rapes because she believed if she made any sound at all the "bad man" would come back and kill her. She didn't scream or shout when he raped her and she didn't cry out loud for her mommy in the next room when it was over. In her heart and in her mind she cried out for her mommy repeatedly until she finally fell asleep.

She must have thought one day her mommy would come and rescue her. No one ever came to rescue her. From the day the violence began until the day it finally ended, no one ever came. She faced the pain alone. My poor precious Angel. I don't want her to ever have to face the pain alone again.

Please God, help me to identify and fully empathize with Angel as I have with the other children. She needs to know she's not alone anymore—the rescue crew has arrived at long last. Let her know Your presence and love in a deep way, too, Lord. She needs to feel the safety and comfort of Your arms holding her.

April 28, 1995 — What did I lose because Mom wasn't there for me? I lost out on having someone there to help me with my pain, to give me comfort, to give me hope that it was going to be all right. I lost out on feeling that I mattered, that I had any value. I lost out on having any feeling that I was a part of something bigger, a sense of belonging. I lost the sense of my own identity and reality and instead I felt I was invisible and unreal—an alien who landed here by mistake.

I didn't have anyone to look into my eyes, to know my name and to hold me in my fear. I don't understand. How could this have happened? Where was she? How could she not notice that something was terribly wrong with me? Not one part of me, not Little One or Fearful One, not Judy Marie or the Lonely Little Girl, not Angel—none of us felt we could go to my mother and tell her what was happening to us in the dark. The feelings of loneliness and abandonment these truths bring to me as an adult are shattering. How did I manage them as a child?

It's hard for me to explore these negative feelings about Mom. Over the years since I grew up we have built a loving relationship. She is the only one in the family who is willing to say she believes me about the incest. I know she loves me now and cares about my pain. I feel if I look my childhood experiences in the eye, I am somehow betraying our relationship today.

As I spoke with Jan about this I realized I didn't want to lose the "beautiful queen" I had admired from afar in my childhood and replace her with a "wicked witch." This is characteristic, black-and-white, all-or-nothing thinking so common to survivors of childhood sexual abuse. My mother is neither all good nor all bad. Facing the impact of my experience of her as a child does not negate the positive aspects of the relationship we now have.

Lord God, please help me to come to terms with all of my feelings about my Mom. I need Your strength to face the whole truth and yet still be able to love. You know the feelings of loss, loneliness and abandonment that I have in relationship to my mother, my father and my siblings. Fill the empty places where they each once stood within me, Lord. Only You can satisfy the aching hunger within me there. I need You, Lord. I need You. Amen.

April 29, 1995 — Today was a true Sabbath Day—a day of rest and restoration. My heart is full of praise to the Lord for His goodness and mercy. As I spoke with people before and after church this morning, I was conscious of a deep sense of peace within, a feeling of fullness, of being in touch with the here and now and of knowing who I am. I'm starting to feel like I'm a real person with a sense of identity, a person I can actually like!

"For you did not receive a spirit that makes you a slave again to fear, but you received the spirit of sonship. And by Him, we cry 'Abba, Father.' The Spirit Himself testifies with our spirit that we are God's children. Now if we are children, then we are heirs—heirs of God and coheirs with Christ, if indeed we share in His sufferings in order that we may also share in His glory." (Romans 8:15-17)

My true identity is found only in Christ and it is created in His image. The closer I draw to Him, the closer I conform to the real me, as He created me to be! My pain and suffering are but vehicles that carry me to His throne of grace. As I bow before Him at the foot of the throne, He gently reaches out and lifts up my head. As I gaze upon His glorious face, He says, "Rise up, my child. Come. Sit here on my knee and rest your head here on my chest. You are my beloved one. I have been waiting for you to come to me. I love you, my child. I always have and I always will. Come and rest in my arms for awhile."

May 1, 1995 — *Father God, please help me to remember that wherever I go in this world Your Holy Spirit comes with me. You are the true Counselor and You have promised me You will not abandon me nor leave me an orphan in the storms of my life. You will come to me. You will pursue me to the ends of the earth because of Your great love. Let me feel Your presence in the loneliest places of my soul always. Lord, when I am a long way from my earthly counselor, help me to focus not on my pain, not even on my healing, but on You, my wonderful and ever-present Counselor. Amen.*

May 5, 1995 — Dear Mary — You stayed and talked to Paul when he came in to visit us. Good for you! He is also kind and gentle, like Jan, and he will be with us all the time we are in America. We won't be all alone! To answer some of your questions, I think Little Judy Marie is right that you will both be stronger when you fuse together. You definitely will not die, I can promise you that! When the Good Mother fused with the host personality "Judy" neither of them died. They just became united. Then Marilyn fused with them, too, and I am now a blend of Judy, the Good Mother and Marilyn. Before you became Mary, you were the Lonely Little Girl and the Fearful One. Their experiences, memories, thoughts and feelings blended to make you who you are. If and when you and Little Judy Marie decide to fuse, the new creation we have decided to call Merry will be all of each of you. You won't be less. You will be more. Can you understand that? — Judy. ☐

☐ Judy — I think I really do want to fuse with Little Judy Marie but I promised Jan I would talk to him again first. I have to ask him if he will still love me and always remember me even when I am not me anymore. If he promises then I think I will be ready to do it. Love, Mary. ☐

☐ None of this is really about Jan. I want it to be. It would be easier if it was. But it's not. It's about being hopelessly devoted to something I will never be able to have—the unconditional love and protection of a mother and a father. It's all about unfulfilled need, overwhelming hunger, starvation. Jan is simply the screen onto which I project all my unmet childhood needs. I want him to be my mother and my father, to somehow miraculously make up for everything I never got from them. He can't do it. Nobody can. Nobody but Jesus.

Oh God, is this emptiness, this terrible longing, ever going to go away? It hurts. So bad. This pit inside of me is so big, and I don't know if it will ever be filled up.

May 6, 1995 — Sank deep into those feelings, what I think of as the "black hole of my soul." It came as a surprise to me, since I've been doing better lately, especially at containing the pain to within the therapy sessions. Everything seems to be a bit too close to the surface suddenly. Last night, in the midst of a playful time of lovemaking with Paul, I was suddenly overwhelmed by feelings of neediness. With the awareness of need came powerful feelings of fear. I told Paul through tears how much I love him and need him. I told him I was "bad" and I would push him away. I begged him not to leave me and made him promise never to go away. Poor Paul. It must be so difficult to be married to me. He must sometimes wish he had chosen a less complex and confused woman. Yet he said he wasn't going anywhere, and he promised he would never abandon me.

It is so hard for me to trust, especially to trust anyone that I really need. To be in any way dependent is to feel fear. I'm afraid of my need for Paul. I'm afraid of my need for Jan. I'm afraid of my need for God. *God, help me overcome my fear! I want to trust but I don't know how!*

"What a wonderful God we have—He is the Father of our Lord Jesus Christ, the source of every mercy, and the one who so wonderfully comforts and strengthens us in our hardship and trials. And why does He do this? So that when others are troubled, needing our sympathy and encouragement, we can pass on to them this same help and comfort God has given us." (2 Corinthians 1:3-4 TLB)

Lord God, You continually comfort me in my grief, hold me up in my fear and fill me in my emptiness. You are the Lord of all my sorrow and tears, the Lord of my laughter and joy, the Lord of all. Loose these hands of mine which hold so tightly to the security of my chains. I want to hold onto only You, Father God, but I can't grasp You as long as I am grasping and holding on for dear life to things that can never satisfy. Gently pry my fingers from their white-knuckled grip on my self-protective strategies and defenses. Instead, hold my hands in your hands, Abba Father. Amen.

May 7, 1995 — Paul and I are celebrating our nineteenth anniversary today. Nineteen years, nearly half of my life, we have been together. It is a miracle to me that Paul has hung in there with me through thick and thin, with all the changing and rearranging I've gone through. He is so faithful, so steady, so very committed and true. How in the world has he managed to survive this wild ride? Only God could have given him the strength and endurance he needed.

For so many years I played the "come closer... go away" game — longing desperately for intimacy but scared to death to let anyone get too close. I still play it sometimes, but I catch myself sooner. I'm more aware of this self-defeating pattern in my life and I know now where it came from.

Paul gave me an anniversary card he made himself. In it he promised me he would love me more and more every day forever. He knew just what I needed to hear.

Lord, help me love him with the same faithful, unfailing love he gives to me. Free me from the terror that keeps me holding back from him. Teach me to trust and to love wholeheartedly. Amen.

May 8, 1995 — It's hard to know where to begin to write about my session with Jan today. Mary spent a long time talking about how guilty she felt because, in a way, she had liked the things her daddy did to her. ☐

☐ He told me it was all my fault what he did and he said only naughty girls liked it. He said if I told anyone they would know how naughty I was. Jan says that's a lie that only naughty girls like that. He said it is natural for the body to like something that feels good. He said my daddy knew that and he also knew that he wasn't supposed to touch me like that. It was his fault. Not mine.

Jan says I was too little to know what the truth was and my daddy made me all mixed up. He said I am not a naughty girl and not to feel guilty cuz of what daddy did to me. I felt better after he told me those things. Then I told him I am going away soon cuz I'm going to join with Little Judy Marie. I told him I want to but I'm scared. I'm scared Little Judy Marie will be sadder but I won't be happier. Jan says it's good that we talked about my guilty feelings cuz he thinks my sad feelings won't be so hard if they aren't all mixed up with the guilty feelings.

I asked him if I go away into Little Judy Marie will he still love me? He said yes! I feel so happy. He said I could still hold his hand, too, even when I'm not sad. It was the first time I ever smiled at him. Inside I could feel how happy Little Judy Marie was cuz she knew I could join with her now. When me and Little Judy Marie become Merry, he will still love us. I have never been so happy before. Love, Mary. ☐

The Shadow Falls

☐ May 9, 1995 — "Merry" was born today! Little Judy Marie and Mary have fused. The fusion was very painful. I experienced it as a loss, having grown to deeply love both of the little girls within me. After the fusion, I was encouraging Merry to go to sleep for awhile and to sort things out when she woke up. She wasn't tired, she wanted to stay awake and she seemed happy. I guess I was the one who was tired and wanted to put off dealing with the changes within. ☐

☐ It worked! It worked! We aren't we anymore—we're me! I can be happy now and sad cuz I have happy and sad inside of me, all together and not apart. I think I am stronger now than when we were apart, too. I don't want to think about what I remember right now. I just want to feel what it feels like to be Merry. I like my name! XOXOXO, Merry. ☐

☐ May 15, 1995 — I'm slipping down, down, down into despair as the time nears for us to leave for two months in the States. I don't want to go. Not a single fiber of my being wants to go. Everything within me screams, "No!" Though I've made a lot of progress on my journey to recovery, I am still very fragile. The children and I are crying ourselves to sleep every night. I am so tired. Jan thinks I'm tired because of my compulsive need to control everything, including the therapy. I think he's frustrated, maybe even angry with me.

I can't think. I can't collect my thoughts. I tried to talk with Paul and explain how impossible it is for me to be in America for such a long time right now. Even Jan thought it was too long. It's more than I can handle and I know it. I am afraid I am going to fall apart and go back into the deep depression or back behind my wall of protection, never to emerge again.

Paul can't hear me. He feels he needs me there the whole time, every minute, every meeting, and if I don't go, I am really abandoning him. I will be a failure as a wife if I don't go and a failure as a human being if I do go. I just wanted to find a way to shorten it down to maybe one month. That's the amount of time I originally told Paul was all that I felt I could handle, but he just said we need to stay longer.

I want out of this pain, out of this conflict, out of this fear. It could all be over if I just swallow those sleeping pills. No more pain. Just go to sleep and never wake up.

May 17, 1995 — That night I took the sleeping pills. Part of me wanted to die so much, just to go to sleep and get out from under the weight of the pain. Part of me wanted to live. I called Jan just before taking the pills but he wasn't home so I said good-bye to his answering machine. After I took them, Hellen called and she started threatening to call the police. That brought out a child in me who complied with her demand to let her talk to Paul. She told him what I had done.

The last thing I remember was watching from a distance as Paul stuck his finger down my throat trying to make me vomit. He held my head over the toilet in a perfect reenactment of what my mother did to the Lonely Little Girl. That's when I "went away" completely. I have no idea "who" went through the trip to the hospital and experienced the process of having my stomach pumped to get rid of the drugs and alcohol. I was completely dissociated and am now amnesic to the whole experience. Angel was the first to wake up in the hospital early the next morning and I was co-conscious with her.

When I woke up I wasn't even glad to be alive. A kind nurse came to talk to me and Angel came out crying, "I want my mommy." Paul took me home and I slept all day. We went together to see Jan last night. Merry came out to explain what had happened. Through tears she said she had tried to talk to Paul about how she couldn't go to America for so long. She was so afraid that she would have to "die" (psychologically) in America and if she had to die, then she wanted everyone to die, but she hadn't been able to explain her fears to Paul. When she had tried, Paul talked on and on about all the reasons why she had to go. If she didn't go, if I didn't go (he didn't realize I was representing Merry's feelings at the time), he couldn't do it alone. The more and the longer he talked, the smaller and muter Merry and I became.

After that conversation, I just got up, robot-like, and performed my daily duties of shopping, cooking dinner, etc. while a plot was formulating on the inside to escape the conflict and pain. I took a giant step backward and abdicated control. I didn't care.

Jan somehow managed to get Merry to explain for all of us the intense internal pressure we feel to get "better" fast and to act like everything's fine when everything is not fine. She told Paul how afraid we are that we will not be able to act "fine" for such a long time in America, especially without Jan to help us. She even expressed her anger a bit. Jan explained to Paul how much anger we have inside because of what was done to us when we were little, how frightening that is to us, and that it is going to take a long time for us to get better. □

131

☐ Jan said he wasn't mad with me cuz I have such a hard time to talk about how mad I am. I thought he didn't like me anymore cuz I didn't get better fast enough. He says I'm getting better as fast as I can and he understands that I am scared that if I am mad he will hate me and so will Paul and I will be all alone. I was really scared to tell Paul so many things and for him to know how I am scared and mad and everything. I didn't tell him everything I think cuz it was not safe. I was afraid I would be in big trouble and he would talk and talk and talk until he made me invisible. But Jan made him promise not to talk to me that way this week. Jan says I can say all my feelings and Paul is not allowed to argue about them this week. We will all talk again with Jan on Friday. I counted how many more times to see Jan until we have to go. Only five! And I counted how many weeks in America and it wasn't only seven, it was eight! I don't wanna go! Merry. ☐

☐ May 18, 1995 — Three days later I am still trying to come to grips with what happened Monday night. I thought I had been doing okay during the week before. Merry, Angel and I were all weepy, but nothing was setting off alarms.

I spent most of the weekend typing the excerpts from my journal along with my book proposal. That may have been part of what triggered Monday's chaos. As I read the excerpts I had selected, they moved in a progression that seemed to tie my struggles up in a neat little package of healing. The contrast between the apparent positive outcome implied by the excerpts, and my awareness of just how far I am from wholeness was pretty painful.

Monday morning when I met with Jan my feelings were, in fact, despair and hopelessness. I felt I was never going to get well, never going to learn to trust, never going to have the courage to go on and face the anger, never going to learn how to let go of my need to be in control. When we talked about America, Guardian came out to say how angry he is that we have to go when Merry and Angel and I are so afraid. He even offered to talk to Paul to try to get the message across of just how serious the problem is. I was sure it wouldn't make any difference no matter what I or any of us said to Paul, but Jan gave me a tiny bit of hope that if I opened my heart and emotions to Paul, he might understand.

I grasped at that straw of hope and went home to talk to Paul about my fears. Unfortunately, Paul came at my tentative exploration of the subject with a long and very rational response that left me mute. I felt angry that I had allowed myself to hope. I felt powerless and victimized by my own foolishness. That's when I shut down. Merry was inside going into her own state of despair and anger. I was feeling de-personalized, a step back from the action, watching myself sink from a disinterested distance.

As I try to reconstruct what followed, I'm not exactly clear on things. Merry's afraid of going to America. She feels she will "die" if we go there. There were voices inside egging her on to kill herself. They were saying to her, "It would be good just to go to sleep and never wake up again—that is a good idea!"

There is at least one part inside of me who is dedicated to keeping the secrets and is very upset about the idea of publishing a book. That part wants to kill all of us who are telling the secrets. It doesn't seem to realize that if one of us dies, all of us die. Now it has become essential to make some contact with that part and to make a contract with all parts regarding the issue of suicide.

Britt asked me to promise never to do it again. I could promise for me but I couldn't promise for the other parts. I don't feel safe from suicidal or homicidal parts right now. Things have become very unstable. I think the fusion of Little Judy Marie and Mary has contributed to this instability. Merry is indeed stronger. She also seems to have little impulse-control, more like five-year-old Little Judy Marie. That wasn't a real problem before because she had no anger to act out. Merry has lots of pain and bad memories and the strength of will to push them to the forefront. Even driving has become a problem in the last few days, as I keep switching into Merry involuntarily when I am behind the wheel. I've had three near misses in as many days.

Lord, I have come to you in repentance for the sinful act of trying to kill myself. I have received Your forgiveness. Yet, Lord, I don't have the confidence to be able to say I won't do it again! I don't trust myself. Father, chase away the confusion and the illusions in my soul. Bring reconciliation and unity to the parts of me in conflict with each other. Forgive us all, Lord, for our blindness and our ingratitude for Your sacrifice for us. We need You, Lord. Hold us close. Keep us safe. Amen.

May 20, 1995 — Paul and I went back to see Jan again yesterday. He encouraged first Merry and then Angel to come talk about their fears and feelings about America. When Angel came, she was so afraid of Paul she hid behind the armrest of the couch and covered her face with her hair. She didn't want him to see her and she was afraid to look at him. Paul is a man and she was afraid he would hurt her. She didn't trust him at all.

Jan explained that Paul had some very good reasons for wanting us to go to America and didn't want to hurt her. She is afraid because she wants to kill the "bad man" and she knows he is in America. She also told Jan, "I want to stay here with you." She feels safe with him and no one else yet.

He asked her to tell Paul how she came into being and why she had to come. She cried and told him she had to come when the "bad man" was doing terrible things because she could keep from crying out or making any noise at all. She did this by shouting the thought "I want to kill you" over and over in her mind. She told Paul if she cried or made noise, he would kill her but even though she never screamed, he still hurt her very much when he raped her.

Then she started to cry for her mommy and suck her thumb. Jan told her she had been very brave to share so much with Paul. He asked if there was anything else she wanted Paul to know. She wanted him to know that she and the others inside are important—not only Judy. She said, "We aren't just little things that are going to go away—we're real!"

Then she left and I came back feeling very exposed and embarrassed that Paul had seen these parts of myself. I said sarcastically, "Well, that was really helpful."

"Was it honest?" Jan asked. I had to say yes but I still didn't see how it could change anything. I was still feeling hopeless. I knew how strongly Paul felt he needed me in America, in spite of the emotional turmoil it was creating in me.

Paul talked for a long time with Jan about trying to be rational and thinking in the long term perspective, etc. I began to lose all hope. Finally, something he said made me angry and I sat up straight and contested it. We needed to end the session and nothing was decided. Jan suggested continuing the dialogue we had just begun and looked me in the eye as if to encourage my assertive response. I felt his advocacy without words.

Yet as we stood up to go, I panicked. We (the girls and I) were afraid because nothing was resolved, nothing was finished, and we were well past our allotted time. We didn't know how to finish it with Paul, but we didn't want him to come to any more sessions. We need time with Jan alone to solve the suicide/homicide issues inside and to create a sense of internal safety.

Jan could feel my panic and confusion and questioned me about it. We were backing into the wall and getting ready to bolt from the room. We couldn't tell him we didn't want Paul to come with us again. I managed to say, "I don't want all my time..." but I couldn't say anymore. Jan repeated it back to me, but we said, "Never mind. I don't want to talk about it."

I was able to ask if I was supposed to come alone or with Paul on Monday. Then Jan understood my panic and said he felt I should come alone. He also got Paul to agree to work on plans for America based on a time frame that I felt comfortable with for now. I opened the door and ran from the room.

Paul has conceded to a compromise. I will go for six weeks instead of eight. That concession has helped me. I have been able to relax enough to actually work with Paul on specific plans for the trip and will do some prep work in the next weeks before we go. We still need to find ways to create a sense of safety and to maintain some therapeutic support for me while we're in the States. Paul now understands how vital this is and has promised to protect us and support us as best he can.

With only a few sessions left before D-day, Jan and I must find a way to create some safety and protection on the inside, too.

A Place of Safety

May 22, 1995 — One of the parts that egged on the suicide attempt came to talk with Jan today. He wouldn't give his name because he believes Jan could control him if he did. He was indeed under the impression that he could "get rid of" me and others and he would be able to live on. He wanted us to die because I have a "big mouth"—I'm telling the secrets. He doesn't want anyone to know the secrets and he is very upset about the book I'm writing. He doesn't trust anyone.

I was able to stay quite close and feel him. He seems to be quite young, maybe eight years old, yet he acts like an adult. He's more like a child playing at being a grown-up. Independence is very important to him. Jan believes at some point he made a vow never to trust anyone again because trust leads to being hurt. He seems to have the ability to turn fear into anger.

As I thought about the things this young boy said, my heart responded with compassion and a desire to give him the love and nurture he needs. What he needs most right now is respect and a voice. I want to give him that. I wish I knew his name and when and why he came.

May 24, 1995 — I seem to have a compulsive need to control all aspects of my life, even the therapy. Jan pointed this out to me saying he thinks it is this need to control that makes me so tired and fills me with despair. That was hard to hear. Only two days prior I had listened to a world-renowned expert on DID say that one sign of a poor prognosis for recovery was the unwillingness to release control of the therapy.

I desperately want to surrender control, to let others like Paul and Jan help me, but being out of control feels terrifying to me. I have, in fact, released a lot of control already in the past year or so, but we are now down to the nitty-gritty issues and my resistance is tough to overcome.

As I ponder how to get past my fears, one of my biggest ones surfaces. I don't feel safe from those parts within me who are motivated by suicidal/homicidal ideas. Merry talked about more than one voice egging her on toward suicide. We have spoken to one of the voices and he has been able to realize that he, too, would die if he killed one of us. Are there others?

Lord Jesus, thank you for protecting me and keeping me alive. Forgive me for my forgetfulness of Your love and sacrifice for me. My time isn't up yet, is it? You're not finished with me yet. Lord, thank You for continuing the work You have begun in me even when I get stuck or bump into walls or fall down deep holes or just give up and drop to the ground in exhaustion. You just keep on molding and shaping my life. I'm not worthy, Lord, but You love me anyway and You never give up on me. You never stop inviting me to take Your yoke upon me, to join You in Your work of re-creating me. I'm a crumpled-up rag doll, Lord.

Not much use to anyone. But You're mending my broken heart, putting a piece of Your own heart of love inside me. May it shine through me.

May 28, 1995 — The hunger in my heart will never be truly satisfied in this life and maybe that's okay. I long so much for love, for fulfillment, for a sense of completion and wholeness. I have, up until now, seen this craving as a liability. Perhaps I've been confused. Perhaps this hunger in my heart is a gift from God. The hunger keeps me seeking Him, keeps me leaning into Him, keeps me reaching for all that He wants to give to me.

Father God, thank You for the hunger, that deep longing for love You have placed in my heart. Without that hunger I might never have sought You. I might never have found the sweetness of Your provision. Jesus, I pray You will keep reminding me that You are my source of satisfaction. You sustain me. You fill me up. You have promised that if I hunger and thirst after Your righteousness, a day will come when I will hunger and thirst no more. Alleluia! □

□ May 29, 1995 — It was time to work on creating some safety on the inside so we let Jan lead us in a deep relaxation exercise as a means of facilitating access to the more antagonistic and uncooperative alters. Judy is so afraid of them because she senses their negative affects—anger, belligerence, homicidal desires and so forth—and she becomes so tense she blocks them from coming forward. At the same time, it's vitally important that we build bridges to them, inviting them to become actively cooperative and involved in the healing process.

When Judy became physically relaxed, Jan encouraged her to go to the safest place in her mind, the meadow in our spirit where Jesus waits. The Lord has given us a visual image of that place in our center where we find Him. We see Him standing in a beautiful open meadow full of wildflowers—red poppies, yellow buttercups, blue bachelor buttons and purple irises. In the meadow is a huge maple tree standing beside a sparkling stream. Far in the distance are purple hills. Jesus waits for us there in the meadow and when we find Him, He is dressed as a shepherd and tending His flock. He often holds a little lamb in His arms.

Today we spent some time there under the shade of the maple tree just resting and watching the fluffy white clouds float by. After awhile a feeling of fear disturbed our tranquility. Suddenly Judy had a feeling of impending doom and the young male alter we are now calling Judah said, "She shouldn't get too comfortable because whenever you get too comfortable you get hurt."

Judah talked for quite a long time, expressing a certainty that people are not to be trusted. He said he needed to be on his guard at all times, always standing with his sword in hand ready to protect and defend. He asserted that the only way to stay safe was to keep your mouth shut and keep your distance.

Jan argued that not all people would hurt you, and some could even help you. He asked Judah, "Have I ever hurt any of you in any way other than in helping you to remember things you had forgotten?" Judah said yes and pointed out that Jan had hurt Judy and the little girls when he had said they could only come once a week (so he's been watching the therapy for a long time). He also said Jan was sure to hurt us again.

At a certain point, a stronger angry voice began to rebuke Judah from inside, telling him to shut up, go back inside and quit "blowing it." Judah was obviously intimidated and told Jan "I think I better go now." Judah is only a child though he talks tough and acts very independent. He is not as tough as he sounds when it comes to standing up to this other part which turned out to be the Gatekeeper. Judah did what he was told and retreated, allowing the Gatekeeper to take executive control of the body.

He spoke with Jan in a cold, angry tone, but listened as Jan explained that a strong, independent person is able to work together with others in a cooperative way while retaining healthy boundaries and separateness. A person becomes truly able to be independent by learning how to decide realistically who he or she can trust and how much, not by refusing to trust anyone.

Jan suggested that perhaps it would be better to allow Judy and the others to learn these things for themselves instead of erecting protective, defensive barriers for them. The Gatekeeper never conceded a point to Jan but he listened and considered all that was said. He went back inside as suddenly as he had appeared. Judy was confused and disoriented when she found herself in the body again. She didn't remember the conversation but she did feel safer.

I don't know where, why or when either Judah or the Gatekeeper were created. They are similar in motivation and style and seem to be connected to each other in some way. Both are convinced that people can't be trusted and independence is vital. I hope they'll come talk some more and come to understand our present reality better. — Observer. □

□ I told Jan I still don't wanna go to America cuz six weeks is a very long time. I miss him even after only a few days like this week I had to wait all the way from Wednesday till Monday. I told him when I miss him I think about him and dream about him that I am his little baby girl and I can crawl up on his lap and he will hold me and keep me safe and love me. I am afraid I will forget what he looks like when I am gone away for so long. I am so afraid he will disappear and me too! I asked him if I can have a picture of him to take with me and he said he would see if maybe he could find one. I hope so with all my heart! He promised me we will meet again and he will make an appointment for me to come back.

He said if I go somewhere deep inside or I go to sleep for the whole time in America, he will find me and call to me until I come back to talk to him. I don't wanna go... I just wanna stay with him. — Merry. □

□ June 1, 1995 — The Gatekeeper might more accurately be called a Safekeeper. It seems he sees himself as standing guard over a large vault. Locked inside are all the secrets. He feels way too many secrets have already leaked out. He doesn't trust anyone and thinks people who trust are stupid.

Jan helped us to relax and go to the meadow where Jesus waits. From there we left and found ourselves in a courtyard in the center of a big house. In the midst of the courtyard was a beautiful fountain. We sat beside it on an old wooden bench and looked around. In the corner of the garden was a tree and a big rock. We could see Jesus kneeling, His arms resting on the rock, His hands clasped together in prayer. He was praying for us. As we looked around we saw many rooms off the courtyard, each with its own door.

Angel noticed a large black metal door "like a very big safe" and she was afraid that "bad things might be in there." Someone was standing in front of the door, guarding it, and he looked angry. Jan asked Angel if she could ask the guard why he was angry. She was afraid to talk to him, but suddenly he took executive control and spoke for himself saying, "It's none of your business!"

It was the Gatekeeper. The whole time he was out he held his fist in a clench. Again, I was far away and not very in touch with the conversation. Later Jan told me he had explained to the Gatekeeper that he was here to help, but he didn't have a strong agenda or any intention of coercing anyone to do anything. He said sometimes a person may try so hard not to feel like a victim that instead they take the opposite stance of being invulnerable, angry and "strong." In a sense though, by doing that, they are still being determined by the things that happened to them, instead of being truly free. The Gatekeeper listened and said he'd think about the things Jan said. In the end he seemed a little less angry.

He admitted he wasn't satisfied with the way things were; he just doubted things could be different. He suddenly retreated and Jan welcomed me back. It was time to end the session. As I left, the tears started to fall. So much brokenness, so much isolation, so much pain, so much more work to be done. Will it ever be over?

June 3, 1995 — I have been keeping busy these past few days as a way to avoid the feelings. Busyness, overeating, running away in as many different ways as I can think of. That's how I am avoiding the pain of facing this awful churning in the stomach, the dryness in the mouth, the tension in the body—in other words, the fear. I'm exhausted from the exertion of the avoidance behaviors.

I have designated next Wednesday from 4-5:30 PM, my last appointment time with Jan, as the time when I am allowed to feel. In the meantime, we drew a picture of how attached Merry and Angel are to Jan. Merry is hugging him and Angel is sitting at his feet, her arms wrapped around his leg. Even Judah is there, a short distance away but looking on from his position on the swing that hangs from the maple tree. I really should be in there, too, sitting under the tree trying to maintain my dignity.

June 4, 1995 — Angel ventured out today to take a closer look at Paul. She spoke a few words to him, told him she was scared he would hurt her, and let him hold her hand. She became quite relaxed with him and closed her eyes to sleep.

June 7, 1995 — We leave tomorrow. I'm exhausted from facing all the intense emotions of our good-bye to Jan today. Now I'm feeling alone and afraid and angry. At the same time, I know the Lord is directing us to take this trip and He has a plan.

Merry is devastated by the idea of an extended separation from Jan. He helped her see that this shorter trip now is important because it will prevent a longer and maybe more permanent trip in a few months. Angel was hurt and angry that Jan didn't rescue her. She felt he could have made it so she didn't have to go.

I was so frightened by my own needs, by the overwhelming hunger rooted in my childhood, that I felt ashamed. I was afraid my need would be so great that Jan wouldn't be able to cope with it—that he would reject me. That fear brought with it the temptation to force him to reject me so that the tension would be over and done with, but the Observer was saying, "Don't do it, Judy," and the little girls were crying out against my self-destructive ideas as well.

Lord God, teach me to trust in Your love more with each passing day. You are faithful but so often I am not. Teach me to trust. Father, I know You have ordained this trip which I travel so hesitantly. Help me rest in You and allow You to guide and carry me through. Let me see Your purposes and Your will and be tuned to Your voice in these coming weeks. Amen.

Going Home

June 10, 1995 — Two days down, about forty to go. I'm feeling okay so far. I've had some good contact with Judah. He is beginning to explore the world for the first time in many years. His natural curiosity is overcoming his defensive barriers. We are building a relationship.

June 12, 1995 — Had another Fugitive-style chase dream last night. I am being chased through one hazardous scene to the next all the while trying to save and safeguard a little baby girl. The dream seems to go on for hours.

June 16, 1995 — Read another survivor's book last night. It was an intense exposure of her pain and struggle to find God in the midst of traumatic memory recovery. It was moving and powerful for me to read her story. Her father claimed to be sleepwalking. It tore me apart. My father claimed to be a sleepwalker, too. I had it all sorted out in my mind that, in a way, he really was sleepwalking—in a dissociated state.

When I read about another father who blatantly explains his "night wanderings" as sleepwalking, my own neat little package begins to unwrap. In the middle of the night, Angel came to the surface for the first time in days. She was sobbing in grief as Paul held her in his arms. She is coming to grips with the reality that the "bad man" was really her daddy. It was the first time she had let Paul hold her. She told him about her pain, about how much she had wanted "him" to stop but she couldn't make him, couldn't make a sound of protest for fear of dying.

Paul held her and promised her no one would ever hurt her like that again. This time, when Angel cried out for someone to help her carry her pain and anger, someone answered her cry. Paul was there for her, for me. We reached for a flower and, this time, we didn't get stung. In the end, she asked him to pray for her and she settled down as the grief and pain slowly abated in the safety of Paul's arms and God's love. She is learning to trust. So am I.

Jesus, how good and kind and faithful You are. Thank You for giving me just the man I needed to be beside me in this life—a very good man, my husband. Help me to love him as he deserves to be loved and to learn to trust him more with each passing day. Amen. □

□ June 18, 1995 — I came out to look at the picture Jan gave me. He smiles at me from the picture. His eyes are soft and warm. I wish he was my daddy. My real daddy did things to me that made me feel afraid but he said they were very special, just for only me. But then he started to hurt me real bad. It wasn't very special anymore so I went away. Angel came then. She hated my daddy. She didn't know he was her daddy, too, but now she knows. When she figured it out it made her very sad and she cried for a long time. She is a very brave and strong girl and some day she and me will join together. But I want to wait so I can go home and see my friend Jan. He is helping me grow up. — Merry. □

□ It's Father's Day. I wonder how Dad is doing. This is the first Father's Day since I started remembering. I thought about making some contact with him, but I'm quite sure Hallmark doesn't have the appropriate sentiment. Besides, the last time I sent him an E-mail, he made it very clear he doesn't want to hear from me. So I guess I'll write my Father's Day thoughts here in my journal instead.

Dear Dad — In spite of everything you did to me, I love you. In spite of the damage to my heart and soul, I love you. In spite of your failure to love and nurture me, in spite of the way you used and abused me, I love you.

I remember the songs you sang to us at bedtime, the stories you told, fireworks on the 4th of July, Christmas traditions, eating corn-on-the-cob fresh-picked from the garden, so many childhood memories... But there are other memories now, too, Dad, memories that belie the idealized picture of life in an American family, memories I can no longer push away because I am learning to love myself. Loving myself means being honest with myself and trusting myself, my thoughts, my feelings, my senses and my God.

Happy Father's Day, God! To the greatest Father of all time and the Father of all. You are my Abba, my Daddy, and You meet all my needs. You will never leave me or forsake me. I will always be your beloved child. I just want to serve and honor You, oh Father. I pray that You will be proud of me and one day say, "Well done!" Hold me close to You forever. With love, Judy.

June 21, 1995 — In a couple of days Paul and I will drive ten hours straight to the small town where I lived from kindergarten through fourth grade—to see the house on North Street. The next day we will go to the house on Riverside Drive. I'm nervous. So is Paul. I know I'm taking a chance by going but I feel compelled to take this trip. My desire to see the forgotten scene of the crimes outweighs my fear of newly triggered memories rising to the surface. Besides, what could be worse than what I already know?

June 23, 1995 — As I looked up at the house, it seemed so different from what I had expected. It was clean and bright, white with black shutters, with a crisply manicured lawn. Looking at it, one would never imagine that anything as evil as incest could have taken place there. We rang the bell and the current owners, who were expecting us, came to the front porch to greet us. As they talked on the porch with Paul, I walked around to the backyard alone. The back porch, the stairs, the garage and the yard I recognized as "home" and welled up with emotion and tears. This was familiar.

Returning to the front of the house, I walked up the stairs to the familiarity of the front porch. I played for many hours on that porch with my sister Jean. We were good friends then.

As I reached for the front door to go inside, I drew back. My heart began to pound. I was about to fill in the blanks and I was scared. I reached for the door again and this time walked through to the front hall. I saw the stairs that led to the bedrooms but I wasn't ready for that yet. Instead I turned to my left and began my exploration of the main floor. All of it seemed alien to me, as if I had never been there before. Only the back porch seemed the same, and I could almost see my mother hanging freshly laundered diapers on the pulley line just outside the back door.

Next I found the door to the basement. I went down the stairs and the emotions began to stir again as I pictured my sister and I acting out scenes from Mary Martin's "Peter Pan" and dancing the Mashed Potato. I was remembering happy, carefree times of joy and spontaneity and little girls' giggles. A safe haven in the house. Dad never came down to the basement.

Reluctantly, I climbed the stairs back up out of the cellar and headed for the front hall and the staircase that would take me to the bedrooms. At the top of the stairs I felt a sense of foreboding. I turned into the room immediately to the left at the top of the stairs, my brother had told me this was his room. The next room, the other front bedroom, was especially hard for me to enter. I sat down on the bed and remembered my father standing in the doorway, light from the hallway behind him, as he sang me a bedtime song. It was that same door that became a source of terror for me in the middle of the night. The door where the "monster" entered.

I glanced at the other two bedrooms and the bathroom and returned once again to the place where my nightmares were born. I sat on the bed and sobbed.

June 24, 1995 — When we left North Street, I knew I'd never go back there again. It was done and I was ready to put it behind me permanently. We drove the eight miles to see the house on Riverside Drive where I lived when I was ten to sixteen years old. It's a beautiful old Victorian home. The giant maple tree that used to grace the front yard was gone and the sky blue house had been painted a dark gray with white trim. I took a slow stroll up the walkway to the stone porch where I had spent so many hours sitting and watching the squirrels scurry up and down the thick trunk of the old maple tree.

I felt calm and relaxed because I was certain the abuse had ended when we had moved to this house. I rang the bell and the owner, a professor who looked the part, came down the regal staircase with a friendly smile. I told him who I was and he immediately welcomed me inside. He and his wife had bought the house from my parents nearly three decades ago. The house was much as I had remembered it—starting with the huge entrance hall with stairs going up from left to right and reversing at the landing where a giant stained glass window sparkled with sunlight.

I walked first into the living room to the left of the entrance hall. With fourteen-foot-high ceilings, beautiful parquet hardwood floors, large windows and carved moldings, the living room extended from the front of the house back into an area we had used as a family room but which the current owners had made into a formal dining room. At the back of the long room was the door to the backyard. A door from the dining room gave entrance to a large breakfast room off to the right with windows facing the garden. I looked out and saw the old barn had been torn down, the play yard was gone and a lovely country garden had been cultivated. Down at the back of the grassy lawn were the woods where I had spent many hours alone with my "friends"—the squirrels, the chipmunks and the birds.

Returning toward the front of the house, passing through the kitchen, I faced the stairs and suddenly, my fears. What would I see when I climbed those stairs? If I was so sure the incest had stopped when we left North Street, why was I so afraid?

Slowly, trembling, I climbed the great staircase. Just at the top and to my left was the "girls dormitory"—formerly (and now once again) the master bedroom. I walked into the room and burst into tears, fear and grief washing over me, as I saw where Jean and I slept, where Ellie slept against another wall, and the entrance to the tiny nursery where April's crib used to be. I saw the closet door so close to where I once laid my head. I felt the fear and the horror and I knew that I had been raped in this room.

I turned away to look at the next bedroom where my parents had slept, and then the room in the left rear of the house. I realized then that I had slept in that room, too, before we moved to the front bedroom. The same rush of horror washed over me as I looked at the position of the door and the closet and knew instinctively that bad things had happened in this room, too. I know now that the abuse did not end when we left North Street. When and how did it end?

June 27, 1995 — I'm on the plane about to take off for Los Angeles. Oh, how I wish I was heading in the other direction back toward Holland and home. They say missionaries never really feel good except when they are on an airplane flying one way or the other between their two cultures. Not me. I feel good when I am home in Holland. I want more than anything to go home but I know I have work to do so I am trying to trust God one day at a time. □

□ I hate our daddy! How could he do such awful things to us? I didn't understand that he was my daddy too but now I do and I hate him even more than before. He hurt me and he scared me and I thought I was going to die. He trapped me. He held my hair so I couldn't turn away. I hated that. I felt so dirty but I couldn't make it go away cuz I was scared to get out of my bed. I was stuck there in that bed just like I was glued there.

Don't tell me what to do! Don't try to control me! Don't trap me! He held my hands together over my head. It hurt me and I felt like an animal in a trap. I felt so small. I couldn't scream. I couldn't cry. I wanted to kill him. I wished he would die so I could be safe. But he didn't die. He came to hurt me again and again. Mommy never came to rescue me. I had to be strong and take care of myself. — Angel. □

143

☐ Angel, today you are no longer alone with no one to call on to rescue you. You no longer have to be so strong. You no longer have to take care of yourself. You are a little girl and little girls shouldn't have to take care of themselves. I'm taking care of you now. Jesus is watching over you, too. You can trust Him. It will feel so good when you can sit back and relax and enjoy the pleasure of trusting others to take care of you. That's what it's supposed to be like for little girls your age. That was stolen from you by our father. I want to give it back to you now. It's not too late to go back to the innocence. You are gradually beginning to trust me and Jesus and Jan and Paul. The more you let yourself trust us, the less trapped you will be by the past and the more real freedom you will experience. I love you, Angel. — Judy. ☐

☐ July 3, 1995 — I am very mad with Jan cuz he is going away and we can't find him. After tomorrow he goes with his real children to vacation and he didn't tell us where! Even though we're in America we might need to call him! What if we get very scared and we can't talk to him? He is leaving us and he doesn't even care what happens to us. He is bad to leave us all alone. I'm going to ask him where he will be. If he won't tell me I will be very mad and I won't talk anymore ever again. *Please God don't let Jan go away where I can't find him! I'm scared.* — Angel. ☐

☐ July 4, 1995 — I'm not feeling very independent on this Independence Day. Merry and Angel talked to Jan on the phone this morning for the last time for three weeks. Both are angry and afraid, feeling they are being abandoned, accusing him of not loving them. Jan refused to own that conclusion, saying they were not being left alone and reminding them they had me, Paul and Sandy to talk to. He reassured them about how well they were doing so far and that they will be able to continue doing well with my help. They cried and told him they wanted to be with him and wished they could be his little girls and how they wanted him to hold them. He agreed that it would be good for them to be held but he felt it would be best for Paul to hold them.

This is a very difficult time for both Merry and Angel, and it's difficult for me to be the loving, nurturing mother they need as I am feeling so needy myself right now. I want to go home! *Father God, please give all of us the strength to make it through these next three weeks in America. We need to rest in you and know that You know our needs. You are not going to abandon us no matter how "bad" we are, no matter if we make mistakes, no matter that we are angry, or weak and helpless, or ugly and stupid. Help us, oh Lord, to stop looking at ourselves and just concentrate on loving You.*

July 5, 1995 — Yesterday afternoon we went to Mom's house for a 4th of July barbecue. I talked to her about my feelings of alienation from my siblings since I confronted Dad. I just don't know how to relate to them anymore. I don't know how to "be" with them. It's like we're all sitting around in a room together and in the middle of the room is a giant pink elephant that everyone pretends isn't there. The pink elephant belongs to me, is attached to me. We all talk around and through the pink elephant but at the end of the day, I have to somehow take it home with me and live with it.

Mom was kind and understanding but she also understands my brothers and sisters and their need to ignore my reality to protect their own fantasies and illusions. I understand it, too, but it still hurts to walk alone with the pink elephant. Mom acknowledged her failure to protect me and asked me to forgive her. My heart melted within me as she spoke these healing words I so desperately longed to hear.

July 6, 1995 — We saw Sandy today. I told her I was uncomfortable and shy about letting switches happen in front of her because I was afraid she would see that I was a fraud. Sandy works with lots of multiples and I was so scared she would find me to be unreal. I continue to doubt myself! She reassured me that I was clearly dissociative and she had met Merry who was very different from me. She confirmed the diagnosis of DID and said I also have all the symptoms of Post Traumatic Stress Disorder. She even said she had suspected DID the last time she had seen me at the end of last summer. I don't know why I needed that validation so much. I guess I just grew up being told that everything that I thought, felt or sensed was not really true so it's still hard to believe myself, to trust my own instincts.

Merry is basking in Sandy's gentle, loving ways. She's soaking up all the loving affection she can get. Sandy's not afraid to hold us and hug us; she's just what the doctor ordered. I hope Angel will venture out and spend some time with her at our next appointment.

July 8, 1995 — Four weeks down, two to go. It's getting harder and harder to play the game, to act the part of the "I've-got-it-all-together" missionary. Yesterday the depression dropped down over me like the LA smog—a combination of gray sorrow and yellow cynicism. Even the meetings I had expected to be encouraging have left me feeling beat-up and misunderstood. I'm just so tired. I want to go home. Only thirteen more days.

July 9, 1995 — I think Paul may be even more tired than I am. I'm worried he is depressed, too. I don't think he has ever really allowed himself to grieve his father's death. The two of us walk around like zombies in between official appointments in which we do our best to communicate our honest enthusiasm for the work God has called us to do. We are excited about it and look forward to doing it. We're just tired of being here!

145

July 10, 1995 — I went shopping today and as I tried on clothes in the dressing room, a little boy talked with his mother in the stall next to mine saying, "Mommy, how much do you love me?"

"I love you from here to the moon and back again," Mommy said.

"That's not very big, Mommy. I love you from here to the moon and back and to the moon and back about 27 million times! That's how much I love you! How much do you love me?" the little boy asked again.

I was reminded about how totally natural and right and BIG is a little child's need to be loved by his or her Mommy and Daddy. God created us with that need for unconditional love and He intended for our parents to provide that love until such time as we are old enough to transfer our dependency from them to Him.

I don't ever remember either of my parents ever saying they loved me and I have no sense of having felt loved by either of them. The closest thing I had to feeling in any way special as a little girl was when my father first began the process of seduction and the milder forms of abuse prior to the start of the violence. No wonder affection, love and sex became so confused in my mind.

July 15, 1995 — I sang my song "Glittering Images" tonight at our home church. It is an incredible experience to get up and sing my own song, my own story. Afterwards, many people came to me to say the song had touched them deeply. I realized that the Singer alter is fully integrated now, spontaneously. She was created the first time I sang a solo on the stage of this same church a few years ago. Now she is no longer needed. Doing a solo is no longer a dissociative, out-of-body experience. It's wonderful to be a singer instead of having a Singer! *Thank You, Lord, for this spontaneous reintegration of a once-separated aspect of myself.*

July 18, 1995 — Had a terrible dream last night. David had been kidnapped, abducted by evil people, and I couldn't seem to get anyone to investigate and find and rescue him. At the same time, I was trying to care for and nurture Britt. All I wanted to do was curl up in the fetal position on the floor and scream out my agony and frustration! This wasn't about my son and daughter. It was about me. It was about extreme helplessness and powerlessness and a deep desire to be rescued, to be nurtured. Will I ever get beyond all of this?

July 20, 1995 — Last night Paul and I tried making love again. Again, things didn't go well. The "monster in the closet" comes between us. I finally told Paul I think we need to take a complete break from any sexual expression of our love for now. He was deeply hurt, but I just can't handle it anymore.

As Sandy would say, "only one more sleep" and I'm on my way home. I woke this morning at five and lay in bed talking to God. I'm grateful to have survived the last six weeks. There have been some good days, especially recently, when I have felt strong and capable rather than weak and helpless. Good things were accomplished and I can see God's hand in the timing and in the contacts we made. I have much to be thankful for when I stop long enough to taste and see that the Lord is good.

I survived. Life goes on. I didn't disintegrate, fall apart, disappear or die. Once again, we are stronger than we thought we were, with God's help. Can't wait to get home. Green fields and gray skies. Sheep on the hillsides. Bicycles. Canals. Ducks on the water. Walks in the wind. Friends around the corner. Solitude. So much. Calling me home. Home to Holland.

Chapter 5 — The River of Shame

Dark Night of the Soul

July 23, 1995 — I am in pain. I am frightened at the prospect of seeing Jan tomorrow after the E-mails we sent him from America accusing him of abandoning us. Anger is close to the surface, too. I went for a walk earlier today and got angrier and angrier. I'm angry at Jan and I'm angry at my father. Instead of getting better, I'm getting worse. Why did Jan ever teach me how to feel?

I was better off when I was numb. I was able to do so much more, to accomplish things, to maintain the status quo in my marriage. Now everything is chaos. I feel useless and a failure. I doubt if I will ever get well. I can never get what I didn't get!

I'm angry at myself for imagining I could write a book that could help anyone else. What's the point of any of this? So much pain. So much fear. So much anger. So much shame. All a waste. My life is not getting better. I'm confused and depressed. Where's the joy? The laughter? The friendship? As always, there is NO ONE! Paul is barely surviving himself. He can't help me and I can't help him. Thoughts of death are dancing, tantalizingly, in my mind. I'm so tired. God calls to me but I turn away in anger. I want this to be over!

July 24, 1995 — All I really want to do is go to sleep and never wake up. I keep praying for God to take me home to Him. I just want to be a little girl and for Jesus to come and take me home—no more tears. No more pain. No more hunger. No more loneliness. No more shame.

My time with Jan today was an ordeal. At first there were too many voices in my head, too much confusion and noise; I actually couldn't speak. Jan asked if I was scared. I managed a nod. He asked if it was because of the E-mails we sent. Another nod. Was I afraid he was angry with me? Again a nod. Then he said, "I'm not mad at you."

For the longest time, I just couldn't talk. I felt humiliated and inadequate. Finally Angel came and said, "You went away for a long time."

"Yes."

"You don't love me."

Silence... Then he said, "You feel that because I went away for a long time and didn't tell you where to find me, I don't love you... Are you angry at me?"

"I can't talk about it."

"I wish you would. I think it would be good."

She sat in silence. Outside a baby started to cry. She was angry with the baby. Jan asked what she felt when she heard the baby cry.

"I don't like it," she said with a scowl.

"All those needs that were more important than your needs..." he responded.

She talked about love and she asked him what love means. He asked her what it means to her to be loved. She said, "That I know the one who loves me won't really go away ever, even when we're not together."

He called that love without boundaries and said he couldn't give her that kind of eternal love. He said he could say he loves her in the sense that he wants good for her. Then she said, "I have to take care of myself, to do it all myself."

When he asked her if she could really do that, she just said, "I have to," and then she started to cry because she could see that Jan wasn't going to save her. I saw it, too, and I switched into executive control in tears of despair. All my hopelessness poured out to Jan as I recognized just how broken I am—how far from being healthy, how useless and worthless I feel.

The dreams about songwriting, about the book, about counseling other women who have been abused, are all just fantasies. Props to try to rebuild the glittering image, to give meaning to a meaningless, painful journey which has resulted in fragmentation and loss, not healing. Worse. Not better. Farther from God than I've been in years. My only prayer—*"Please, let me die."*

Merry came to relieve me. Merry loves him so and I think he's very fond of her, too. He almost always has occasion to smile once or twice when she is out. He didn't make things easy on her today though. She asked him if he would hug her, ever, and he said he didn't think so because she really isn't a little girl even though she feels like one. He said it wouldn't be good to hug her because we are a grown woman with a strong sex drive and he is a man.

She told him she wanted him to sit closer. He said if she wanted him to hold her hand, she needed to ask for it. He didn't want it to be something that could happen spontaneously. He said some of the other alters wouldn't want him to sit too close. She said, "I don't care."

That made him smile. We love it so when Jan smiles. I wish I could make him smile more. Then Merry told him that when she asks him to hold her hand, she wishes he would come very close and hold it so she didn't have to go "all the way to the end of the couch" and he said he would do that. She tested it to see if he really would. She asked to hold his hand and he moved across to the closer chair beside her and took her hand.

Holding his hand is a powerful experience for Merry. She usually cries. She says she feels like a real person when he holds her hand, and stronger somehow. She closes her eyes and drinks it in. Nobody ever touched her like that. She is so hungry. She whispered, "I will understand if you don't want to hold my hand because of all the ugly things."

"The ugly things happened to you. They are not you. You are not the ugly things. Sometimes when ugly things happen to people they get confused. They think they are ugly or bad or stupid but they're not. You are not the things that happened to you."

She cried and held his hand and said, "Thank you." He couldn't say he loves her but he acts like he does. She loves him.

I don't want another damn birthday. *Please, God, please! Can't you please take me home? Please! I hate birthdays. I should never have been born. Birthdays are just days to remind you of how worthless you are, of how unloved and unlovable and unimportant you are. God, take me away. Please, God. I don't want to go on. I don't want another birthday.*

July 25, 1995 — Like it or not, I got the birthday anyway. Woke up at four this morning and couldn't get back to sleep after crying myself to sleep last night at midnight. Angel and I cried together over our need to be rescued from the pain. "I want my Mommy!" she cried over and over again. Me, too. This is just another dark night of the soul—another layer of grief over the losses—the irreplaceable losses my father brought into my life when he decided to place his needs above mine.

Will I ever be well? If I do get well, who will I be? What kind of person will I be? Will it be worth it? I dream of writing songs that will penetrate hearts. I dream of writing a book that will help someone along the way. I dream of a ministry of comfort and encouragement to others who must walk the path I am walking today. Are they all just pipe dreams? Just further proof of my mental instability and my dissociation from the real world? What good am I?

I'm 43 years old. My life is more than half over now. I spent the first half running frantically from the truth, living a half-life, pretending to be... Somewhere amidst all the fragmentation there's a real person. She's starting to show herself now. She's the one who cries, who feels all the desperate longings, all the doubts. She's no good at pretending and she's finding it hard to hide these days.

July 26, 1995 — Had the "chase" dream this morning. Once again, I'm a fugitive—on the run with a precious, innocent baby girl. Once again, no matter how far and fast I run, no matter where I hide, the bad men find us. There's no escaping them. And they always come to take the little girl away. I woke up in tears which led me down the pathway to Angel, scared and alone, crying out, "I want my Mommy..." And I said, "Me, too."

I told Jan about the dream and he said it sounded like I was blaming myself for what happened to the "little girl". I said there were voices that were blaming me.

"I think it would be a good idea to listen to those voices and try to understand what they're really saying. I think their focus is very narrow. They are concentrated on trying to avoid pain at all cost. It would be good if we could hear from them."

While Jan was saying this an angry voice was making threats in the background and Judah was pushed forward. He began voicing contempt for me for letting the bad things happen. He said he would have kicked and scratched and fought back and I was stupid and powerless to let it happen like I did—to run away (like in the dream).

Jan asked him, "Would it have been smart to fight back even if you would have gotten killed?"

Judah said, "Death is better than pain and powerlessness."

As Judah was expressing his anger at the father, he began to be afraid. He told Jan the father wouldn't like the things he was saying and he could try to hurt him. Jan said the father couldn't hurt him because he wasn't close at hand, but Judah informed Jan that the father was indeed close at hand.

"You don't understand. The father is right here now. Inside the body. He is like us but he is different."

Jan agreed, saying, "He is foreign. He doesn't belong there. It's as if he has gathered up all the anger and he is using it for his own unrighteous purposes, to try to hurt you and Judy and the little girls."

"He shouldn't be here," said Judah. "We should make him go away. How can we do that?"

"We need to take away his power which is based on anger that isn't rightfully his. He is using your anger and everyone else's anger to be powerful, but if everyone takes their anger back from him, owns it and exercises it in good ways, he will no longer have any power over any of you. He is a weak imposter and you can stand up to him with your anger."

"Yes," replied Judah. "I want to do that. I don't want him to use me anymore."

Then I burst back onto the scene as if I had never been gone, talking about the dream again and crying, "I want the dream to have a different ending! I don't want to be a victim anymore! I want to stand and fight!"

"Good," said Jan. "You can do that. You're not a helpless little girl anymore. You're a grown woman with a lot of power. You can stop him by using your anger."

The introject of my father has been with me ever since I was a very little girl. Very much like an alter, he has a voice and a life of his own, but he is not an alter. I mistakenly labeled him the Gatekeeper, but his agenda has been to maintain the secrets and punish any of us who told. He is closely linked to Judah who he uses to accomplish his purposes. He was the influence behind Judah's attempt to persuade Merry to kill herself, but Judah's real anger is against my father, the introject of my father and probably my mother as well.

151

Up to now, the "inside father" has been able to overpower and intimidate Judah, who is just a young boy, but Jan has deflated some of the introject's power in Judah's eyes. I don't think Judah will be so easily manipulated from now on. He is going to direct his anger where it belongs.

We learned a lot today. I lost time again though. It felt like five minutes had passed when I was shocked by Jan saying our time was up. Judah's time is foggy to me. Once again, I retreat from the anger.

July 27, 1995 — Today when I look in the mirror I'm ugly again. So I run from the ugliness. From the hopelessness and despair. From the loneliness and isolation. From the stinking ugly facts of life, my life, an empty wasteland. I walk and walk, and as I walk I listen to music—sometimes loud music to cover up the voices that accuse me or so that I won't hear my own voice of anger. I'm afraid to face the anger all alone. Sometimes I listen to sad music—it lets me feel the grief but it masks the anger. That kind of sadness can be a satisfying punishment for daring to be angry. It's ever so much safer to feel sad than to be mad.

Did a crazy thing tonight. Took a long walk in the midst of a major electrical storm. As the thunder crashed and the lightening flashed I sought out the dark pathways of a forest, almost daring someone to come and try to hurt me. This time I would take a stand, fight back, have a different outcome than in the past. Instead of a dangerous attacker, I was confronted by a cold, soaking downpour of rain. Once out of the trees and walking beside open fields, my bravado faded fast. I was frightened by the storm and felt small and vulnerable and foolish in my soaked t-shirt and jeans.

I prayed the cleansing rain would be enough to wash away all the dirt deposits left by the incest but no. It wasn't enough. Nothing will ever be enough to wash away the fifth and ugliness my father bequeathed to me—my inheritance of guilt and shame.

Part of me was hoping to be struck by lightening. It seems an appropriate way for me to die. I had a traumatic start. I should have a traumatic finish. I am living daily with the death wish.

Gimme Some Space, Man!

July 28, 1995 — When we arrived in the waiting room, we realized the intern was there. We hadn't seen him since returning from America and we all thought that he was gone and we were glad. His presence today was unexpected and frightening. Angel immediately came out in the waiting room and she was very agitated. When Jan invited us in he asked how we'd feel about the intern sitting in on our session. Angel said, "No, I don't want him here."

Jan could see Angel was very upset and he asked her what was wrong. She talked more about the intern, about how she thought he was gone and how big he is. Jan asked her who he reminded her of but she was afraid to say. He asked if the intern reminded her of the bad man who had hurt her. She only nodded.

"What are you seeing? What are you remembering?"

Shaking her head, Angel said, "I'm not allowed to say."

"Yes, you are allowed. I think it's good for you to tell me, to talk about it."

There's a long pause while Angel tries to decide if it's safe, then, "He's standing by the bed and he's very mad at me. I don't know why."

"You have no idea why he's mad at you."

"I don't know what I did wrong!"

"You didn't do anything wrong. He is very angry, but not at you. He has a lot of anger inside but it is something wrong with him, not with you. What does he do?"

Angel shakes her head "no."

Jan gently reminds her, "It is not happening now. It's only a memory. It's not going to happen again. It's good to try to remember what happened."

"He is so big! He takes my hands and he holds them and he hurts them. I try to pull my hands away but his hand is so big and he is so big and he is so strong!"

"You want to get away but he is too big and strong."

Angel continues, "He climbs onto the bed and he... he... he pulls my legs apart and he puts his knees on top of them so I can't pull them together again! It hurts me! So much!"

"It hurts terribly and you try to squirm away but you can't. What he did to you was very evil and wrong and he should not have done it. It was so unfair! You didn't do anything to deserve it. He was very bad. It was not your fault. You didn't want him to do it. You were angry with him but you were more scared than mad."

"I couldn't let him see how mad I was cuz he would kill me!"

"You didn't want to die. You did well. You hid your anger very well and you were able to stay alive. You did the right thing, the best thing. I'm glad you survived. You did well."

Suddenly Angel is watching the daddy walk away from the bed and she begins to sob. "It's too big. Too much hurting. I want my Mommy... I want my Mommy..."

"You were frightened and so hurt in so many places and now you are remembering how you felt after and how you wished your mommy would come and take away the hurt and wash away the dirt. It was right that you would want mommy to come. That was good. But mommy didn't come, did she..."

Angel shook her head, "I couldn't cry out to her cuz he would come and kill me. Why did he do that to me? What did I do?"

"You didn't do anything wrong. He wasn't doing it as a punishment. He was full of his own anger at other people, not at you. You didn't deserve it but you thought you must be very bad or ugly or stupid if he would hurt you like that.

153

That was the only way you could make sense out of what was happening. But that's just not true. It's a lie. You are not bad or ugly or stupid or anything like that. He was the bad one, not you! It's very important for you to understand this because it is the truth. Knowing this truth can help you feel much better. It is going to take time and lots of talking for you to change your thinking, but you will. In time."

"You're so far away."

"Yes. You want me to come closer?"

She nods and Jan moves to the chair right beside her. Angel asks, "Are you going to hurt me?"

"No. I won't hurt you."

"Even if you get mad at me?"

"I don't get mad easily. We might see things differently from time-to-time, but no, I won't hurt you."

"You're not like my daddy, are you."

"No. Your daddy had something really wrong with him. Most people aren't like your daddy."

"I don't want to go away but I'm too tired to stay."

"You'll be back."

Nodding, she said good-bye. I came out sobbing and Jan said, "That was you."

First came grief, followed by anger. Anger not just about what he did to the little girl physically, but even more about the deposit of guilt and shame he left behind. How could he have looked at that little girl's face and done what he did? The confusion, guilt and shame did their damage to the personality for a lifetime.

I admitted I feel so dirty, I don't believe I'll ever be clean, that the rain couldn't wash me clean. Nothing can. He said we can do a lot about changing those feelings because they're firmly based in wrong thinking. He really believes we can work together to conquer the feelings of badness, ugliness and dirtiness. He pointed out that we have done a lot already. Before I couldn't even face the awful shame I felt, it was so overwhelming. Now I can bring the feelings to the surface, talk about them and look at them. And, Jan reminded me, there is a God in heaven who can cleanse me not only from my sins but from every unclean thing, every sin that was committed against me. I needed so much to be reminded of that. Sometimes walking through thunderstorms can lead you to a cleansing stream.

July 30, 1995 — The depression is deepening, or maybe it's just grief. I don't know. I can't seem to bring myself to do anything other than walk. Important tasks that need doing are piling up everywhere but I can't concentrate, can't get going on anything. I'm preoccupied with thoughts of death. I'm not thinking about killing myself (much) but I keep thinking how nice it would be to die.

Went to church this morning. It was too hard. I tried to worship but it didn't come. I'm so tired. No energy to do anything. I couldn't even stay standing for the singing. I felt so sad. I feel so isolated from the others because of my emotional state and my inability to share my burden of pain with them. Missionary churchplanters aren't supposed to want to die and they definitely aren't allowed to have MPD. I left immediately after the service without talking with anyone. I feel so alone.

I took my daily walk. The death wish is my constant companion. They say suicidal ideation is almost always associated with anger. Actually, I don't consider this death wish to be suicidal in nature. The wish contains threads of true compassion. I watch myself suffer and sink down into drowning pain and I want to put myself out of my misery—they shoot horses, don't they? I would see it as a mercy killing. Just like the wishes we have for someone who is dying a slow, painful death, my death wish is a desire to obtain merciful release. Heaven waits for me and I long for it.

Three days ago, I walked in the thunderstorm, hoping to be struck by lightening. I didn't consciously realize it was the anniversary of my first memory of incest. Exactly one year ago I began to remember. I am not yet well. Will I ever be?

August 3, 1995 — Paul came home today. We had a long talk in which he shared with me in tears his sense that we are growing farther and farther apart. He doesn't feel loved by me and hasn't for a long time. He wants us to be working on our relationship, having intimate times, laughing, working together on our mission. I understand what he is feeling and why. I felt sad to see him in such pain. I assured him that I do love him and I want our relationship to be more satisfying for both of us. I asked what specifically I could do to help him feel more loved, more connected.

He wasn't able to really articulate what he wanted. I sense what he really wants is for things to go back to the way they were before—before I started to face my history. He felt safe and comfortable and satisfied with the glittering image. He's been waiting patiently for that "me" to return. I pray to God she won't. Whoever I am, whoever I end up being, I want to be real. No more glitter. No more masks. Never again.

I couldn't offer much consolation to Paul because there are no easy answers. I'm tired. I'm depressed. I'm using most of my energy to deal with my journey to recovery. I don't have much to give. I want space. I want some distance between us. I care about him, love him enough to try to meet his needs, but maybe for the first time in our twenty years together, I am in touch with my own needs and I want to act in response to them.

I can't just say "I trust you" and magically make it so. I feel fear, not trust. I'm so confused. I love him. I'm scared of losing him and I keep fantasizing about running away from home and starting a new life. Hopeless.

August 4, 1995 — Told Jan about my desire to run away from home, to start all over without any of the shackles and restraints of my past. Jan said it is not clear yet whether those demands and expectations that I chafe against now are really coming from the outside or if they are internally generated and are only being expressed in the transference. He cautioned me that I am probably projecting a lot of transference onto Paul just as I do on him. Now is not the time to make any life changes that are not absolutely necessary. I may find that I can discover who I am, become who I want to be, and still remain in the context of my existing roles and commitments.

Jan admits that there is a risk that, even after I unravel the transference and patiently wait to see what reveals itself, I may decide that I can't "unfold" and discover myself in the context of my relationship with Paul. I said I was sure that wouldn't be God's will and Jan agreed with me. Yet, he said, I may still choose to go the way of the prodigal—as if God wouldn't severely punish me if I ever dared deliberately to step out of His will!

This is one reason why I feel far from God right now. I am resisting loving Paul as I feel I "should" and I am resisting the mission-based expectations. I think God may be unhappy with me and standing in judgement over me. I feel Him sitting on His throne, looking down His nose at me, saying, "You can't come into heaven. You suck your thumb!"— just like in the nightmare of my childhood.

I know I am transferring my father's attitudes onto God. What is God really like? If He loves me, does that mean He would love me even if I didn't spend the rest of my life with Paul? I'm not saying I want to do that. I'm only saying, "What if?" When I imagine the possibility of making a freewill choice to go against what I think are God's expectations, my stomach ties up in a tight knot and I feel afraid.

Today I felt angry at God and at Paul for "their" expectations on me. Right now I don't want anyone telling me what to do. It's a bit like a very delayed adolescence. I want to do things my way, I want to find myself, to make my own rules, and I want somebody else to pay the bills! Since I never had this opportunity for freedom with security in my teens, it makes sense that I would be going through this developmental stage now... Gimme some space, man! But instead of breaking the parental bonds, I'm messing with marital, familial and spiritual attachments. I need to be careful that I don't lose things that are very important and valuable to me—like Paul and my kids and my faith. I don't really want to burn my bridges. All I really want is some room to breathe.

The Cave of Mirrors

August 5, 1995 — Paul sees the distance between us. He believes he is losing me, that the relationship is already dead. He is in so much pain. I feel compassion and sorrow and guilt but I am powerless to say the things he wants me to say. I told him I love him because it's true that I do. It's true that I believe God brought us together and it is His will for us to stay together. It is also true that I am very confused and ambivalent about our relationship. I am profoundly unable to make promises or guarantees. I am hurting Paul. I wish I wasn't. I can't pretend that I really know what I want. I am trying to just let my honest emotions wash over me without censorship. I need to face them and their roots but avoid drawing any rash conclusions based on them because I am convinced they are both transitory and transference-based. In other words, this phase, too, shall pass.

My life is in chaos, Lord. In the pit. Will I ever laugh again? Will I ever know joy? Or peace? Help me, God. My faith is like a fine thread now. Don't let me go, Lord. I need You. Amen.

August 8, 1995 — Angel brought a memory to our session today. Jan saw her beginning to abreact and asked her to describe what she was seeing. She shook her head, saying, "No, I'm not allowed to."

"Who says you're not allowed to?"

"You know."

"I'd like to talk to the voice who tells you that. How would you feel about that?"

Angel again shook her head no, saying, "I don't think he will want to talk to you." She drew her knees into her chest and began to tremble.

Responding to her body language, Jan asked, "Can you tell me what you are remembering?"

"He punished me with making me remember. I don't want to remember."

Jan actively contradicted her misperceptions, saying, "He might tell you he's making you remember to try to scare you, but he really doesn't have the power to make you remember. The memories are not a punishment. They come to help you heal and get better. He doesn't control them but he might want you to think he does."

"How do you know?"

"Because I understand some things about him now; Judy understood some things about him. He's not as powerful as he seems. Can you tell me what you're remembering?"

"I can show you," Angel replied.

Reaching for the teddy bear on the chair, she said, "You have to pretend that this is the little girl. She is in her bed and the covers are over her head so only her eyes and nose are showing and she is laying very still and watching the closet to see if she is safe. Then she hears the noise of the door click and she is very scared. He comes to her bed and he starts to touch her in gentle ways and he is saying, 'You like this, don't you? Only naughty little girls like this.' But she doesn't like it even if it feels good cuz she already knows that the good stuff comes before the bad stuff and he is going to hurt her soon! He starts to touch her in the bad place..." Angel began to cringe and whimper.

Jan said, "He touches her vagina."

'Yeah, and then he takes her arms like this... (She holds the teddy bear with its arms pressed against its sides.)... and picks her up on his lap and he pushes into her and does like this... (She begins bouncing the bear up and down against her own groin.)... and he hurts her very bad!" Angel began to sob and bow her head in shame.

Leaning toward her, Jan said, "I'm so sorry that happened to you. It was so wrong. It never should have happened. It was not your fault."

Angel cried out, "I let him do it! I could have kicked him!"

"You were too little. You couldn't have really kicked him hard enough to stop him. You knew that. You did well to survive. To stay alive."

As Jan spoke words of comfort and empowerment, Angel went in and I came out, holding the teddy lovingly as a tangible, kinesthetic way of nurturing Angel who had projected herself into the bear. I saw that it made sense that all of my life, whenever something felt good, I felt afraid. I was always waiting for the pain that comes on the heels of every good feeling. No wonder I have no basic trust in goodness. I was taught that goodness inevitably turns to badness. Loving tenderness turns to pain. Laughter to tears.

Later in the session, Jan led Angel into a full abreaction of this memory. Just as she was going into it, he asked her if she wanted to hold his hand. She nodded and he moved to the chair close to her and clasped her hand tightly in both of his. As she abreacted the rape, she cried out her anger saying, "He didn't have to do that. It was enough what he was doing before."

"You were willing to accept that, but this was too much. It made you angry that he was never satisfied when it should have been enough. This was too much."

"He shouldn't have done it!" she protested.

As she visualized the rape she said, "He made a noise. An ugly noise with his mouth. It went faster and faster and I was glad when it was faster cuz then I knew it was over soon."

Then she saw him leave her bed and she curled up in all the pain. Angel doesn't feel the pain of the actual rapes. She had some way of numbing out during the penetration. But when it was over, after he left her alone, she was flooded with pain everywhere. So when she sees him leave, she feels the pain in her arms, in her legs and groin, in her stomach and abdomen, and she curls up sobbing from the overwhelming physical and emotional trauma. This time she cried for a very long time while Jan held her hand and offered words of comfort. When it was time to wrap things up she said, "I don't wanna go away."

"You'd like to just stay here where you feel safe."

Nodding, she said, "I'm scared."

"What scares you?"

"He will hurt me with the memories."

Jan knew she was again talking about the introject of my father and he said, "The memories aren't under his control. They are not a punishment. But when they come, you don't have to go through them. You can ask the memories to wait and you can bring them here so we can look at them together. I think that's the best way. Will you do that?"

She nodded and said okay and they said their good-byes. She closed her eyes and I came back. I spent a moment or two in silent contemplation of the depth of her pain, which is my pain, too. I put on my shoes, thanked Jan and left.

August 11, 1995 — My sister wrote and said she thinks it's as if I am in a cave of mirrors, looking at myself, and I need to get out of that cave and start looking at others instead. Jan thinks it is good that I am in the cave of mirrors and looking at myself. He says it is necessary and important for me to take this time.

August 13, 1995 — Joined Paul here in Germany for our mission agency's annual conference. It was good to see him after three days apart. He has had a revelation about his anger and has gotten hold of a godly principle that may be lifechanging for him if he can hold onto it. After he told me what he learned, he began to talk to me about my healing journey and how he thinks his revelation applies to me. I got defensive and a lot happened between us but now I can't remember much of it. (I ran from the anger in it.) I know I cried a lot and felt guilty and he said I was a godly woman, but I said no, I'm not. I was full of shame. He sat on the bed and put his face close to mine and looked right into my eyes and communicated his love and commitment. I was overwhelmed. He is such a good and faithful man and I know I'm not worthy of him. I want to be well and be able to return the love he gives to me. I'm so tired.

August 17, 1995 — Made a new friend. Cathy is a missionary doing church planting in Russia and a survivor of incest. It was incredible to finally be able to talk to someone who knows and understands, who doesn't recoil in shock or require lengthy explanations. She's been there. She knows the guilt, the shame, the loneliness, the terror, the anger, the grief.

Getting to know her, sharing our realities and suffering, and encouraging each other has been a joy to me! I have seen myself reflected in her eyes and I have gained new hope for healing. We have met for at least one hour each day here at the conference. She has been a gift from God to me. I am thankful and my desire is to honor God by letting go of a bit more of my fear and mistrust. I think I'm getting ready to make another step forward on my healing journey.

August 18, 1995 — The message this morning was on Jesus in the Garden of Gethsemane. It penetrated deep into my soul. I understood once again and more deeply how Jesus can identify with me in my suffering. As He prayed in the Garden, asking His Father to remove the cup of suffering from Him, He knew He was facing immanent betrayal by one whom He loved. He was facing abandonment by His closest friends. He was facing the burdens of guilt and shame that weren't rightfully His to carry. He was facing the devastation of separation from the Father He loved. Betrayal, abandonment, guilt, shame and loneliness along with the physical suffering of the beating, the crown of thorns and the nails and suffocation of the Cross were His cup of suffering. He cried out—begged His Father, the Almighty God—to remove this cup from Him. Yet, He prayed, "Thy will, not mine, be done."

He suffered every possible emotional and physical agony. Nothing I have experienced or am now experiencing is beyond His understanding in a very personal way. He even understands my desire to escape the suffering, to be "well" instantly. His commitment to fulfill His ministry according to God's will never wavered. His feelings about the commitment, that desire to let the cup pass, were legitimate and acceptable. He deemed it appropriate to beg His Father three times to take the cup from Him, knowing full well His Father had the power to do so. But God so loved me, His child, that He restrained that power in the face of His beloved, pleading Son, in order that I might know Him and be adopted into His family.

Jesus surrendered to God's will because Jesus never doubted that God is good. Do I doubt that God is good? Sometimes. But as I look at the truth of Gethsemane and the Cross, the doubts fade. *Father God, You are good. You know the suffering I have faced in the past and what awaits me in the future. You are good and Your love never fails. You know that I would prefer that my cup of sorrow would pass from me. You have the power to take away the pain and struggle I'm facing. If You restrain Your power in the face of my strong desire to avoid the suffering, I know You do it because of Your love. You are good. Your love never changes. Teach me, oh God, to trust in You. Amen.*

August 19, 1995 — We head back to Holland today. This week in Germany has been a strengthening time and a blessing to me. I feel renewed and restored—close to the Lord again after a long time away. Aaaah! I needed that. *Thank You, Lord.*

"None of those who have faith in God will ever be disgraced by trusting Him." (Psalm 25:3 TLB) *"My eyes are ever looking to the Lord for help, for He*

alone can rescue me. Come, Lord, and show me Your mercy, for I am helpless, overwhelmed, in deep distress; my problems go from bad to worse. Oh, save me from them all! See my sorrows, feel my pain, forgive my sins." (Psalm 25:15-18 TLB)

I am stronger from having turned my eyes and my faith back toward Jesus. Once again, after several weeks of feeling far from God, I am aware of His presence and guidance. I am moving forward and upward at least for now. I'm hoping that the downward spiral I have been on has come to an end. Just maybe the worst is over now. I want to believe this but I am tentative because I still find myself hungering for heaven. I'd gladly give up my life in this cave of mirrors in an instant, if God offered to let me come home to Him.

The Black Hole

August 20, 1995 — I've been thinking about fusing Merry and Angel. They know a lot about each other's traumatic memories already. It might be easier to retrieve the memories if we combine the pieces of the puzzle for a clearer, more accurate and complete picture. Maybe it would be good to let Judah fuse with Guardian, too, because they are similar except in age. Fusion would end the inside father's manipulation of Judah.

Just as the Singer spontaneously integrated with me over the summer, I think the Observer and I are almost totally united now. If we all agree to do the fusions, we will be less complicated. The father introject will be contained and out of action here pretty soon, too. I don't see any reason not to do the fusions, but I want to hear from everyone on the inside re: pros and cons. So let's all begin to think and pray about it and we'll talk to Jan about it, too, okay? Remember, nobody dies. Nobody gets lost. We just join together in deeper unity and harmony, as we gradually become one whole and integrated person.

August 21, 1995 — Jan and I talked about the pros and cons of fusion and he asked me what my first impressions were from the rest of the gang. I think Angel is scared. She has no personal experience with fusion and I don't think she understands it. Jan will talk with her about it. Merry has mixed feelings. On the one hand, she loves Angel and wants to help her by giving her the capacity to feel happy, to smile. On the other hand, she is afraid she will be overpowered by the painful feelings Angel carries.

I see Judah as not very fully developed. He had a limited role to play in my childhood as a protector before the Guardian came along. Eventually he became a pawn used by the father introject. He doesn't want to be used like that anymore, so I think he would gladly fuse with the older, stronger Guardian.

Guardian, however, wants to be a man. He may not like the idea of fusing with an eight-year-old boy because it represents a threat to his manhood. My idea is to reward Guardian's cooperation by age-progressing Judah to Guardian's age and then age-progressing them both to my age for fusion. I imagine that it won't be long after that fusion takes place that it will be time to pull that part of myself all the way in. I'm getting stronger now. The Guardian has some capacities that I want to own and I see no reason to keep him separate if he becomes willing to fuse. We'll see.

The internal processing of these options will continue. I think a good name for Judah/Guardian is Jude. It's one of the names we used a lot when I was a teenager. It's a good strong name.

Merry started talking about how much she wants to go where Jesus is. Jan asked what she would do there.

"I'd crawl up into His lap and He would hold me and I would just stay there forever and ever and he wouldn't make me go away ever."

He suggested, "If you stayed on Jesus' lap for long enough, you could get filled up and you might want to do some things."

"I would run and play and swing on the swings in the sunshine but I would not go far away from Jesus. I would stay where I could see him so if I make a mistake I could run back to Him and He would help me... I don't ever want to stop coming here ever. If I get well will you make me go away even if I really, really, really want to still come here?" Merry asked him.

"If the feeling of staying here was still that strong, I would think there was still something we needed to work on together. Right now you feel you don't ever want to leave here, but feelings change and you are growing up. There will come a time when you will feel right about no longer coming here, but you can't feel that right now and that's okay."

Merry shook her head and answered, "I love you. I love you so much it makes me almost cry. How did that happen?"

"I listened to you. I gave you attention. I was the first adult male you ever started to trust. You opened your heart to me. You will open your heart to others—Paul for one, and Jesus, so that the strong feelings you now focus on me will be diffused."

I don't think Merry believed that she would ever stop loving him so deeply. When I came out, after Merry reluctantly said good-bye, I was once again ashamed of the depth of my need and the way it is being focused on Jan. I asked him if the need would ever diminish. He said the hole is deep but the fantasy that a good daddy is going to come along and fill it up makes it even deeper.

"So I get to give up the fantasy and keep the hole, right?" I said with despair.

August 22, 1995 — I'm beginning to realize Jan is just an instrument God is using, a vessel to pour out His loving tenderness to me. I believe God wants me to recognize Him—to look past His messenger Jan—to know He is the source of the safety, comfort and security I find in Jan's presence. God is calling me to let go of the fantasy that Jan can be my daddy and make up for the losses in my life. He is calling me to acknowledge my dependence on Him. To give up the fantasy and grasp the reality of His amazing love. He can and will fill my empty places if I will allow Him.

Will I? It is hard to give up the desire for a physical, material fulfillment; an external fix. Jan suggested that I may be holding onto the fantasy as an escape from the pain I must yet face. Ever since the day Angel curled up in agonized sobbing as she held his hand and remembered the awful despair, the little girls and I have been on the run. We've all been thinking constantly about Jan and our desire to be rescued. "No more pain!" we seem to cry out in unison. "Save me!"

But Jan isn't going to save us from the pain. No one is. In fact, our only hope for freedom is to walk right through the fire. Jan knows that and he won't allow us to dance around it's edges too much longer. We're going to have to face the anger and frustration connected to his refusal to erase the boundaries of therapy, and come to a place of acceptance, in order to move on. *Lord God, help us to do what we need to do.*

August 23, 1995 — At the end of July, Angel had a session with Jan in which she exposed the very depths of the pain she is carrying. She sobbed long and hard, curled up like a wounded kitten on the couch as Jan held her hands and comforted her. I watched the agony and despair wash over her from a slight distance, but I couldn't escape its intensity. I have been running from it ever since.

From that day nearly four weeks ago I have immersed myself in the fantasy of Jan, my hero, my rescuer, miraculously saving me from my past. I realize this now and I try to stop the fantasy but it seems almost to have a life of its own. Oh, the comfort I find in imagining myself as a little girl on his lap, nestled in his arms, safe and secure at last... It's not going to be that way ever! Get a grip, Judy!

August 25, 1995 — I admitted to Jan I have been trying to escape the horrible despair Angel revealed a few weeks ago. I'm afraid of sinking in that bottomless pit—the black hole. As we began to talk about those dark feelings, Angel switched in and she was terrified to let the feelings come over her. Jan helped her understand they were a memory; she was safe with him in the here and now and it was okay to let the memory come. She talked about how big and frightening it was, how lost and alone she was, how there was nobody, no one who even cared if she disappeared forever in the black hole at the bottom of the pit, shattered into a million shards in the darkness.

She howled in agonized abandonment. My heart was breaking. I couldn't let her carry this pain alone anymore. In my mind, I wrapped my arms lovingly around her and pulled her inside while I took her place. I integrated a portion of the pain and isolation, the rejection and abandonment. It was almost like dying.

Jan helped me see that I could invite Jesus into the black hole with me. Jesus understands abandonment. He felt the abandonment of His Father as He took the sins of the world upon His shoulders on the Cross that day. I thought He wouldn't want to come to me in the black hole because of the dirtiness, the ugliness, the unlovableness of me. Jan assured me that I was clean and beautiful in the eyes of Jesus.

I thought I had been abandoned because of me, because I was inherently, irrevocably unlovable to the very core and fiber of my being. Jan said that's a lie and I need to work hard to fully realize it's a lie. The truth is my father didn't love me because of him—he was sick, he was obsessed, he was unable to differentiate intimacy from sex. He never loved and he never will because he never had the capacity to love. It wasn't my fault. I was just an ordinary little girl. I didn't seduce him. I wasn't ugly or stupid or unlovable. I was just a child.

Fully accepting that truth will gradually cause the black hole to shrink, reducing the terror of my life. It will also mean giving up on the idea, the fantasy, that I will ever receive the love I want from my father—a painful loss, but a necessary one.

Jan says I am lovable. He has never lied to me. I am beginning to learn how to trust him now and I want to trust him on this issue. I am lovable, and I am clean and beautiful to Jesus. I am lovable not because of what I do or because of how I look, but just because of who I am on the inside. He really believes I am lovable!

Today I followed Angel into the black hole. I took her place there. I talked about what it is like in there and I stayed with the feelings for a long time. I am making progress. I even talked about my childhood experiences in the first person singular as if they had happened to me, not to Merry or Angel. More progress.

Jan assured me that each time I rework an issue, I learn it on a deeper level. It's okay to talk about things again and again. Sometimes going forward feels like going downward as we enter deeper layers of pain and process them. Jan says I have grown and changed and I am moving forward at a satisfactory pace. He says he doesn't measure time, he measures the work we are doing. He says I'm right on schedule.

Now we are at the point where we are mostly dealing with the issues from early childhood neglect and abandonment by both of my parents. The memories of hopelessness and despair, of feeling I must be bad and stupid and worthless and to blame are also affecting my interpretation of the therapy. Thus I am thinking I'm stupid and worthless because I have to keep learning the same things over again. I am thinking I am hopeless and to blame and I'll never change because what's wrong with me is an indivisible part of who I am. So many negative concepts and emotional memories are chewing away at my ability to see clearly the progress I am making and at my ability to own the hard work I am doing in therapy.

After all that I have confessed to Jan, all the ugliness of my childhood and the years following, could I possibly be clean and beautiful in his eyes? I doubt it. When I think of everything he knows about me, my hands cover my face in shame.

Abba Father, purify my soul. Make me clean. Take away the filth and grime that seem to cling to me, to my face, to my body, to my heart and mind. Father, wash me in Your Son's blood and make me holy as You are holy. Amen.

You Don't Love Me!

August 27, 1995 — I wonder what it will be like to be fully integrated? Sometimes I think I will be lonely without my inside family. These days, whenever I see a gorgeous sunset, or a beautiful tree, or a graceful bird or a giggling child, I always have someone to share the wonder with. I call on Angel and Merry and Judah and Guardian to come quickly and look! What will it be like when there is no one there? The thought makes me shiver. I will be lonely but I will be whole. The shiver is mixed fear and anticipation. I want to know what it is like to have all of my identity available to me at once and for all time.

August 28, 1995 — Wow! What an incredible morning! With the help of Jan and the Lord's blessing, Judah and Guardian grew up and fused to become Jude. Besides that major transformation, Angel also had a transformational encounter with Jesus.

Jan helped us enter a state of deep relaxation and encouraged us all to go the meadow where Jesus waits. We saw the intense beauty and safety of this place within our spirit. I was touched by how much I love each member of my inside family and by how much Jesus loves us all. Tears flowed as I experienced the intensity of safety I was feeling. Jan must have wondered what the tears were about but I wasn't talking. We were all "inside" just enjoying being together in the presence of the Lord.

Then Jan began to sensitively facilitate the fusion ceremony. I really enjoyed watching Judah go through the process of catching up in age with Guardian. He was so excited and proud and he kept saying, "Wow! This is so cool!" Then Guardian and Judah progressed together to age 43. Guardian was so happy to finally get his heart's desire to be a man, not a boy. I felt so proud of him and it seemed so right for him to grow up. He deserved it!

Finally, Judah and Guardian joined hands and they became one. Jude was born. The first thing he said was, "I don't think we should wait too long to fuse with Judy."

He talked to Jan saying it was good to be a man, and he thought Jesus was "pretty amazing" the way He was able to make the alters grow up. He believes Jesus is who He says He is and he wanted to thank Him for helping him grow up to be a man. Jan prayed first, to show Jude it wasn't difficult. Then Jude prayed.

Merry came out to ask if the age-progression was going to happen to her and Angel. She was trembling in fear. Jan said maybe or maybe not and it wouldn't be right away. She didn't need to be afraid. She talked for awhile but she wanted to go back into the meadow.

She told him what it was like for her in the meadow and then what it was like for Angel. She said Angel is afraid, even of Jesus. Jan suggested Merry help Angel approach Jesus and touch His robe. Angel came out then crying, "He's the judge! He's the judge!"

Jan spoke to her about the character of Jesus and His love. He encouraged her to look at His face and reach out for Him or at least move closer to Him. Angel said, "He might not like it."

Then Jan told her the story of the woman condemned because of adultery. Jesus had not judged her but He had defended her and looked kindly on her and set her free. Angel cried. She moved closer to Jesus to touch and then cling to His robe. He looked gently down upon her, sat down on a rock and invited her into His lap where He held her and comforted her as her tears fell.

She looked at Jan and asked him to hold her hand. He came over beside her and held her hand in both of his hands asking, "Is there something you are afraid of?"

"No," she said, "I just want to remember this feeling of Jesus holding me. He doesn't mind the dirtiness." She touched her face where she feels the dirt shows the most.

"No, He sees right through it. You are clean and pure in His eyes."

August 29, 1995 — Jude and I agree that we should fuse soon. We are so close now, there's nothing to keep us apart but I'd like to stay separate long enough to face down the father-introject. I want the little girls shielded from that confrontation, especially since I want to ask the inside father for an accounting of what was done to us. I've asked Jude to be available to take them to the meadow and keep them there until it's safe to come back.

The introject has already lost much of his power. Now it's time to find out all that he knows and then send him away where he can no longer harass us. Have to admit I'm still pretty scared of him, not so much him as of what he knows. I think he knows the whole ugly saga of the incest. Do I really want to know?

August 31, 1995 — The trip to Germany for the conference was a turning point. Sharing with Cathy every day during that week was such an encouragement to me. Seeing how truly clean and beautiful she is, in spite of all that was done to her, made me begin to believe I could be clean and beautiful, too. The peace and love of Jesus radiated like the noonday sun on her face. She gave me the gift of hope.

The morning messages focused on the final few days of Christ's ministry on earth. Jesus drew me into His arms during that week and I have been walking close to Him each day, listening for His voice, almost feeling His hand holding mine. I am learning to trust Him in a deeper way. All of my parts within are learning to trust Him. I'm beginning to understand what the word "safety" really means, what it really feels like.

Father God, I want You to fill every moment of my life with Yourself. Let me know more consistently and more deeply the nurture that can only be found in You. Yours is the only well that offers Living Water. I drink of You and I am satisfied. Amen.

September 1, 1995 — Today I realized for the first time how literally I took my mother's place when I was eleven or twelve. When the bedrooms on Riverside Drive were rearranged, suddenly I was sleeping where my mother had slept before me. Soon my father made me his wife, having sexual intercourse with me instead of Mom. It's so unfair. I was still just a child—not a woman!

My life has been lived in a state of terror. That's why when I enter deeply into the "meadow where Jesus waits" I weep. When I enter into His presence, His love, His safety, I am overwhelmed by the beauty that is Him and the contrast to my life here in the tomb.

Lord God, please help me to give up the terror. I've grown so accustomed to it that it has become like a blanket pulled over my head against the darkness. Help me release it, and to reach instead for your hand of mercy which will enfold me in Your safety and Your love. Amen.

September 2, 1995 — A cloud has hung over me since yesterday's session. It was a confusing kaleidoscope of images and scenes from my childhood with many blank screens in between.

At the end of the session hour, I was realizing how terribly afraid I was as a child and have been all my life. I dropped into grief, but it was time to stop, so I gathered my strength so I could leave. The moment I walked out the door, my hastily constructed defensive wall came crumbling down and I was flooded with pain. I could barely walk to my car. I wanted to just drop to the ground in front of the office door and weep. The sorrow clings to me still.

11:30 PM — I'm finding refuge in fantasies about Jan again. Whenever the despair threatens to surface and overwhelm me, I run to dreams, wishes and magical thinking. By now I am seeing the futility of hoping for Jan to rescue me, so I find little comfort there, but where else can I go? My only true hope is in

Christ but I know that means facing and feeling the terror of those awful feelings of abandonment, rejection and loneliness. Do I dare? Do I trust God enough to let go of fantasies and illusions and drop to the bottom of a seemingly bottomless pit? Will He cushion my fall? Will He catch me before I am smashed to smithereens or lost forever in the void of nothingness?

September 3, 1995 — I am angry with Jan for letting me leave on Friday when he could see I was in distress. Is it so easy for him to shut me out? To turn away from my pain?

Fridays are so hard sometimes. Fifty minutes is never enough time. I'm always afraid to let anything happen on Fridays because I am so afraid of falling apart and not being able to pull things back together again in time. Mustn't let Humpty Dumpty fall down on Fridays. I want to meet with Jan for ninety minutes on Fridays like I do on Mondays, but I am afraid to ask him for the time. His "no" answer would hurt so much. He's probably thinking he is giving me too much time already. I'm going to risk asking anyway.

I wonder what he feels, how it is for him, when he sends me out the door with tears running down my face, vision blurred, staggering in pain? How does it feel, Jan? Do you want to know how it makes me feel? Afraid, abandoned and angry.

As I pondered this reality, Angel came out to express her own anger at our father, the anger which is the root of my anger with Jan. □

□ He doesn't own me! He doesn't own me! He's not my daddy. He's not! And I'm not his little girl either! Go away! Go away! You don't own me. Leave me alone. I don't have to. You're not my daddy! I don't want to. No! No! No! You can't make me cuz I'm not your little girl anymore! I hate you! I HATE YOU! GO AWAY! You don't love me! You don't love me! You don't love me! You hurt me then you go away and leave me alone. I hate you. I hate you! □

□ 9:30 PM — After that Angel broke down in sobs because of the realization that the father didn't love her. We find that so incomprehensible. How could he look into our eyes of terror and do what he did? Why did he not love us? Were we bad? Were we ugly? Were we stupid? Were we dirty?

As Angel cried, she rose from the bed and went and stood by Paul until he looked up from his computer to see her tears. He stood up and put his arms around her and held her as ragged sobs racked her body. Finally he took her back to the bed and laid down beside her. She began to talk through her tears.

"He didn't love me... I don't understand... He hurt me and then he left me all alone... I was nobody's little girl... Nobody loved me."

"You are loved now," Paul said tenderly.

"You won't leave me, will you?

"No, I won't leave you."

Her breathing settled down, she cuddled her teddy bear and sucked her thumb and rested peacefully at last.

September 5, 1995 — Paul is convinced he is losing me. He told me he feels as if I have already left. I hate seeing him in so much pain—so full of the fear of losing it all, again. This is the theme of his pain. He expresses over and over his frustration about how he has worked so hard to build things only to have them taken away. He doesn't want to have to start over again.

My "celibacy" didn't last long. I found I'm not cut out to be a monk, so I initiated sexual intimacy back into the relationship but so far, it's still problematic. Flashbacks and fears on my side. Pain and frustration on both sides. Sometimes it seems counterproductive to the relationship and hardly worth it.

We have decided we are going to start praying aloud together again every day. We have always found that to be a very intimate experience of sharing and God knows we need the prayer.

Please, God, restore us and renew and freshen our love for each other. Strengthen our commitment and our communication. Help us to rededicate ourselves to our relationship vision. Most of all, be at the very heart of our marriage.

Good Riddance to Bad Rubbish!

September 7, 1995 — *"The Lord is close to the brokenhearted and saves those who are crushed in spirit."* (Psalm 34:18)

I desperately want my father to acknowledge what he did to me and to say he is sorry. My father is a narcissistic sociopath, no more capable of remorse or empathy or repentance than he was when I was a child. I long so much for a "happy ending" that I find it hard to accept that truth.

Clinging to the fantasy that I might be able to do or say something that would change him and make him genuinely sorry is simply another facet of the "good daddy" fantasy. I have to let go of my father! How? How do I let go? The dream is slow to die...

Jan says there is another happy ending I can reach for. He was speaking with Angel. He said she could let go of her daddy and go on with life. She is strong and she has survived many awful things and, though it will be painful and feel very empty for awhile, she could begin to just enjoy rest and rain, trees and birds, life and happiness without her daddy.

Angel said she is tired from being afraid all the time. Jan asked what she is afraid of and, of course, it was rejection and abandonment. He asked why people would reject her.

"Because I am a bad girl."

169

"You're not a bad girl. Not from anything I've seen. You didn't want to do the bad things your daddy did."

"No, but I wanted to kill my daddy."

'Your daddy hurt you. He treated you like you were his possession. He didn't respect you. You had good reasons to be very angry. You didn't kill him so you aren't bad because of your anger."

"If I'm not bad, then why did he hurt me?"

"Your daddy had big problems of his own. He didn't know how to love or be tender. He knew how to have sex and he just let his lust control him. It was not your fault. You were just an ordinary, normal little girl."

"I always thought I am not normal. I am a horrible, ugly monster."

"You are nothing like that. Not at all. You have a nice body, a nice face, just an ordinary little girl. It's hard for you to believe that, isn't it? But it's true."

Angel spent a long time just resting, cuddling her teddy bear. She is just beginning to understand that she doesn't have to go into traumatic memories in order to come talk to Jan. It's okay just to come and be at rest, even to be resistant to the work of therapy sometimes for awhile. I guess Angel and I both need to learn this lesson.

September 9, 1995 — Jude says the reason I'm sad and agitated and resistant to therapy right now is that I'm afraid of the father introject. I think Jude is right except it's not the introject I'm afraid of—it's what he knows. If he has been around as long as I think he has, since the first sexual assault when I was two-and-a-half years old, he knows every sordid detail of what happened to me. That really scares me.

Jude says I should stay in the "meadow" with the little girls and let him be the one that stays co-conscious while Jan calls out and questions the introject. That would be strange for me because I'm not used to consciously choosing to give up conscious awareness, but it might be a good idea. Jude could gradually and gently release the information revealed by the introject to me at a pace I could handle. He would just be functioning in his role as protector, as always.

I'm in a lot of physical pain these past several days, too, and I think there's some connection to the introject. I sense he is causing the pain to punish me for daring to even think about confronting him. My back, my hips and my knees are all in pain. Everything hurts, a lot.

Lord God, I pray you will show me what I need to do. I need Your wisdom to know how to deal with this entity in my mind which has caused so much confusion and pain. I want to be released from bondage to my father and I believe this introject is part of what binds me to him. Please guide me, guide Jan, direct the therapy to accomplish Your will. Amen.

September 10, 1995 — Jan agreed that Jude should be the co-conscious one during the intervention with the father introject. We talked about our strategy and Jan suggested that the introject be asked to move to a different chair when he surfaces, to emphasize the fact that he isn't really a legitimate part of me.

We talked about deepening the relaxation so the little girls and I would be more securely shielded from the confrontation. Jan doesn't have a problem with trance states in that he feels they are a natural phenomenon. He said he doesn't initiate trance with his clients through hypnosis, but if it happens naturally he will work with it. Since I, like many multiples, go spontaneously in and out of trance during our sessions as part of the dissociative process, he is willing to formalize it a bit during certain difficult and complicated interventions if I want him to. In this case, because of the nature of what may be revealed and my need to protect the little girls and myself from re-traumatization, I do.

We worked out all the details and then I said, "We don't have enough time to do it today." Jan disagreed. I got really scared, mostly because I was afraid it wouldn't go as planned—that I wouldn't "perform" properly. Suddenly I was filled with doubts about the veracity of both the incest and the DID. I was afraid I was wrong about the "father" being an introject. I was afraid I would be proven to be a fraud.

If it was all a fantasy, all a lie, then I didn't belong here; I didn't belong anywhere. I became so frightened I jumped up and left the room to go get a drink of water. But when I came back I said, "All right, Jan." I sat on the couch, laid back and closed my eyes. I decided to trust.

Jan helped us to relax and guided us into the "meadow where Jesus waits."

After spending some time together just enjoying being in the presence of Jesus, Jan asked Jude to say good-bye to the rest of us and join him in the office. Jude opened his eyes and looked at Jan to let him know he was with him. Then he closed his eyes again and Jan asked to speak with the "father." When the introject appeared, Jan asked him to take the appropriate chair. Jude was right there watching. I was in the meadow but I was vaguely aware of what was going on in the office. I think it might be more accurate if Jude would be willing to write about what happened. ☐

☐ He sat in the chair and he wasn't in a real cooperative mood so he was trying to refuse to answer any questions. But Jan didn't put up with any crap from him. Jan told him, "Hey, you've got a choice. You either cooperate or you'll be dissolved right now. You know that. You know you don't belong here and you have no right to be here, so you can cooperate and end up going somewhere nice of your choosing or you can get locked up in an unpleasant place."

Well, then the "father" began to spill the beans. He said he was created the first time Judy was abused by the real father when she was a toddler. He and the

Little One came at the same time. He explained that the ongoing sexual abuse started up when the little girl was five and she had a room of her own for almost a year. By the time the sister was moved in there with her, things had already progressed to oral rapes. He continually abused her, especially on weekends.

He was drunk the first time he hurt her and most of the times he did it. The introject said the real father started initially with fondling and told her it was something special just for her because she was his special little girl but that was only so he could set her up. He wanted to make her believe she was the guilty one, and he did! Since her body responded to the fondling, he was able to persuade her that she was naughty and that she made him do what he did.

Apparently, it was during that first year that the Fearful One came into existence and then Angel, when he started the violent oral rapes. All that stuff continued until she was eleven when the father decided she was mature enough for intercourse. She was close to twelve when the more severe rapes began to occur. These rapes started up not long after she stopped wetting the bed and went on until her period started when she was around fourteen. None of us had heard about the sodomy before this.

I'm furious at the way he degraded her and made her feel like a non-person. To him she was simply a repository for his sexual release. He obviously wanted maximum control, maximum helplessness on her part. She was only a little girl—not a woman! A five-year-old girl in an eleven-year-old body. She was terrified, completely overpowered, helpless. I'd like to kill him. He deserves to die.

The inside father said it would take maybe as long as five minutes for the real father to reach a climax. That's a long time to endure shock, pain and horror. The first time he raped her was especially shocking because she had no idea what was coming—knew nothing at all about the concept of intercourse. That slime!

The "father" said he saw his role as keeping the secrets and he would use whatever it took to keep everyone quiet including triggering memories of physical pain and mental torture. He didn't like being there, didn't like the people inside, didn't like Judy's husband or children. He said he did whatever he could do to sabotage Judy's marriage since he had no respect for Paul and didn't want Judy to be married. She belongs to the father. He owns her. The introject would put negative thoughts into Judy's mind about Paul, saying he was stupid, he was a jerk, etc., to influence her against him.

After Jan got everything he wanted, he asked the "father" where he'd rather be and sent him away to a place in the mind where he could go bass fishing day after day and not have to or be able to interfere with the system anymore. Good riddance to bad rubbish!

I hope it worked! It seems like it did because it feels different inside—there's a new sense of freedom that wasn't there before. We'll see. — Jude. □

☐ Thanks, Jude. I'm so glad you're here with me. I don't remember very much of what happened today, but I did understand about two things. Though I have no memories yet of having been sodomized, I now know that my father did that. This just showed me that there were no limits. There was no love. As I understood from the inside father that even the early tenderness was calculated to set me up, I saw ever so clearly that there was no love at any point in time. My father had no love for me ever and he never will love me. As I came out of the meadow, I immediately began to grieve. All I ever wanted him to do was love me. I just wanted someone to love me... He didn't. Not at all. I have to fully comprehend that.

He made me feel like a nothing, nothing more than a set of openings for him to use. I'm angry. I'm furious with him. He is a man without a heart. A man without compassion. A man without tenderness. I want to break the bondage, to be free from his lies. It's going to happen. It's happening now.

Abba Father, thank You for Your work of healing and hope within me. You are teaching me how to trust, a hard lesson for one such as I, but a vital one. Keep me in close and precious communion with You, My Father.

New Beginnings

September 14, 1995 — I'm exhausted. The house is in utter chaos as we are packing for our move to a different city here in Holland to begin a new church. I did manage to take the time to walk this morning and it was a beautiful day. As I walked along the canal I drank in the sparkling beauty of the sunlight dancing on the water. A pair of white swans floated lazily downstream. Sheep chewed on the long grass on the bank across the way. It was a scene that hinted of the "meadow" within. Suddenly tears began to fall as my heart filled with a longing to leave this world and go home to heaven, to Jesus.

I guess I've always longed for and searched for that place of peace and contentment. As I walked on, I heard the voice of Jesus saying, "That place you long to go is yours. I'm preparing it especially for you. But not yet, Judy. It's not time. You must be patient and trust Me. Your meadow awaits you when the time is right."

September 15, 1995 — Since becoming aware of the fact that my father sodomized me, I have felt so ashamed. I can't really think about what he did because I immediately get such a strong response of fear and degradation it pushes all thoughts of the act of abuse away. There were no limits, no boundaries, no place where he stopped and I began! I was degraded by him. Dehumanized. Made into an animal or something less than an animal—a creature!

Today I feel the evil and filth he put on me can never be removed. It's like indelible ink; I am forever stained. As I confessed my shame to Jan he reminded me that Jesus died for me, to make me clean, to remove all the ugly stains of my own sins and the sins committed against me. It is so hard for me to really believe this ugliness can be removed from me. Jan says it will. He says I can keep bringing it to Jesus and He will wash it all away with His loving hands, His tender eyes, His compassionate tears. *Jesus, I need You so much. So much!*

September 16, 1995 — I was so depressed this afternoon, I crawled under my blankets with my teddy bear and cried. Paul came in and sat down beside me and I started to talk more honestly than perhaps ever before. I told him about my shame because of the sodomy. I told him how degraded I felt.

I admitted my fear that I will never be well, that the filth will never be cleansed away, that I'll never be healthy and whole. It was hard to share so intimately with him, to be so vulnerable. He just held me, told me I was clean, that Jesus had already cleansed all the dirt away, and that he loves me.

This morning we were holding and kissing each other, being loving, tender and intimate for the longest time. It felt so good. After awhile Paul said, "Do you want me to stop?"

I said, "I don't want you to stop but I don't want you to go further either."

He answered, "Okay. I just want to know my limits. I don't want to hurt you."

Then he looked me in the eyes and said, "You're in control."

Tears filled my eyes as I realized, yes, he understood. My heart beat with gratitude to my Lord, who hears my prayers and grants me favor and grace. There is hope.

"Who would dare to accuse us whom God has chosen? The judge himself has declared us free from sin. Who is in a position to condemn? Only Christ, and Christ died for us, Christ rose for us, Christ reigns in power for us! Who can separate us from the love of Christ?" (Romans 8:33-35 Phillips)

September 19, 1995 — Been thinking about next steps on the healing path. It's so good to see Angel getting some release from the legacy of shame she was handed. She has begun to trust Jesus, to be able to approach Him and receive His love and comfort and cleansing. I'd like Angel to experience baptism or something like that because I feel she might be able to more readily grasp the concept of the washing away of sin in this symbolic form. It would also be good for Merry and Jude to experience such a ceremony; me, too, for that matter. A cleansing ritual of some sort. Let's all think, talk and pray about it.

Jude and I should fuse soon. We are so close now, so much integration has already taken place, fusion is the natural next step. Merry and Angel are close to being ready for fusion, too. Angel is getting much stronger and is even beginning to smile. Together they would form a child who had more complete memories of the incest and also had the strength to face them and discharge them.

Lord, please lead us all in these next steps. You are our Shepherd.

September 20, 1995 — Paul and I will be seeing Jan together once every other week after we move into our new home. It's difficult for me to surrender any of my private time with Jan and share him with Paul. It is going to be difficult for me to sit with the two men, for both of whom I have such ambivalent feelings. I can't imagine what it will be like and I wonder if it will be productive. However, I think it is important for Paul and me to actively work on our relationship together and we need help to do that, so we've agreed to give it a try.

I have moments of loneliness and feelings of abandonment off and on throughout the day. As they wash over me, I think of Jan and the comfort and security I know when I am with him. I think what I need to do at those moments is to make contact with Jesus. Maybe I can begin to transfer my dependence on Jan for dependence on God. *Lord, help me look beyond Your messenger, Jan, to see You—to love and trust and depend on You.*

September 21, 1995 — Today as I walked alone in the rain the little girls began expressing their desire to be with Jan and their discomfort about his trip next week (we won't see him for ten days). I was able to encourage them, instead of having fantasies about Jan, to go inward to the place where Jesus is always waiting to give them the love and nurture they crave. They went to the meadow and crawled into His lap and stayed there for awhile.

Looking to Jan to satisfy our deepest longings is largely clinging to a fantasy—he can only do so very little. Looking to Jesus for fulfillment is reality-based. Jesus has the power and the love in unending supply and only Jesus is always right there when we need Him.

September 22, 1995 — I told Jan he is my escape route from the terror of abandonment. I told him I am now trying to turn instead to Jesus for the safety and security I crave. He suggested I try staying with the feelings for awhile. But I'm afraid! Going into those feelings is like sinking in black quicksand in a dark and evil forest. I don't even want to go near the abandonment.

When he saw how frightened I became, he suggested I go to the meadow. Almost immediately a calm came over me and my breathing slowed as I began to look inside for the sunlight on the water, the green leaves of the maple tree above me, the colors, the wildflowers everywhere. Within minutes I was in a deep state of natural trance. Jan let me rest there for awhile and just enjoy the luxurious comfort and safety I find in the presence of Jesus.

I opened my eyes and spoke with sadness about forty-three years without ever knowing safety. Jan encouraged me to try to develop a strong sense of

175

myself when I come to the meadow, a sense of who I am, a sense of my wants and needs, a sense of my thoughts and feelings. Jesus loves me exactly as I am, with all my wants and needs and thoughts and feelings. His acceptance is unconditional. I never knew unconditional acceptance. It's not easy to reverse the perspective that I was taught in the crucible of the abuse and neglect. But Jesus will help me.

September 28, 1995 — Oh, my aching feet! All day from six in the morning 'til ten at night I'm standing, walking and lifting as we settle into our new home. I can barely move now but we got a lot done today. I went for a walk, too, around the outside edge of our new community. It's beautiful here. As I walked along a canal with gorgeous white swans floating gracefully, I came to an open field with brown horses grazing. We are in the middle of a large metropolitan city but we are surrounded by green pastures and, at the heart of the community is a spacious park with tree-lined paths.

I felt as if I had come home again, not to a house or a town, but to a feeling— a feeling called joy. Haven't had much joy in recent times, but today for a little while, I knew joy! There is hope and a new horizon just around the bend. *Thank You, Lord, for loving me and for giving me this gift of joy.*

September 29, 1995 — Moving takes its toll physically and emotionally. Add the fact that it's been over a week since we last saw Jan and you've got a recipe for trouble. While Angel was out, she put an open pen down on the quilt and I now have two big, black ink spots that I'll never get rid of... Sometimes we all feel like we are permanently stained.

October 1, 1995 — Much work has been done toward settling in but many boxes have yet to be unpacked. My healing is like that. A lot has been done toward facing and grieving the things of the past and I have one foot in the present now and an eye on the future, but there are still a few "packed boxes" yet. I'm tired now from working so hard. I peek into a box, see things I'm not sure what to do with, and set the box aside to unpack later, when I feel stronger and more energetic.

I know before too long I'm going to have to look closely at certain memories, to touch them, to explore them, to grieve them and let them go.

October 3, 1995 — Friday Paul and I are supposed to go together to see Jan, but none of "us" feel comfortable about it. I know it could be very good for our marriage and I want that, but I feel so nervous about the idea. I'm afraid each of the two men will be watching how I interact with the other. □

☐ I don't want him to come! Why does he have to? Jan is my friend not his! I don't want Paul to see me cuz what if he thinks I am ugly and stupid? We don't need to bring him. He can stay home. I want to see Jan and talk to him but if Paul comes he will have to talk to him and I won't get a turn! He will be mad with us and maybe he will be like Ivan the terrible big brown bear again and I will feel so small and scared. Please Judy can we go without him? Please? Love, Angel. ☐

☐ Dearest Angel — It is scary to bring Paul with us to see Jan. At the same time, Paul is my husband, whom I love, and with whom I plan to spend the rest of my life. He deserves to be able to work through his struggles about the way we are put together and the things that happened to us. It hurts him and he needs to be able to talk about it and get some help with it.

Even though you are sometimes afraid of Paul, I think you know Paul is a good man, not a bad man. He has done a very good job of taking care of us for nearly twenty years! We need to also take care of him and be kind to him. With love, Judy.

Father God, help me be willing to do what is needed to renew and strengthen my marriage. Right now it's sometimes hard for me to see hope and a future for Paul and me. Yet I know it was Your hand that joined us together and it is Your will that we honor our commitment to each other and grow in our love. Sometimes I don't have enough love, enough strength, enough goodness within myself. I need You, Jesus. Amen.

October 5, 1995 — Paul said he didn't want to go see Jan, said he couldn't remember why we were going and didn't know what he would do there. I told him if he didn't want to come, I didn't want to drag him there against his will. I reminded him we had agreed we needed to work on our relationship and we needed Jan to help us, but I also gave him an out. He decided to do it after all. Angel is not happy. I am ambivalent, but I'm committed to Paul. God is in control.

Absolute Truths

October 9, 1995 — I said, "I've been wanting to bring some closure to things with Dad including writing to him the details of what I have remembered. Every time I think about it, I start to doubt all that I think I know."

There followed a painful process of evaluation of my doubts. Jan let me hang there on a limb with them, refusing to offer any reassurances. When I contemplated the possibility that I could have made everything up in order to avoid becoming independent and growing up, I entered a severe state of anxiety and Jan asked me to tell him my thoughts and feelings. That's when Angel took over.

"Tell me," Jan said, leaning forward in his chair.

Angel shook her head no several times and said, "I can't talk to you."

"Why not?" he questioned.

"If you don't believe me I can't talk to you cuz it's stupid."

Jan said, "It's strange. You can doubt but I can't. Is that right?"

She wasn't the doubter, I was, but she nodded her head anyway, "If you don't believe me I can't talk to you. It's stupid."

"You want me to believe you, but even if I didn't believe you, it wouldn't mean that what you said wasn't true. Do you really doubt all the things you remember?"

Angel said, "I know what I remember. But nobody believes me. Nobody. Nobody. Somebody should have known! Nobody knows what's true. There was no one. So many people in that house and no one saw. No one heard."

What a horribly engulfing feeling of loneliness, rejection and abandonment! I felt Angel's pain in all of its intensity and came forward to help her carry it. Jan recognized the switch, of course, and he said, "So alone. Angel was so alone for so many years. There was no one to validate what she knew. Even the ones on the inside turned away and denied her truth. She was so alone."

I cried guilty and sorrowful tears as I recognized that once again I had turned away from her and doubted her truth. Jan asked, "What do you feel toward Angel?"

"I love her."

"What were you doing when you were doubting and thinking how you wanted your daddy back?" he asked me.

"I was abandoning and rejecting her again. Turning away." I turned inward to give words of comfort to Angel, and tell her how sorry I was for what I had done. To Jan I said, "I don't ever want to do that again. I don't care if nobody believes me, I won't abandon Angel like that again."

10:15 PM — I went back down into the feelings with Angel again late this afternoon. At the bottom of the Pit of Longing we peered into the black hole. I was able to tell Angel I knew what she had experienced was real—it's more than just believing her. In my heart, in the deepest place, I know, just as she knows, what really happened. I told her she is the important one, not my father. She is the one that matters! □

□ I wish I could go outside with Jan one day. I wish we could go together to a park or a animal farm or even only for a little walk together. I hardly ever get to talk to him anymore cuz Angel always needs to now and that's all right but I know I will be joining with Angel soon and then I will be different. Maybe not so happy for awhile. Before we do that I wish I could just have Jan all for myself for just one time and we could go outside. I want to show him how pretty everything is. All the trees and the water and the sun and the sky. I will ask him soon, but I think he will say no. It is probably some kind of law or something. I hope not. I want to show him all the things on the outside. I hope he will say yes! Merry. □

□ October 11, 1995 — I think it's time for Jude and me to fuse. There is no longer any reason for us to be separate. We are very much integrated now and fusion is just the final step to complete the process.

Dear Jude — I love you so much. You have had such a vital role to play. You've saved our lives, been our protector, carried some of our anger, acted in powerful ways throughout the years to insure our safety. I love and respect you beyond words. Now that you are my age, you are not only strong, you are wise as well. You and I are so close now, closer than twins. I believe the time has come for us to fuse our individual strengths together. The whole will be greater than the sum of its parts. I will miss you, Jude, but though it's making me cry to say this, I believe it is time to close the gap between us once and for all. — Judy. □

□ Judy, don't worry. It's gonna be all right. You'll still feel me in you. You'll feel my strength and my power. You'll feel my awareness of boundaries and my determination to safeguard them. You haven't lost the Good Mother or Marilyn or the Observer. They're just not separate anymore. They're not gone— they're just totally included in you and I will be, too. It'll be cool. Don't worry. And if things ever get so out of control that you really need me to be separate again, I'll do it. I don't think that will happen though. You've gotten a lot stronger than you used to be and you and me united will be invincible! — Jude. □

□ October 13, 1995 — Susan Howatch is absolutely my favorite author. I've just now finished reading <u>Absolute Truths</u> —a tremendously satisfying read. I was struck in the final paragraphs by these beautiful words:

"...How little we know, how limited we are, how puny are our words as they strain to describe the truth which lies beyond all truths, the final truth which is God. Indeed, in the end there are no words, only Christ on the cross symbolizing God's agonizing involvement with his creation, Christ rising from the dead symbolizing God's creative promise to redeem and renew, Christ enacting in flesh and blood the absolute truths for all mankind to see."

And that, I believe, is the ultimate meaning of Romans 8:28 which tells us we know that all things intermingle for good to them that love God. The bad things that happen are bad, the good things are good, but by the grace of God, the evil, the errors, the ugliness, the darkness is intermingled with the light of His resurrection, His redemption and His renewal. Those patterns of light in the darkness bring restored faith, hope and love in our lives. The suffering is given meaning.

Father God, in my search for truth, let me never, ever forget that You are the absolute truth as revealed through Your Son, Jesus Christ. As I face those memories of pain and suffering hidden away so long ago, help me to remember also the suffering of the Cross and its meaning—Your promise of redemption, renewal and rebirth. No acts of evil or injustice can compare with the Cross, the agony of the Lamb that was slain. And no evil, no error, no injustice is beyond Your power to redeem. Be my Redeemer, oh God. Deliver me from evil. For Yours is the Kingdom and the power and the glory forever.

10:45 PM — Jude is no longer separate. We are one. We just went together to the meadow, along with Merry and Angel. We held hands in a circle with Jesus and prayed and worshipped him. We confessed our sins and received His forgiveness, then we stood before Him and were joined together as Merry and Angel looked on.

It was a poignant moment as we grieved the loss of our separate identities and our friendship but also rejoiced in our union and integration. I now feel the power to protect Merry and Angel. I pulled them to me and held them as I cried, promising them my protection and strong love. The strength of my love is Jude's contribution.

Thank You, Lord, for your miracle tonight—the miracle of unity. You are fulfilling Your promise to make us one.

So now it appears to be only me and Merry and Angel. There may be others we don't know yet, but maybe not! I sometimes wonder if there may be one more traumatized child because of the way Angel's memories skip from initial penetration directly to the aftermath of the rapes. Time will tell. It's all in my Father's hands. He is the one who knows the absolute truth and I trust Him to show me that truth as He determines I'm ready to see it.

Chapter 6 — A Place In This World

The Heart's True Home

October 15, 1995 — After nearly four decades, I am facing at last the devastating isolation and loneliness I experienced in a house surrounded by people who couldn't see my invisible tears, couldn't hear my silent screams— shattering loneliness in a house of ten where everyone seemed to have someone except me. That little girl, called Angel now, was me, or at least a part of me. I can't turn my back on her cries.

At the moment, Angel trusts Jan more than she trusts me, and I confess, so do I. But in the end, it is I who must be faithful to her. I am the one human being in this world who can love, nurture and protect her, and I can only do that with the help of Jesus who loves us both. As He gives me the courage to look upon her with His love and to accept all that she represents, she will learn to trust me more and I will learn to be more worthy of her trust.

We entered the Pit of Longing together again this afternoon, letting the sorrow wash over us in waves. Together we were brave. No longer Daddy's slave, helpless and ashamed. We stood our ground, faced our fears and found that in our weakness, we are strong. We are not to blame. Our anger was not wrong.

Yet, in spite of our time together and what we learned about the rightness of our feelings and the strength we have in unity, in the end both of us turned our thoughts to Jan. The fantasy that he might take us home and let us be his little girl is a potent one for Angel (Merry, too). It gives the little girls a respite from the pain for just a little while. For me, well, I know I don't know him at all except in his "therapist mode" but he represents the closest embodiment of First Corinthians 13 that I know. He is patient, he is kind. It is comforting to think about him when I hurt because I know he would help me feel strong enough to make it through the pain all the way to the hope.

October 16, 1995 — It's been many months since I've been here by the sea. I arrived two hours ago and was drawn inevitably to the water. The sun was high, the sea shimmering, and my heart danced with hope and passion like one of the many colorful kites playing in the breeze above my head. Angel, Merry and I walked and talked together on the sand, and later, in the little park where the animals stood waiting to welcome us home.

Merry is still basking in the afterglow of having gone for a walk with Jan this morning. □

☐ I really liked that! I didn't really think Jan would go with me but today I decided to ask him anyway. And he did! I'm so happy! I was wanting to talk to him for a very long time but he never called to me but today I was talking to him sorta through Judy and he called to me. Not like "Merry! Merry! Come out!" He didn't say that but I knew he knew I was there and he found a special way to tell me I could come so I did.

I wanted to talk to him in a happy way and tell him about some things but mostly I wanted him to smile at me. But I was feeling so sad and ugly when I first came today because I did something very bad this morning and I was ashamed. Jan talked to me about it so I could understand it and he said I could confess it to Jesus and Jesus would make me clean again.

At first I was afraid to tell Jesus cuz I was scared he would be mad with me but Jan said to try. When I went to the meadow where Jesus waits, he saw me coming and he opened his arms wide and said "Come to me." I ran to him crying and told him I was sorry and he just held me close. He said next time I want to do something to make me feel better and not to be lonely come to him! I love Jesus so much and he loves me, too.

I told everything that happened with Jesus to Jan. Then I said I wish I could go outside with him. At first he kept saying uh-huh or mm-hmm to everything I said so I asked him "How come you always say uh-huh or mm-hmm to what I say but you don't give me a real answer? If I say will you go outside with me will you say mm-hmm?" (That means yes.) I said that for a joke and he laughed but then he said no, not necessarily. I said how come? Then he talked again about boundaries and clients (I hate that) and I said I don't understand. Then I felt sad and I said "I just wanted to go outside and spend some time with you before me and Angel become one and I'm so different. I didn't think you would go. It's very pretty outside."

But then I guess he understood it was just a way to say good-bye, a short little good-bye walk. So he said let's go for it and I said really? And we did! We walked in the woods and I showed him the trees and the ducks and the sheep and I told him about the woods in my backyard when I lived in America and about how Judy is afraid our daddy is going to die and how Angel wishes he would because she is afraid of him, and lots of other things. I talked and talked and we walked in a big round circle all the way back home. It was so wonderful and I said thank you and told Jan I can remember this for a very long time. I will never forget it. I love him so. — Merry. ☐

☐ 11:00 PM — It's been a beautiful day. I am feeling secure in God's perfect love, love with the power to cast out fear. Merry was so afraid to go to Jesus with her confession, but when she risked drawing near to Him, He drew near to her. With open arms He welcomed her, saying, "Come to me..." And she ran into His outstretched arms to be enfolded by His perfect love—no longer afraid.

Lord Jesus, thank You for Your love. In its beautiful perfection, it casts out all fear. Thank You for Your forgiveness for our sins, won at so high a cost yet so freely given. We just have to ask. I love You and give You my heart. Your will be done. Amen.

October 17, 1995 — Dear Merry and Angel — We had a great walk on the beach today. I especially liked it when all those horses came galloping down the beach toward us. That was an exciting surprise, wasn't it?

I've been wondering if maybe it's time for the two of you to join together into one. What do you think about that idea? I want to ask you both to pray about it with me and to spend some time thinking and talking together about it. We will only do it if it seems right to all of us. Love, Judy.

October 18, 1995 — We can run into the outstretched arms of Jesus, our Rescuer and Redeemer. We are no longer alone with what we know and when we tell our stories to Jesus we are surprised to discover He has known them all along. He has waited so patiently for us to come to Him. He knows our fears. He knows our sorrow. He knows our shame. And He never turns away from our truth. He reaches out and touches our wounds and brings wholeness, healing and a tender love.

Once again today Jesus brought His healing hand to bear in my life. Merry, Angel and I lifted our hearts to Him in grateful praise as we entered the "meadow within" which is our spiritual core. As we worshipped Him, the Lord gave us a "picture" of Merry and Angel kneeling side-by-side in prayer. We all saw how connected and united they already were. We felt the Lord saying now is the time, so we gathered under the maple tree in the meadow for the fusion ceremony. As the three of us knelt before Jesus, I told each little girl I loved her and Jesus loved her even more. She didn't need to be afraid. She would be safe with Jesus.

Then Jesus joined their hands together as He placed His hands on their heads in a blessing. They turned to each other and hugged as they became one child. As the fusion was taking place, we began to sob uncontrollably. It was hard for me to respond effectively at first to the new child's needs because I found myself grieving their loss, but soon I was able to point out to Merriel (Merry/Angel) that she was with Jesus and He was holding her and she was safe.

Father God, it seems You are speaking to me so clearly now. I can see Your desire for me. You stand and wait so patiently, calling out my name and saying "Come to me."

Those words, "come to me" have echoed down through the hours and days of this retreat. Then today I finally opened the book I brought to read called <u>Prayer</u>

— Finding the Heart's True Home by Richard Foster, only to find these opening words:

"Today the heart of God is an open wound of love. He aches over our distance and preoccupation. He mourns that we do not draw near to him. He grieves that we have forgotten him... He longs for our presence.

And He is inviting you—and me—to come home, to come home to where we belong, to come home to that for which we were created. His arms are stretched out wide to receive us. His heart is enlarged to take us in...

For too long we have been in a far country: a country of noise and hurry and crowds, a country of climb and push and shove, a country of frustration and fear and intimidation. And he welcomes us home: home to serenity and peace and joy, home to friendship and fellowship and openness, home to intimacy and acceptance and affirmation... where we can be naked and vulnerable and free. It is also a place of deepest intimacy, where we know and are known to the fullest."

I want to come home to You, Lord. To find myself in You. Keep calling me to come to You. Amen.

9:00 PM — In contemplating the cost to Jesus on the Cross to enable my forgiveness, I couldn't help but think about my father. I have forgiven him much but more is as yet unforgiven. This week I have seen that I must keep on forgiving day-by-day until the work of forgiveness is complete, first by choosing as an act of my will to forgive all that my father did to me, then by forgiving each day all that I know thus far.

October 19, 1995 — The Lord impressed on my heart this morning that His call to forgiveness goes beyond my father and my mother. He is calling me to forgive my husband. He showed me how angry and disappointed I have been because Paul is not the invincibly strong and independent man I imagined him to be in my childlike fantasies. I have been bitter toward him because he has failed to live up to my ideal and I have come face to face with his humanity.

Jesus wants me to forgive him for his weakness and his neediness. He is weak and needy, just as I am! Just as we all are. I thought he would be my rescuer, but he can't be! I must let go of this unrealistic expectation and the disappointment associated with it and forgive him for being human. I must learn how to love the Paul that exists in reality, not some fantasy hero that he could never be.

Only God can be my Rescuer, the unfailing Lover of my soul. I choose this day to release Paul from responsibility for fulfilling this impossible task. I choose to forgive. *Father God, help me to live out this decision and teach me how to really love Paul. Show me his neediness and his weakness and help me respond with love and compassion. Father, You are strong and You are loving. In my own quest to become strong, to attain a sense of identity apart from Paul, I have failed in my loving. Teach me how to love Paul with a strong love as You love us. You have shown me the strength of Your love as You have brought healing to my fragmented soul. Just one year ago I was broken, shattered into a dozen separate pieces. Piece by precious piece, you have been putting me back together again. Today, it's just Merriel and me. You are fulfilling your promise to me to make us one. I'm learning to trust You, Lord. Amen.*

Never Enough!

October 23, 1995 — I am finding it almost impossible to accept the reality of the sodomy. I'm beginning to have flashbacks and visual images now but I can't talk about them with Jan. I can't describe what I'm seeing and I can't say the words "anal rape"—when Jan said those words today, I winced and turned away in shame and fear.

Jan saw my fear and he said, "It's okay. You're safe now. It's not happening now. It's never going to happen to you again. You're safe..."

As my breathing began to normalize a bit, he said, "I want to say to you that you did not do anything to cause this or to deserve it. It was not your fault. It was completely unfair and you were not the bad one or the guilty one or the dirty one."

As he talked, Merriel came to the surface sobbing, saying, "I did everything he wanted me to do. I did everything but it was never enough! He just kept hurting me more and more. I couldn't do enough... He always wanted more! When I would think this is the worst thing then something even more worse would happen... I would think I must be a very bad girl that he would hurt me so much. He kept hurting me..."

Jan actively contradicted her misperceptions and the shame and told her she had done well. She had done the best she could. When she began to settle down, she asked him to come closer and hold her hand. She asked him if he knew her name, and he said, "Yes—Merriel. I like it!" She smiled and said, "Me, too. I'm going to go now."

And she went. I struggled to remember what had gone on while she was out. I felt numb. Much of what had happened with Merriel in the session was in a fog. I had distanced myself from her but I need to have the courage to come closer to this terrible truth.

October 24, 1995 — After writing that entry in my journal, I spent some time talking with Merriel. I told her how good it was that she had shared with Jan yesterday. I apologized for having been unable to stay close to her in the session.

I felt I had let both of us down. Then I allowed myself to go with Merriel to the feelings connected to the sodomy. This time I stayed with them for a long time.

It was as if I was an animal or less than an animal. The ugliness of it! The filthiness of it! The physical pain and the fear of suffocation, my face in the pillow, my body held immobilized by his huge hands. I was eleven or twelve but the child who "stayed"—Angel—was developmentally a helpless five-year-old. I was completely powerless to prevent this degradation of my body and soul.

Shame, inadequacy, powerlessness, helplessness, pain, fear, anger, and, of course, betrayal. Always the question, "Why?" Merriel cannot contain all those feelings alone anymore. Last night we went into them together and we carried them to Jesus. He took us into His arms and tenderly comforted us, soothing our wounded heart with his love and peace. We belong to Him and in Him we will rest. He is our heart's true home.

October 27, 1995 — I wanted to find a symbolic way to be cleansed from the filth and the dirt and the shame that has clung to me for forty years in all the places where my father defiled me. Jan invited me to go into the meadow and see what Jesus would do. Merriel and I went together into the warmth and safety. We lay down side-by-side under the tree in the tall grass. We closed our eyes and entered into that powerful peace which is generated by the presence of Jesus.

When we were very peaceful Jan suggested we open our eyes and look around. We saw Jesus sitting on a large rock. He smiled at us and called to us to join Him. Merriel ran to Him and fell to the ground before Him, wrapping her arms around His leg and clinging to His robe. I sat down at His feet and rested my head on His knee. He gently brushed my hair from my face with a tender touch of His hand. As I looked up into His eyes, I saw His love for me and I cried because I need Him so. We need Him so. And He loves us with all our dirtiness and shame. He loves us.

Jan said, "Is there a question you wanted to ask Jesus?"

I nodded my head, but I found it hard to ask for what I wanted because I felt so unworthy.

Jan encouraged me, saying, "It's okay. Take your time. Why don't you just try saying one word at a time. It's okay."

Finally, I said to my Lord, "Jesus, I feel so dirty. I want You to wash me clean. Will you?"

He smiled at me and said, "Yes, my child. Come with me."

Merriel and I took His hands and He led us to the stream that flows through the meadow, a sparkling, crystal-clear stream of pure, cool water. He took Merriel down into the water first. He held her close and secure as the water flowed over her chest and down her body while she floated there. He cupped some water in His hand and cleansed her face and hair. Eventually, He let her go under the flowing stream completely but only for a moment so she wouldn't be

187

afraid. She came up smiling and He was smiling, too, as He carried her to the bank of the stream and set her down in the warm sun.

Then it was my turn. I was afraid He wouldn't be able to make my face clean but I was wrong. As the water gently caressed my body, every part of me was made clean and fresh. It was a miracle of His love and something only He could have done. Afterwards I lay close to Merriel and prayed a prayer of thanksgiving. Now when Merriel or I begin to feel dirty and ashamed because of the incest, we can remember what Jesus did and know that it's a lie.

In a little while I opened my eyes and looked at Jan. I told him how lonely I have been this week. I said, "Sometimes I really don't understand myself. Why, when I've experienced so many beautiful, intimate times with Jesus, do I still find myself running to you in my mind when I'm lonely or afraid?"

He said it has to do with the age at which I was hurt, an age when a child needs physical and emotional support in the most tangible forms. My wounds are not just spiritual, so the fact that I seek a physical, material source of comfort is not strange, but makes perfect sense. He seems quite certain I will grow beyond this hunger for him, but not without some pain. What does that mean? What form will the pain take? I can't think about that now.

Oh, Lord, words fail me. How can I ever say how grateful I am for Your love and grace which You pour out over me day-by-day. You never stop loving me! You are so awesome. So beautiful. So gracious, loving and kind. When I look into Your eyes, I know love. You cleanse me, Lord. You don't just cover my shame— you annihilate it! Your streams of Living Water purify me. Thank You, Jesus. Thank You, Jesus. You are my Healer and my Deliverer. In You will I trust. Amen.

October 30, 1995 — Merriel came out today and told Jan through tears that she didn't feel good. "My tummy hurts," she said. It was the pain of the unfulfilled desire to be held and touched in a loving, non-sexual way—a powerful sensation of both loneliness and longing. She wanted him to hold her close so she could be safe. She wanted him to touch her hair and her eyes.

"I don't want to do anything bad," she said.

And he answered, "I know. I know that."

Merriel lowered her head and turned her eyes away from him, saying, "You won't hold me, will you?"

"No,' he answered gently.

"Why?" she asked him.

"I feel it's crossing a boundary and in the end it would make things harder for you, even though it seems like it would make things easier for the moment. It would make it harder in the long run for you to grow up and learn to deal with the feelings of loneliness and desire."

Merriel answered, 'I don't care."

188

And Jan responded, "I know you don't, but that's my job—to keep the longer view and help you see beyond what seems good for the moment."

Merriel looked into his eyes and asked, "Don't you want to hold me?"

Jan paused before responding, then he said, "There are times when I instinctively would like to hold you, but I choose not to."

She said, "I just want to be close to you."

"I know. You want someone to be like a mommy or a daddy to you."

"I love you," she spoke softly and her eyes implored him to love her back.

He only said, "I know."

She began to grieve.

I couldn't bear to see her grieving alone with no one to hold her, no one to love her. I came to join her in her grief and sorrow. I held her in my mind and drew her back inside. I took the grief upon myself but it was hard for me to bear. I could only hold it for a couple of minutes before I pushed it away.

Jan helped me to see that there is much anger within that pain as well. Deep, deep anger that terrifies me. Part of the reason I can't remember the worst abuse is my fear of the anger that is sure to be attached to it. I let just a tiny bit of pressure off of that anger today.

Lord, I'm so tired and so lonely, and I need You so much. Help me to find myself in You again. These last few days I feel I've been looking at You in the far-off distance. I see You there, waiting for me, calling to me, longing for intimacy, but I hold back, I keep my distance. I long for You but I can't seem to still my restless soul long enough to enter into Your presence. You are so unchanging and true and I am so impossibly foolish and fickle. Spare me from my own inconsistency and draw me back to You, oh Lord. I need You more than anyone or anything in this world. Amen.

November 3, 1995 — I was in the bedroom when Paul came in to ask how I was doing. I began to share openly with him the struggles and the pain I was dealing with, the anger and the loneliness. Merriel came out and told him how much she wishes for a mommy and a daddy. She really opened up her heart to Paul, trusting him with her deepest longing and her darkest disappointment and despair. As she began to cry with deep, wrenching sobs, he lay down beside her and put his arms around her. She felt comforted and safe. I was so glad we had risked the vulnerability and intimacy of that moment. Paul came shining through.

But we feel differently today. Today has changed things. Today Paul told Jan in our "joint" session how uncomfortable he feels when anyone else comes to the surface, especially a child. He considers it a purely one-way conversation since he says he doesn't know what to do or say when it happens. It was clear he would prefer it didn't happen at all. He didn't say he didn't like Merriel but I couldn't help but feel some rejection. Merriel is a part of me! She is as much a part of the whole as I am! Her feelings are important and sharing them with Paul was a stunning act of intimacy on both her part and my part.

I've asked Merriel not to draw any hasty conclusions based on today but she is angry and disappointed. She had been thinking that Paul loved her and she now feels he can't love her if he doesn't want to listen to her or talk to her. She is pulling way back from him, saying she won't ever again talk to him. □

□ Dear Jan — I don't care if you are mad at me cuz I am mad at you too! Why did you tell me that I can talk to other people cuz it's not true! Nobody wants to listen to me. I thought that Paul loved me but he only pretended that he loved me. He held me and I thought he could be my daddy now but he told you he didn't like it. He lied to me when he made me think that he loves me! He only loves Judy but not me. Nobody wants to talk to me. Maybe not even you. I don't want him to come to see you anymore. He is not my friend. It is bad. I have so many things to say to you and there is never enough time. Anyway now you won't even listen to me cuz I broke the rules and you will be mad with me and I was mad at you which is not allowed either! I don't care. I don't need you or anybody else. I hate you and I hate Paul and I hate all the bad men!!!!!!!!!!!!!!!! Leave me alone! — Merriel. □

□ November 4, 1995 — Obviously Merriel is very angry with both Paul and Jan. I feel like I should be trying to talk her out of her feelings, but then I think, "No, it's good for her to wrestle with this anger which is rooted in the past." I think it will be good for her to face Jan with her feelings of anger and betrayal and have the chance to connect these feelings with events and people of the past. I have assured her that both of the men do care about her, and I pointed out that she can be angry with someone and still be friends. She is quite afraid of going to see Jan on Monday since sending the e-mail, but we'll go and ride out the consequences together.

"For the Lord God, the Holy One of Israel, says: Only in returning to Me and waiting for me will you be saved; in quietness and confidence is your strength." (Isaiah 30:15 TLB)

"Yet the Lord still waits for you to come to him so he can show you his love; he will conquer you to bless you, just as he said. For the Lord is faithful to his promises. Blessed are all those who wait for him to help them." (Isaiah 30:18 TLB)

Daddy God, I know without Your help I will never have the courage to face the great Cave of Anger in my soul. Only if I rest in you in quietness and confidence will I be able to venture into the murky blackness of my rage. Father, empower me to come to You and allow You to be my strength.

November 6, 1995 — Merriel was scared to see Jan today. She tried to talk me out of it and resisted walking toward his office. As we waited our turn in the waiting room, she was like a frightened kitten in a corner. She kept looking at the door—her escape route. I think she really thought Jan was going to physically punish her for being angry with him.

When she entered his office, she grabbed her teddy bear, curled up facing away from him, and said not a word. Jan spoke, "You look frightened. Are you?"

She said, "If I take care of myself, then no one can hurt me."

After she had let Paul care for her and hold her, she thought he loved her. She felt betrayed and rejected. Jan helped her understand that Paul could find it hard to talk with her even if he loved her. He wasn't really like her daddy who had purposely deceived her into believing he loved her. Merriel began to talk about how her daddy had touched her and held her and made her think he loved her but then he hurt her. As she talked about this she began to relive the sodomy. She described in detail what happened right up to the point of penetration when she said, "I can't remember!"

It was the worst abreaction we've ever had, perhaps because all of the memory is tightly compressed within one individual identity rather than safely split among several. When it was over, Jan helped her untangle the thoughts and emotions and see where she was confused in her thinking.

10:30 PM — I just fell into the pain so deeply I almost couldn't get back out. When Merriel came in and I went out, the memory of the rape was so close I entered into it, crying out, "I don't understand! How could he do that to me? I wanted to make him happy but I never could! It was never enough!"

I covered my face with my hands in shame deeper than I had ever before experienced. I was feeling everything like it had really happened to me—not to some other little girl! It was awful because it was nearly unbearable pain but it was wonderful because it was a testimony to my growing strength and integration. Then I began to face and feel the rage I am carrying against my father.

A Lioness on the Loose

November 7, 1995 — Today I hate him. I really do hate him. He stole everything from me. What he did to me has affected my entire life. I had so much potential but he twisted and broke me. Things could have been so different—I could have loved and trusted so much more. Could have been a better wife and mother and minister. Now more than half my life is gone and so much damage already done that can never be undone.

The deepest damage flows from the way he betrayed me. He started by making me believe that I was special, that he loved me. He never brutalized me without first getting my hopes up that this time, he would be the good daddy of my dreams. Every rape was preceded by gentle caresses, pleasurable sensations. Each time he pushed the boundary one step further, I adjusted and accommodated to the new level of degradation and pain, always hoping that this time it would be enough—this time he would be satisfied.

With the shock of the first anal rape came the realization that it was hopeless, that I was hopelessly incompetent to make him happy, to make him change. Nothing would ever be enough! With that came the rage, the fury so great and terrifying it had to be completely erased, though it couldn't be eradicated.

We are entering the darkest places of the tomb now. Jan and Merriel and I have hit pay dirt. The feelings of rage and shame I am experiencing now just may be the sources of my lifetime of running and hiding—the saboteurs of all of my hopes and dreams. Each time I would begin to feel hope and a little bit of confidence, that glimmer of hope would trigger my awareness of the River of Shame and the Cave of Anger within me and the light would be snuffed out.

Last night's abreaction and the subsequent panic attack shattered me enough that I called Jan. I am beginning to feel everything as if it actually happened to me which, of course, it did! I was never strong enough to really let myself feel it that way, that's all. Now the things my father did, the things my mother didn't do, the things that other men did to me are all coming to me as my own memories. They happened to me! I don't just know it now, I feel it, I remember it.

"We live within the shadow of the Almighty; sheltered by the God who is above all gods. This I declare, that he alone is my refuge, my place of safety; he is my God and I am trusting him. For he rescues you from every trap and protects you from the fatal plague. He will shield you with his wings! They will shelter you. His faithful promises are your armor. Now you don't need to be afraid of the dark anymore, nor fear the dangers of the day, nor dread the plagues of darkness, nor disasters in the morning." (Psalm 91:1-6 TLB)

Abba Father, You are indeed my refuge and my place of safety. You have become my confidence and my hope. Because of You I will not fear. My father taught me that faith, hope and love lead to pain and betrayal. He lied to me so many times I began to believe his lies. I need to embrace the truth now, Lord, and cling to it tenaciously. You are the truth. Your love is graceful. If I put my faith and hope in You, Your love will not betray me. You will not forsake me. I put my trust in You.

November 9, 1995 — I dreamed once again I was being chased, pursued by someone or something intent on hurting the tiny baby I held in my arms. Clutching the baby desperately to my breast, I was scrambling up the sheer side of a steep, snow-covered canyon wall, my feet slipping and stumbling in the icy snow. Below us was a dark, swirling river of slime and I was terrified that we would fall to our deaths. Suddenly a huge lioness came bounding out of the black waters up the sheer incline and pounced on top of the baby and me. The lioness was covered from head to toe with the filth and slime of the river below. She pressed down upon us and opened her huge jaws to encircle my neck... And I woke up.

November 10, 1995 — "She pressed down upon us and opened her huge jaws to encircle my neck." Usually the chase dreams end when the bad men catch up with the baby and me. They take her away and I cry as I wake up with a feeling of helplessness and shame. This time it was different. Jan helped me to see how very different it was. Just as the baby represents the vulnerable, needy part of me, the Lioness is an image of me as well. She comes bounding out of the river of black slime so she is coated with slime, but the slime is not who she is. It isn't inside of her, isn't really part of her. It's only there because of where she's been. The shame is covering her but she actually embodies my anger. Her essence is power.

As I huddled hunched over the baby and the Lioness pounced on top of me, I felt afraid but I also remember feeling bewildered, unsure of her intentions for us. When her jaws opened around the back of my neck, I woke myself up.

Jan suggested that just possibly the Lioness was about to lift me by the scruff of the neck like a lion cub and carry me and the baby to the top of the mountain and safety. Underneath the coating of shame is a powerful and beautiful Lioness who is angry but is also on my side! Because of the strength of her anger and her instinct for survival, instead of falling into the river of slime, we could come bounding upward and out of the shame to the top of the mountain where we can become clean and beautiful at last.

November 13, 1995 — Merriel was moving into and out of the memories. When things became overwhelming she would stop and take a deep breath or a short break, but then she would move back into the memories again. She is getting so strong now. So brave.

Afterwards, Jan talked to her for a long time, helping her to sort through and understand what had happened, untangling truth from lies and distortion. She began to settle down and he asked her how she was doing now and if the memory work had been manageable for her. She replied, "It scares me but I know I have to remember so I can get better so I won't always be so afraid."

Jan asked, "Do you feel okay about what we did today?

Nodding her head, she said, "I think I am really very strong."

With a gentle smile, he said, "You're a lioness."

Smiling back, she said, "Sometimes we feel like a little lamb, but I think it's good for us to be a lion, too. We can be both!"

Lord, help me. I so often feel childlike and helpless and dependent. It is hard to really own the Lioness in me who holds the power, strength and determination to rise victorious from the ashes of the abuse and neglect. I need You, Lord. Amen.

The Pit, the Pendulum and the Rose

November 15, 1995 — *"No temptation has seized you except what is common to man. And God is faithful; he will not let you be tempted beyond what you can bear. But when you are tempted, he will also provide a way out so that you can stand up under it. Therefore... flee from idolatry."* (I Corinthians 10:13-14)

Lord, You have once again reminded me that each time I return to broken cisterns to draw water seeking to fill my deepest longings, I am falling into temptation and out of Your will. No one can give me the desire of my heart except You. I can never go back and relive my childhood in such as way as to meet my childhood needs. It's too late to crawl back up into my mother's womb and start again. I must find a way to accept the losses in order to thoroughly grieve them. This is the healing path. Every false hope that I cling to is an obstacle on that path, an attempt to detour around the legitimate pain and necessary grieving. Every fantasy is an idol I am calling upon, a broken cistern I'm drawing from, instead of depending on You — the only True Hope. God, forgive me for my cowardice, for my lack of faith. Be my strength in the face of temptation. May my thoughts and dreams and desires be pleasing and acceptable in Your sight. I love You, Lord.

November 17, 1995 — Jan was kind enough to provide Merry and Angel with a picture of himself to take with us to the States last summer. We promised to give it back after the summer. Instead I kept it and we frequently turned to it for comfort.

I realized I had to give it back as a symbol of my willingness to see him realistically. I returned the photograph today along with a note telling him I'm committed to letting go of the fantasy and false hope I have attached to him. Since making that decision, every time I start to fantasize about him, I stop the fantasy and look behind it to the pain I am attempting to avoid.

Paul and I had a joint session today. I want so much for us to share on a deep, intimate level. I want to know and understand him and what threatens or hurts him about me. Today he said he felt I was abandoning him. I feel sad when I see him in pain but I also feel threatened when he says I'm abandoning him. I feel afraid that if I remain true to myself and my healing journey, I will become unacceptable in his eyes and I will lose him.

He talked about the "old" me and the "new" me and how he feels the old me is being thrown away and he is being asked to give a "blank check" of approval, love and acceptance to the new me, whoever that may be or may become. There isn't an old me and a new me. I'm not tossing one away and creating another. Jan asked me to create a different metaphor to replace "old and new."

It's more like I've been a rosebud—for years and years, only certain aspects of myself could be seen by others or by me. Now at last, the bud is beginning to blossom forth into a blooming rose with so much more to show, to see, to smell, to feel, to reveal. It was all there hidden within the rosebud. As I spoke about this imagery, I realized how much I long for Paul to love and accept the rose that I really am.

We talked about the distance I have put between us by frequently withdrawing to my room to do things that don't involve Paul. He worries we will end up being nothing more than roommates. Jan talked about a pendulum, saying I have spent my whole life motivated to try to please everyone in order to avoid rejection and abandonment. Now I am seeking a balanced, healthy position. In order to attain that dynamic balance of good, healthy boundaries, I must swing to the opposite side of the pendulum first. It's unavoidable that I want to listen only to my own wants and needs for awhile. It's unavoidable that I would need to create some space between myself and the people I'm closest to so that I can begin to hear the voices of my own identity and discover where I end and other people begin.

Eventually I will come down to that center point on the pendulum. There I will be able to know what I want and to hear also what Paul wants and to make choices. I will choose sometimes to yield to Paul's wishes out of love for him and sometimes to hold to my wishes when it's important for me to do so.

I'm afraid he'll keep on wishing I'd go back to being the rosebud, quietly fading, never having reached my full potential. I'm afraid when I am well I might not like who he is. In my heart, I'm quite sure my commitment to Paul and my commitment to God are strong enough to hold me in the relationship, but Paul's ability to love me as I really am will be an important factor.

Paul is afraid of the unknown that I am becoming. Me, too, but I won't turn back. I know that where I am going will be true, real, honest—and I've had enough of lies and pretending. I can't go back. My only real hope is in going forward no matter what lies ahead.

Lord Jesus, I praise you and thank You for my husband who loves and cares for me deeply and has remained loyal and faithful through many trials. Jesus, help me to see him through Your eyes and love him with Your love. Bless him, oh God, and continue the work you have begun in him. Bless our marriage. Help me to be a loving wife to Paul, to give him honor and respect and to cherish him more each day. Amen.

November 24, 1995 — I have failed to stay close to Merriel in her pain twice in a row now. I think she is losing her trust in me. She is not happy that I am working so hard to see Jan realistically either. She has expressed anger at me and her disbelief when I try to tell her he can't be our forever friend or her daddy. She seems to be pulling away from me.

I try to comfort and nurture her but she resists. It's as if she believes if she takes the love I want to give her, she will be admitting she isn't going to get it from Jan.

But, Merriel, it's okay. I won't rush you. Take your time. I want you to have all the time you need to grow up. I know that you, too, want to grow up and you are indeed already very strong and capable, more than you realize. I love you and I only want to help you, to be there for you. I know I disappoint you and fail you at times, but I'm getting stronger, too. And I will always be here for you. Please be patient with me and don't give up on me. Love, Judy.

November 29, 1995 — Last night, in the middle of a dream, I suddenly looked around and saw my father. I was standing and I turned around to see him sitting behind me. He looked up at me with so much love in his eyes and I reached out to him, bending down to give him a long, affectionate hug. I woke up in tears. Why did I dream that now? A dream of love and reconciliation—the impossible dream. I really believed I had reached a point of accepting that my father never loved me and he never will. Perhaps I have, but clearly the desire still remains. The longing for the good daddy dies so hard.

December 2, 1995 — Yesterday Merriel talked with Jan about the dream. She was sad but mostly she was angry at herself and her daddy because she knew the dream was a lie—a seductive lie. She no longer wants to dream or imagine that he is a good daddy, because to do so, she must again become the bad girl. She told Jan, "I'm not a bad little girl."

Joy and Laughter

December 3, 1995 — This weekend I have been attending a women's retreat. The theme of the weekend is joy. Last night's worship was a wonderful time of refreshing and intimacy with the Lord. I felt so full. Late in the evening as my roommates and I shared in the dark coziness of our room, I began to tell them about the healing God has done in my life.

The more I proclaimed Christ's glory and acknowledged my total dependence on Him for my healing, the deeper the sense of joy that flowed through my spirit. I was overwhelmed by His loving kindness and His unmerited favor and grace. I tasted a joy so intense I couldn't stop crying. Just last year, at this same annual retreat, I was in pain I thought would never end, sinking down into the deepest depression I'd ever known. At this year's retreat I am crying almost as much, but now they are tears of joy and my heart is lifted up in hope and gratitude for the healing work that the Lord has done.

I have been made new! Alleluia! After all the tears came laughter—my spirit overflowed with giggling laughter for some minutes. In the end, I just had to shout, "Praise the Lord! God is so good! Alleluia!" *Let me keep this joy as a treasure in my heart. May I always remember it. I love you, Father. Amen.*

December 4, 1995 — I told Jan about the art project we did on the retreat. We were supposed to paint a picture of joy. I was afraid of the paint because once you put paint on the brush and the brush to canvas, it's there. You can't erase it and do it again and again until it's right. So first I decided not to paint. I pulled out my sketch pad and watercolor pencils and drew Merriel. Then I walked around the room looking at other women's paintings. I decided to be brave and try painting after all.

As soon as I picked up the brush I knew I had to paint the first rape. I started with a pool of red blood in the center surrounded by a sea of deep blue, purple and brown shame. Then I painted the central figures in mud black—the angry father, the helpless child beneath him. Above the figures in a murky ether of mustard, blue and brown, two ghostlike figures, eyes averted away from the rape scene, rushed away from the swirling red vortex of pain and anger.

As I showed the painting to Jan and talked about it, I realized that all the figures except the "perpetrator" were me—the me that stayed and the me that ran away. I went into the feelings then. I had said he was the "perpetrator" but he was my father! The anger at the time was so overpowering it blew me to pieces. My father's anger and my anger fused together into a fury so powerful, I was split apart—shattered into fragments. The intense fury made a vast contribution to the dissociative process. My rage during the rape was unbearable. Parts of me had to flee, but there was nowhere to go except the nether reaches of my own mind.

All I could do was to pull all that explosive rage inward and hold it tightly there, turning it against myself. Every time he came to me, I kept hoping this time it would be different—this time he would come to meet my needs instead of his own. The false hope was connected to the anger. I needed to hold onto the false hope. Without it, the anger would burst in an annihilating explosion which no one would survive.

So I survived on false hope. The hope that somewhere, somehow, I'd get to be a little girl with a good daddy, kept me alive but it cost me everything I had. I refuse to worship that idol anymore. I'm letting go of the false hope and clinging at last to the real hope, the only hope, Jesus Christ and the Cross of salvation. Jesus is my Hope and my Redeemer, my Deliverer and the Healer of my heart. He is everything I need. He is enough. He longs to satisfy my soul.

I remember last year at the women's retreat crying out in hopeless despair that I wanted my stolen childhood back! I wanted to go back to the innocence and the joy of my childhood as it should have been! Merriel, though she has seen much pain and sorrow, still retains a spark of innocence and unfettered joy. She never had the chance to be a little girl but now she does! Now at last... she does. Through Merriel, God is allowing me to go back and taste joy through the eyes of a child.

When asked to make a painting about "joy" I painted the scene of a terrible crime against an innocent child. If I had never faced the pain and horror of that experience, I could never have experienced the joy of this past weekend. The pain is part of the joy. I can rejoice in the suffering because through it, the Lord has given me a special gift—a measure of love and joy and grace I could never have known without first knowing the pain and suffering. It is worth it. It is!

December 6, 1995 — I know I'm getting better because I don't need to write in my journal as much as I once did. I know I'm getting better because I have whole days of living in the here and now. I know I'm getting better because I am overflowing with creative energy and ideas. I know I'm getting better because I can contemplate reducing the amount of therapy without feeling nauseated. I know I'm getting better because I can stay close to Merriel when she remembers and I can even remember on my own.

I am beginning to fully own everything that happened and even the emotions that came as a result of the abuse. I'm finally beginning to face and feel the rage—the Lioness sleeps no more. She is growling in angry protest at last and it feels good! It feels strong and powerful and righteous. I no longer feel I am a victim. I'm a survivor who is beginning to thrive.

No Longer an Orphan

December 9, 1995 — Lots of stuff is stirring beneath the surface right now. One way I know something's happening is Merriel's drive to cuddle the teddy bear and suck her thumb. She is resorting to these methods of self-soothing for a reason. I don't know if a new breakthrough is coming in the memories or if this is about unresolved aspects of existing memories. I keep flashing on the image of my father pulling me onto his lap to rape me. This memory, retrieved weeks ago, has barely been addressed. I have never experienced it in the first person, only as an observer of Angel's abreaction. Maybe it is time for me to deal with this trauma.

I feel frustrated that Paul is coming to the session with me on Monday. I'm too much in the midst of things now and don't want the interruption to the process. Soon Jan will be on two weeks of vacation, too, and I have so little time before then to work. I have this constant sense of urgency and the feeling there won't be enough time. I know it's a memory. There was never enough time for my needs to be taken care of, and now it's so hard to share because the needs are still there—reaching, grasping, hungering, devouring. So little time...

December 11, 1995 — I was talking about the anger I feel toward my father when Merriel became afraid. She was remembering another time, another place, when she felt angry at her daddy. At first, we pulled away from the memory. We are so afraid of the anger, but Jan helped us to go forward.

I was lying in my bed in the dark, feeling small and so lonely. He sat on the side of the bed. I was afraid but as always I was hoping this time would be different. He reached out to me and began to gently caress and fondle me and then he pulled me toward himself. For just one brief moment, I imagined that he was going to hold me close, to hug me, to give me the kind of love I desperately needed. That hope was shattered when he lifted me onto his lap and raped me.

Merriel and I were remembering this betrayal together. She cried out, "I thought he was going to love me! How could I be so stupid to believe, to hope such a thing! My hope is what made it hurt so bad... again."

Jan told her not to blame the hope. It wasn't stupid. The hope was not to blame. The father was to blame. He was at fault. He was evil but not everyone is evil and hope is good if it's realistic. "'I'm glad you've stopped hoping in your father," he said, "That's good. That's realistic. But you don't need to stop hoping altogether."

"But every time I hope, I get scared," she answered.

Merriel and I held each other inside and cried as we realized he had tricked us. He knew how much we wanted his love and he used our longing against us time after time after time. He tricked us! Playing on our need for nurturing love and using it for his own satisfaction—the love he dangled before us was only an evil lie.

By manipulating me and causing me to hope, he got me to receive him in some way, to open myself to him so that when my hopes were dashed once again, I thought it was my fault. I was powerless to fight back because the betrayal I felt was a crushing blow.

This time all the pain, all the betrayal, all the anguish was mine. It happened to me. Merriel is now helping me to remember so I know on a heart level the truth of what happened to me. The feelings were so powerful I couldn't stop crying.

I looked at Jan and said, 'I don't know how I lived..."

"The important thing is you did live. You survived. You didn't kill him. You didn't kill yourself. You didn't let him kill you. You survived. And that's good. You did well."

December 15, 1995 — I told Jan about the agitation and restlessness I've been experiencing lately. He put his finger on the anger and I had to admit that was the feeling behind the feelings. I'm in touch with my sense of betrayal by my mother. My abuse took place in the bedroom next door to where my mother slept. It happened over and over again for twelve years! My mother lost interest in me and withdrew her protection from me when I was a little girl. My father knew that. When he began to hurt me, I already knew that Mom wasn't there for me. He didn't have to work hard to convince me there was no use in telling her.

Fragile and fatally flawed, I faced life an orphaned child. I took care of myself using whatever means of survival I could find and expected little from the world. I believed my only value was that I could be used. By the grace of God I discovered that was a lie.

It is a lie I believed very deeply, but it is only a terrible, evil lie. The truth is I am precious in God's eyes. Psalm 27:10 says, *"Though my father and mother forsake me, the Lord will receive me,"* and Jesus Himself said, *"I will not leave you as orphans. I will come to you."*

My value is not determined by how useful I am to others, sexually or otherwise. My value is not determined by how my parents abused or neglected me. My value is determined by the reality that Jesus believed I was worth dying for. He loved me even before I knew Him, before I ever served Him in any way. He was nailed to a cross for my sake. I am no longer an orphan. I am a beloved child of the Most High God. He will never leave me or forsake me. I am no longer that lost and lonely little girl. I have found shelter and a safe haven within His arms of love.

Enough is Enough

December 29, 1995 — Paul and I arrived here at my little sanctuary in Bergen-aan-Zee in the early afternoon yesterday. We had a pleasant walk on the boardwalk at sunset and I read all of Hemingway's <u>The Old Man and the Sea</u> while curled snugly under a blanket. I think the change of scenery is doing Paul some good. He seems less brooding and depressed. Today we walked for an hour to Egmond on frozen sand, had a long lunch and walked back again. It was a beautiful winter day. The sea was a calm, deep blue. Sea foam was frozen where the tide had come in to kiss the icy-lipped shore. The dunes were a frosty white, sparkling in the bright sun perched low in a crisp, blue sky. All was cold but dry, with only a touch of breeze to brighten our cheeks and ears with chill.

Though I ended up with a blistered toe and Paul's legs wobbled and collapsed like a newborn colt's when we arrived home, both of us were satisfied with the day. Tonight a comfortable silence lays between us. We listen to our music and read our books and ease gently into the companionable quiet of the evening, content with ourselves and with each other.

Paul will stay with me tomorrow night as well and then go home on Sunday. I will remain here alone until Thursday afternoon. I wonder what the Lord has for me but I'm not looking ahead too far. I want to really be here for Paul right now, enjoying his company and this little respite from the challenges of our daily lives and ministry.

December 30, 1995 — Decadently we lay in bed until eleven this morning. When we finally ventured out from under our duvet, we took a short, cold but very pleasant walk to the park and the animal farm beyond the tiny post office in town. Paul especially enjoyed the aviary where various birds were huddled with feathers fluffed in a futile attempt to keep warm. Further along, the animal pen held two sad-looking sheep and a single white goat. Once, in the spring, there was a llama in the yard and it made a great mountain, lying piled on the ground, as goat kids leapt onto its back and danced around its face. This time the animals stood forlornly in the frosted grass and I wished I had brought them something fresh to eat. They stood like statues frozen in place and I wondered if even a handful of lovely fresh lettuce would have moved them from their appointed positions.

When we returned to the cottage, it was so warm and inviting I was tempted to crawl once again underneath the duvet for a long winter's nap, but Paul needed a good dose of my loving attention before returning to an empty house and five days of unwelcome solitude.

Romantic music played in the background and I persuaded Paul to dance with me for awhile. Eventually we cuddled together on the bed and he told me I'm everything to him—that I am his life. My heart was so full. I thought about our nearly twenty-two years together, more than half my life. I began to realize that the love I have always longed for, that loyal love that would never leave me, the one that I thought was over the rainbow, was right here in my own backyard, right here in my arms.

Paul's love for me is immeasurably faithful, safe and secure. Just like he always says, he's "in for the duration." Why has it been so difficult for me to believe in his love? So hard to see how precious, deep and loyal is his commitment to me? For a few moments as we lay side-by-side, I tasted the beauty of his love and tears fell. They were tears of gratitude for this gift from God and tears of grief that my brokenness has kept me from recognizing pure gold held in my hands for so many years. Paul's amazingly steadfast love makes him one of the few true heroes in this world.

Father God, help me hold onto these truths about my husband. Help me to love him in a way he deserves to be loved. Teach me to trust and teach me to love. Amen.

11:45 PM — Eight hours into my solitary retreat, I've spent some time in praise and worship but I was conscious of a drive within to express some of my anger from the past. I painted the face of a winter-white wolf, eyes full of fury, mouth aggressively wide open and within its jaws, a man, arms raised in a gesture of helplessness as flames of rage devour him. It's a picture of revenge and I find it quite satisfying to behold but also unnerving.

I spent the rest of the evening reviewing my journals from last December through March of last year. So many things have changed. So many things have stayed the same. I struggled a lot more in those days with doubt, doubts about myself, doubts about the memories. I don't doubt as much now. I carried the burden of a lot more shame and guilt a year ago. The Lord has released me from so much of that burden.

A year ago last Christmas I was still very fragmented as fusions had only just begun. Today I'm nearly integrated. But there are two things I continue to struggle with—anger and trust. I still haven't faced the deepest places in the Cave of Anger but I am getting closer and the time is coming when the Lioness will roar.

New Year's Day 1996 — *"'Let the children come to me, for the Kingdom of God belongs to such as they. Don't send them away! I tell you as seriously as I know how that anyone who refuses to come to God as a little child will never be allowed into His Kingdom.' Then He took the children into His arms and placed His hands on their heads and He blessed them."* (Mark 10: 14b-16 TLB)

Part of my difficulty in letting go of my dependency on Jan is a refusal to recognize that I am (still) powerless to make someone satisfy my hunger for parental love. I still want to gain control over something I cannot change. To let go of the fantasy of Jan becoming the good daddy and mommy is to face my powerlessness. Accepting that very powerlessness is the path to dependence on God alone. But I know powerlessness, and I fear it and I grasp at any means of gaining control.

I'm a grown woman now, not a helpless child. I have many resources including my own ability to nurture and care for myself. I need to own and embrace the memory of the unmet needs. I need to face the reality that only God can satisfy my deepest desire for unconditional love. I need to go to Him as a little child, defenseless and hungry, and lift up my arms and cry, "Daddy!" Then He will place His hand on my head and bless me.

January 2, 1996 — I spent five hours working on a painting depicting the sodomy. I didn't feel anything about the painting while I was doing it; I stayed disconnected from my feelings. But later, as I tried with all my will to worship God, I got in touch with angry feelings—big angry feelings. I kept thinking about Jan and how frustrated and angry I was at him for not meeting my huge want. I began fantasizing how I would make him pay, right in the middle of trying to worship!

Finally Jesus broke through, revealing to me clearly that I was really angry with my mother. I let myself begin to feel the overwhelming frustration and anger I felt as a child toward her. I cried out and shouted my anger up to God. I was furious that she didn't love me like I needed to be loved. I wanted her to adore me, to hold me and comfort me, to look into my eyes and tell me everything would be okay, to protect me, to rescue me!

I was angry for every time I had to lay in my bed after the abuse and cry for her while she slept in the next room. I was angry for the time she tried to push my head in the toilet, for making me feel like I belonged in the toilet. And for all the times she turned her back on me and gave her attention to another baby. I wanted her to see I was still a baby, too! I wanted her to be my mommy, too! I had to be my father's wife! I just wanted her to be my mommy! It wasn't too much to ask. I'm so angry! *Thank You, Jesus, for letting me be angry and for understanding. You were angry, too.*

After the anger, grief followed. I will never have that mother-love I needed so. I sobbed and cried out, "I need You, Lord! I need You." As I grieved, letting go of at least some of my demanding desire for a mommy, I felt my Lord holding me and comforting me like the mother I never had. He is big enough to handle my anger and tender enough to gentle me afterwards.

After the grief, the worship in me was released. Merriel was afraid after all the anger and grief and she wanted to call Jan. I asked her to wait and to trust Jesus and take a walk in the "meadow." We closed our eyes and went to the place in our spirit where Jesus waits. Merriel and I sat on the old wooden swing in the maple tree and soon Jesus joined us, sitting between us with His arms around us. Swinging and laughing together, we began to sing songs of praise. For an hour, we experienced some of the most joyful yet humbling worship ever. At one point, I fell to my knees and felt Jesus washing me in His blood, purifying me and making me more like Him. To be more like Him—that is my prayer. *Make me like You, Jesus.*

January 3, 1996 — I was drawn to the ocean by the pink sky I glimpsed as I glanced out the window. I wanted to see the sunset. The water shimmered like ice-blue satin, smooth and rippling beneath a giant topaz sun that hung low over the horizon, its golden necklace stretching down the bodice of the sea. I stood in awe in the frozen sand as a single white seabird invited the sea to join him in a waltz, celebrating the end of another beautiful day to the glory of God.

The Sea knows her Creator and she gives Him glory every moment of every day just by being all that He created her to be—reflecting Him, being as much like Him as she can be. Sometimes she is gentle, calm and caressing. Sometimes she is powerful, strong and angry. Always she is her true self and a reflection of Him.

I, too, want to reflect You, Lord. I, too, am coming to know You, my Creator, in all Your tenderness, in all Your strength. May I be like You, Lord. May I be like You.

7:15 PM — Once again the Lord reached down into the brokenness of my heart with His healing touch. After a period of joyful singing, my spirit stood before the Lord like a little child and I confessed, *"You are my Father now. You are my Mother. I need You so much and You are enough!"*

I was filled to overflowing with a new awareness: Everything I ever needed, everything I ever hungered for as a little girl, everything I long for and desire now, is all to be found in Jesus and He is enough! No matter how much I need, no matter how vast the black hole of emptiness within me, He can just keep on pouring out His love and His Spirit to fill me. His supply is always greater than my need. He is enough! It is the first time in my life I have ever believed in "enough"—I never thought there was enough and I never thought there would be. *I was wrong. Jesus, You are enough!*

Scarcity has been my closest friend. I lived in scarcity all my life. Never enough love, never enough attention, never enough safety, comfort and protection, never even enough food for all. Never enough good mommy and daddy. Never enough time. Never enough of me! If I could somehow be more—more pretty, more clever, more talented, more intelligent, more "good"—maybe then I could get enough of what I needed and hungered for so hopelessly.

I moved into adulthood with all that scarcity, all that "not-enoughness." I worked hard to be productive enough; let my kids walk on me trying to be a good enough mother; gave just enough love to my husband to try to guarantee he loved me more, since there is never enough love for everyone; polished up my best "glittering image" in hopes of getting friends and even God to love me enough. I never knew what "enough" felt like. Never believed I would. I just knew I wanted it.

Today I understood what enough is. As I prayed, Jesus poured His love into me until I was overflowing. I can never ask for more of His love than He is willing and able to give. As I empty myself more and more, letting go of all the pain, all the rage, all the shame, all the sorrow—as I reach into the black hole and bring forth my fears, touching them and letting them go—He will fill every empty place with His Spirit and His love. He has enough. He is enough!

Last night I had a joyful dream. I could fly! I could just raise my arms heavenward, think of my Savior and fly! No wings or magic carpet needed, I could glide and soar as free as a bird above the lake, above the grassy hillsides, and up, up into the bluest of blue skies. Oh, what joy to be so free, so light, so unfettered! What a glorious dream and what a glorious hope I have.

I painted that hope today. I painted myself rising from the ocean of anger, fear and shame that was my past. Though the clawing hands of the past still try to hold me back, I am slipping through their fingers as I raise my arms toward the bright sun and a new day. A dove flies just above me in the blue sky, giving me courage and faith, believing in me and my future.

I know these images of hope are two steps ahead of me on my journey. Just as the dream about the Lioness pointed to the place where I could finally take hold of my anger, I believe this dream of flying free points to the place where I will be freed from my past—free to live in the present moment and to trust in the future without the specter of the past always haunting me. I will be free!

"But look! God will not cast away a good man, nor prosper evildoers. He will yet fill your mouth with laughter and your lips with shouts of joy. Those who hate you shall be clothed with shame, and the wicked destroyed." (Job 8:20-22 TLB)

Patterns of Pain

January 7, 1996 — I keep having this feeling that someone is coming at me from behind and pressing down on me. I've had many similar experiences over the past twenty years—feeling a presence in the room with me, an evil, aggressive, shadowy figure, and then the tactile, kinesthetic sense of being trapped, held down against my will, terrified and barely able to breathe. I always thought it was demonic but today I am wondering if it's just another kind of flashback.

Tomorrow I see Jan for the first time in almost three weeks. I told him on the phone I wanted to access and express my feelings of rage at my mother tomorrow. I wonder if I will dare.

January 8, 1996 — I dared. I remembered and was able to express my outrage at my mother for her abandonment, for her demands that I grow up and take care of her children. I didn't want to take care of her children! I was already taking care of her husband against my will! I wanted her to be my mommy. I wanted her to take care of me! While she was asleep in the bedroom on the other side of the wall, her husband was raping me.

After awhile I reached the limits of my tolerance for anger and I began to feel afraid. Merriel came then to talk about her fear that she was bad to be angry with mommy and daddy. She believed that giving voice to her anger was naughty and no one would like her if she did that and then she'd be all alone. Jan assured her that she had good reason to be angry and let her know her anger was good and good to talk about.

She began to explore her anger toward her father. She talked about being angry with Jan because they had to be apart for so long and angry at me because I wouldn't let her call him. She asked him to hold her hand and talked to him about her desire to live in his house and always be with him. She clearly understands that it isn't possible and she is not angry or hurt by it anymore—just saddened. She is coming to a place of acceptance.

She talked about Jesus and how she can feel Him holding her in His arms when she goes to the meadow, but she can't really look into His eyes. Jan promised her that one day in heaven she would be able to see Jesus face-to-face and look into His eyes.

Merriel said, "I have hungry eyes. I always wanted my mommy and daddy to look into my eyes and know me. To know who I am so they could tell me. But they never did, and now my eyes are always hungry."

The last few minutes were mine and I spent them celebrating the victories of the past week or two. I told Jan I was falling in love with my husband again. I told him about my new awareness of Jesus as enough. I said I always wanted to be an artist, a poet, a singer—and he said, "Who said you're not?"

I am realizing that I am all those things and more. Potentials I thought were lost forever are not really gone. They are simply undeveloped, but I have time! I am beginning to have hope and a sense of who I am and who I can become. I'm beginning to live in the present more and more and to believe in the future. I am learning how to untangle the past and all it's memories from the present moment's realities. I said to Jan, "See, you're doing a good job!" And he said, "So are you."

January 9, 1996 — Late last night I was overwhelmed with feelings of loss connected to my mother. Paul heard my sobs and came to comfort me. At first I was inconsolable, but he lay down next to me and I rested my head on his chest, and in time, as I talked to him about my pain, it began to resolve and I settled down.

Still later in my bed, I had flashbacks of the rapes. I was fearful and restless and found it hard to fall asleep. I dreamed about fat, yellow hoses in my mouth and my vagina. I also dreamed of being dragged along by a large, barrel-chested man who was going to rape me and I couldn't stop him.

I keep having shooting pains in my head and feelings of dizziness. This is what usually happens when more memories or new alters are surfacing. I feel so tired. Enough is enough. I don't want more memories. I don't want new alters. Today I barely left my bed. It is clear to me that as long as I continue to have tactile hallucinations, flashbacks and rape dreams there is still stuff to be worked through and resolved.

January 10, 1996 — I feel surrounded by pain, loss and grief. I wonder, too, when I will be done doing the work of the anger. I want to be done with it. I want to be done with it all. It seems as though every time I have a glimpse or a taste of real hope and a sense that I am on the mend, making real progress on my healing journey, I get caught once again in a swirling cauldron of pain and confusion. It almost feels like it is a punishment for daring to hope, for daring to believe I could be like other people. Will I ever truly be free?

January 11, 1996 — Why do I do this to myself? It's a pattern in my life—feel hope, get punished. A moment of freedom, a day of joy, must be paid for in pain. Not an equal amount of pain, but pain that overpowers the freedom, joy or hope, burying any trace of the positive or pleasurable experience. This week I am paying for both the hope I found on my retreat and the anger I dared to let myself express.

How dare I feel hope? How dare I feel anger? Naughty, naughty girl. Stupid, stupid girl. I learned so well that hope is foolish and anger is bad and both are dangerous and likely to bring pain. If the pain doesn't come from the outside, I create it on the inside. The pain I create disconnects me from the hope and the anger thereby protecting me from worse dangers like daddy's abuse or mommy's neglect.

I have well-worn patterns in my mind, Lord. A word, a gesture, even a hope can send me running down one of those paths that lead me toward despair and away from You, toward pain and away from Love. Sometimes, I can wander for days, even weeks, on some twisted trail I've traveled many times and yet have forgotten. Once again I'm on a path to nowhere.

These paths were created as I searched for places of safety with a child's frightened eyes. At one time they offered me some shelter, an occasional pocket of warm security along the way among the hedges. But as a woman I no longer fit where the child once hid and the brambles and bushes scratch at my hands and feet, leaving me freshly wounded by their thorns. I don't want to walk these paths anymore.

You have shown me another path—a path of love and gentleness and patience. A path that, while sometimes dark, is never completely without Your light, while sometimes sorrowful is never completely without joy. You have shown me a path where I never walk alone, where You set a gentle pace and hold my hand when darkness falls, faithfully bringing me to a new dawn of hope. This is the path I desire to follow. Help me, Father God. Amen.

The Break-In and the Body

January 14, 1996 — I had a dream last night. Today I wrote a poem about it called "The Break-In":

> He broke into her building.
> He broke into her home.
> He broke into her bedroom.
> He broke into her body.
> He broke into her mind.
> Sitting upright in the bed
> Her back against the wall
> She touched the wounded place
> and said, "It's broken..."
> And blood began to flow.

January 15, 1996 — And Jesus said, *"This is my body, broken for you. This is my blood, poured out for you."*

I have been in so much pain for the past few hours I don't know if I can even face writing about it. It began with a dream early this morning. It was not such an unusual dream. I've had similar dreams many times before. I dreamed I was being raped by the devil himself. What upset me about it this time was the realization that I had an orgasm as a result of the rape. As soon as I woke up, I pushed the dream away and forgot about it.

I was restless and depressed and Merriel was anxious and feeling abandoned because Paul left this morning for a month in the States. She kept saying, "I want my daddy to come back!"

And I kept reminding her Paul isn't the good daddy. Shortly before it was time to leave for my session with Jan, I remembered the dream and my sexual response to it with a groan, saying, "Oh, no... Not again."

Yesterday's rape dream and the poem I wrote, followed by today's dream, made me despair of ever getting free of the victim role. By the time I settled on the couch in front of Jan I was depressed, discouraged and highly anxious. I told him about the two dreams over the weekend and wondered aloud if it would ever stop.

Jan encouraged me to try to remember, that is, to look into the face of the devil in my dream. I didn't have to try to remember the image. I knew who he looked like. I said, "He looks like my father."

At that moment, I realized a horrible truth. My body had orgasms when my father was raping me. I can't possibly describe the agony of shame that flooded my soul at this revelation. I cried out, "No! No! I don't want this! Nooooooo!"

"Why? What does it mean to you?" Jan questioned.

And I cried out in horror, "It means I wanted him to do it!"

"No, it does not!" he responded firmly. "That's not true. That is a lie. You did not want him to do it."

Jan worked hard to try to convince me that my body hadn't betrayed me but I was not easily persuaded. The pain! The shame! The revulsion! Suddenly I understood why I could never remember anything past the point of initial penetration. To remember the physical pain, to remember the anger, is to remember the orgasm, the sexual response. I left my body back there where my father had raped me because I couldn't integrate the sensations of pleasure with the emotions of terror and rage.

He stole my body from me! I didn't get to choose. I was just a little girl! He took my orgasm from me against my will. I didn't understand, I didn't even know what it was. I had no words for it.

I made it almost halfway home before I started to scream and cry in the car. The only word I could manage to get out was, "Nooooooo!"

When I got home, I grabbed my walkman, turned the volume up to the max and took a hard, two-hour walk, only stopping once to double over in pain when I heard the Lord break through all the noise to say ever so softly to me, "I was broken, too. I bled, too."

10:45 PM — *"I will be a father to you, and you will be my sons and daughters, says the Lord Almighty."* (2 Corinthians 6:18) *"How great is the love the Father has lavished on us, that we should be called children of God! And that is what we are!"* (1 John 3:1)

My body responded like a body is supposed to respond. The mechanisms which God put in place so we might experience pleasure in our sexuality worked like they were supposed to work. I didn't do anything wrong. There is no sin for me to confess. It was my father who was wrong. He never should have touched me. I didn't want him to do it. The fact that my body responded in the natural way bodies respond to sexual stimulation does not mean I wanted him to do it. I was an innocent child. *God, help me to grasp and hold onto this truth.*

The shame and the thought that my father was probably aware of my body's response was so terrible I couldn't contain it on my own. I wanted to go to the meadow. I tried to take my feelings to Jesus during the session and again after my walk when they hit me full force a second time. I couldn't seem to find Him though I knew He was there. I needed to talk with someone, to break out of the isolation. It was scary to call a woman from my DID support group. I didn't know her well but I knew she'd understand at least some of what I was going through.

At first all I could do was cry.

It was hard to tell her what I was experiencing but she was patient and a good listener. When I confessed about the orgasms during rape, she told me the same

209

thing had happened to her with her father. I am the first person she ever told this to. I felt honored to receive her trust and I saw clearly how innocent of wrong we both were.

As I told her of the guilt and shame I had been feeling I began to tap into righteous anger about the abuse and its long-term effects. The anger was good and it helped me to feel stronger and less like a victim. I am not powerless anymore. I am not a helpless little girl. I don't have to accept the abuse or the false guilt or the shame that I don't deserve.

I am not just a little lamb anymore. I am a lioness, too. I can and will fight back now. I will reclaim my power. I will reclaim my body. I will reclaim my rightful place in this world as a child of God!

January 16, 1996 — I'm not doing as well as I thought I was with this newest revelation. I have been unable to stop moving or running the entire day. I really need to see Jan but I didn't call for an extra appointment. Instead I wrote him this e-mail:

Dear Jan — I don't know what's real. I didn't sleep at all last night. I was a high-speed train at a million miles an hour through the day. I can't seem to slow down. I thought I was handling this but now I don't think so. I can't remember what we talked about at the last session—all the things I thought I was figuring out. All I remember is remembering the orgasms. I wish I didn't remember that part either. I need to go into the meadow but I can't find it anymore. Want to come and see you but I don't feel I deserve it. I shouldn't send this but I will anyway. Judy.

January 17, 1996 — All I want to do is lie down on his couch, hold his hand, and enter deep into the meadow where Jesus waits. I want to be told over and over again that I am clean and beautiful and I didn't want him to do it! I don't want to remember. In fact, I want to forget, and earlier I started to repeatedly deny that I could have had an orgasm while being raped. I couldn't convince myself of the lie though. I'm too committed to knowing the truth, no matter how repulsive.

January 18, 1996 — Worked on the book all day today. It is keeping my mind occupied so I can avoid dealing with what happened on Monday. I have no idea how I'm really doing about that. I imagine myself going in to see Jan tomorrow and saying, "I'm doing fine." (This is always a sure sign that something is seriously wrong.) Then I get angry at myself because I don't believe my own lie. On some level I feel terribly ashamed. I thought I was done with the shame. Guess not.

Looking closely at the earlier stages of my healing journey these last few days while I've worked on the book has been interesting. I am amazed at the work the Lord did to prepare me for the realities of the incest and DID. So much groundwork had to be laid before I could face these truths. My heavenly Father was so patient and thorough. I know this latest awareness has not come sooner than I was made ready to take it in. I know God has a plan to make it possible for me to integrate this memory, to come to terms with it.

Father God, it's been hard to find You these past few days. You haven't gone away, I know, but I seem to have moved off the path and gotten a bit lost. It seems I've forgotten the way to the meadow where Jesus waits. Or maybe I'm just scared to enter because of my shame. I can't imagine much of anything more repulsive and ugly than this last memory. I don't even want to think about it. I withdraw from the thought. I withdraw from myself. I withdraw from You. You know all the confusion and pain I'm running from right now. You know what is needed. Find me, Lord. I need You. Amen.

January 19, 1996 — I was battling dissociation and anxiety. It was difficult to either talk or think. I felt deeply ashamed and afraid—afraid of being overwhelmed by the same feelings I had on Monday. Jan was talking about Jesus, about how God could help me to see if I had really done something wrong or not. A voice within said angrily, "There is no Jesus." I was scared when I heard that voice of an angry child. It made me think there was another alter, perhaps one that remembers the actual rapes after penetration. I was afraid to know, afraid to see. I didn't want to look. New alters mean new memories. I didn't feel safe. I wasn't ready. I sat up straight quite suddenly and said, "I don't want to talk about this anymore. Okay? Can we talk about something else? Please?"

Then I didn't know what to talk about. Jan bailed me out by asking me about my progress on the book. That was good. I could talk about that and feel like a grown-up, like a competent human being. He asked me if I was developing an alter that was a writer as a way of coping with this latest crisis. I don't need a writer alter. I am the writer. I am consciously tuning in to the integrated "Observer" aspect of myself in order to focus my attention on the writing, but it is my writing work. I am the writer.

I said, "Looking back over the years, I realize the Lord has always prepared me for everything He has revealed to me. When something comes, I know I have been given the strength to handle it. Even this time. But I seem to have lost my way to the meadow."

Jan said, "Maybe Merriel knows the way."

That was his way of inviting Merriel to enter into the session. She felt ashamed and bad for feeling something good when she knew what was happening was wrong.

She said Angel was there, and Angel saw what he was doing but she only remembered the initial physical pain of the first rape. Then she stopped feeling the body. She was only "in the head" when the rapes were occurring. She always thought he must be hurting us because she remembered the slashing pain of that first rape. She had to cut herself off from the body so that she could endure the rapes without screaming or crying. Her focus was on her desire to kill him and on staying alive.

Now Merriel has memories of all the different kinds of rapes right up to the point of penetration and then continuing at the point where he leaves the room and she is left alone with her pain. We have still not remembered the actual rapes with all the physical and emotional responses connected to them—the pain, the anger, and now I realize, the sexual response as well. I think it is because of the sense of being betrayed by our own body that we have been unable to remember this portion of our experience. How will I ever integrate this? It is so ugly.

Merriel asked Jan if he would help her find Jesus. Jan held her hand and prayed for her and encouraged her to pray for herself. She cried and confessed her "badness" to Jesus, saying she didn't mean to do anything bad but she was sorry. Afterwards, Jan prayed for her and for me that we would understand that Jesus never goes away from us, that He loves us, and He wants to stay close to us, right inside of us. It was such a relief to make contact with the Lord again. I have been feeling so untouchable. I needed to come back into His presence, to be His beloved child again.

Lord, I have felt so ashamed, so dirty again. How often I forget Your work of atonement for me. You knew about this awful truth the day You took Merriel and I to the cleansing stream. This has not come as a shock to You as it did to me. Still, I feel so defiled, Lord. Realizing that he even claimed control over my orgasms—not just my body, but my sexual responses. I feel angry and powerless and guilty and filthy. I don't understand, God, how I could feel pleasure of any kind in the midst of my pain, terror and revulsion!

That he stole my orgasms, meant to be experienced only in the most intimate and loving relationships—I can't accept this. My mind screams "No!" I don't want this to be the truth! It seems more than I can bear—the worst memory of them all. I don't care about the rapes, the way he hurt me leaving bruises and scars on my body and mind, but he stole my orgasms. Intimate, precious, private, mine! They were supposed to be mine and now they aren't mine. He took from me what I never wanted to give. It's so wrong! Nooooooo!

See, Lord, still I am in turmoil and I can't find the meadow of peace You long to show me. I can't enter that place yet, Lord. I'm too full of anger and shame and fear. Come with me into this valley, Lord, that seems so far removed from the meadow of peace and safety. I must pass through this valley before I can go there again. I want to leave the anger and shame and fear on the floor of the valley. I don't wish to defile the meadow with these things. I can't come to You there, Jesus. Not yet. Will You come to me here?

The Lioness and the Lamb

January 22, 1996 — I was so tense when I sat down on his couch I wanted to crawl right out of my skin. I tucked my legs up underneath myself Indian-style and held my arms tightly against my sides, but my hands betrayed my anxiety. They just wouldn't keep still. Why was I so terrified?

We decided to see if Jan could help me find a way to relax my muscles before we tried to talk. As I laid back on the couch and tried to stretch myself out of my withdrawn and defensive posture, I was embarrassed by my lack of control over my own body. My legs refused to lie down flat, but kept wiggling and twitching and curling at the knees. My arms remained tense and my hands clasped and unclasped the hem of my shirt and flailed about aimlessly.

Jan was using verbal suggestions to breathe deeply, to tighten and then relax my leg muscles, etc., but mostly all that did was get me into my body when everything in me wanted to get out of my body.

Then Jan tried another approach, encouraging me to visualize the meadow. That got me out of my body and into my head which helped a lot. I began to feel calmer. Tears fell and Jan asked what the feeling was.

"Longing... I'm longing for the safety of the meadow. I can see the meadow now... the field of wildflowers... red, yellow, blue... waving in the soft breeze... and a very big tree... big and strong... stretching out her arms to offer shelter... in the distance I see hills and mountains... I can see the meadow but it is very far away..."

"Can you see what is between you and the meadow?" Jan asked me.

I began to regress into a childlike state as fear was rising within me, "Yes, there is a canyon... big and deep and dark and I can't get across!"

"Can you look at the canyon? What is at the edge of the canyon?"

"Nothing! It is a sheer drop! At the edge is a wall... straight down... down and down into a black river... Ugly things are floating in the river... They float by, but more keep coming!"

"Can you look across the canyon to the other side? What do you see there?"

Starting to weep, I said, "I see the meadow... I want to go there but I can't get across! I can't go there with this body. I want to make the body go away..."

Jan asked, "Why do you want to make the body go away?"

"It is black and broken and ugly and bent... I can't get across the black river... I don't know how!"

"Do you see anything else across the canyon that could maybe help you get across?"

213

Nodding, I answered, "I see a Lioness... She is calling to me to come over... But I can't!"

I began to sob. "I am scared. She doesn't understand... The black river is my home... It is where I belong... The ugly things in the river look like me... I look like them... It is my home..."

Jan countered, "But the Lioness wants you to come over. She doesn't see it that way. She has good, sharp eyes. Did you always look black and broken and bent?"

"No. I was a baby once and I was clean and bright and I could smile and belong in the world... But not anymore."

"Who did that to you? Who made you get black and broken?" Jan asked gently.

"The man... He made me all dirty and no one came to make me clean again!"

"So you really didn't come from the black river and you don't belong there now. The Lioness sees that with her good, sharp eyes. She can help you get across the canyon. Is there something you want her to do?"

Plaintively, the child in me responded, "I want her to come back and get me... but I'm scared. I'm afraid she will drop me into the black river. She is big and strong but she doesn't understand how small and weak I am... I don't want to fall in the river and drown! I'm scared!"

"Can you ask the Lioness to come back and get you? She is strong enough to carry you and she won't let you fall."

A calm fell over the child, "Yes... She is back with me now... She says we can just rest here on the edge of the canyon for awhile and she won't let me fall in... I can curl up next to her... She is really my friend... almost like a mother... She says we can look at the canyon from here and when I am ready, we can cross to the other side where the meadow is."

For a few minutes my little girl's heart rested close to the heart of the Lioness within me. Then Jan asked me to let go of the image and come back and talk to him. I pulled myself out of the imagery but held onto the feeling of peaceful rest. I looked at Jan and he said, "The big issue is trust."

It is so hard for me to trust myself and the Lioness within me, my righteous anger. I need to see clearly that my anger has a great deal of merit and a lot more legitimacy than the guilt and shame—no matter how deep that river runs.

I began to count the cost as I took a walk through my history of sexual experiences. The damage done to my sexuality by my father is beyond measurement. It has affected my entire life. Jan says it's not too late. I can't change the past but I can change the present and the future. I have a loving and generous husband who desires a full and satisfying sexual intimacy as much as I do. I can find ways to reclaim my body and I'm going to do it. My father has stolen enough.

I went a half-hour over my allotted time today without realizing it. When I suddenly noticed the time, I was panicked, but Jan said, "Don't be afraid. That's my responsibility. I could have stopped it. I was very aware of the time. It's not your fault. It's my little gift to you."

January 23, 1996 — I bought a little pink doll for Merriel the other day. Just a soft little squeezable fuzzy pink doll with a simple happy-face stitched in place. I am falling in love with this doll. She's about six inches tall and all she can do is smile. When I hold her in my hand, she fits just right.

When I look into her eyes, Merriel and I can see one another smiling back at each other. It's hard to explain how that works, but it does. Best of all, this little doll reaches into a place deep in my heart where a baby lives. There is a baby inside of me who is clean and pure and innocent and who has a place in this world. She wasn't born in the River of Shame and she knows she belongs in this world. She can hope, she can believe, she can love, she can trust.

That innocence, that sense of being one with the world, is still alive somewhere within me. She is still there and I am finding her with the help of a little pink doll.

January 24, 1996 — Working on the book is good for me right now. I am remembering all the pain and confusion, the nightmares, the flashbacks, all the evidence and effects of the incest. Today I wrote about the dream of my father and sour pickles. It was about how desperately I needed his love and I was willing to do anything to get it.

As I thought about this dream, I started screaming "No!" And in my mind, I pushed my father away angrily and said, "I don't want to!" and called him a liar! The anger is there and it needs to be given its voice. The Lioness is my ally and my friend. She will carry me across the River of Shame to the safety of the meadow. I didn't come from the slime. I was pushed into it by my father. My righteous anger at his sinful behavior will empower me to escape the guilt and shame that try to hold me.

January 26, 1996 — Found myself apologizing to Jan for taking the extra time last session. I felt unworthy of the gift. It is hard for me to receive gifts. I'm suspicious of the nice things people do for me because I think they must have strings attached to them. I will owe them something, some unexplained and unexpected cost that I don't want to pay. Or on the other hand, they may suddenly realize I don't deserve the gift and they will take it away from me. I don't trust.

Part of me feels so unworthy, as if it is too much even that my body takes up space in the air. This is why I so often feel I want to crawl out of my body, so I can take up less space in this world where I don't belong. I have to find a way to believe I have a right to be here. I start to believe it when I let the Lioness roar, but then I get so scared, I run back down into the safety of this tiny hole where I huddle trembling.

Merriel and I wanted to go see Jesus in the meadow. Far off in the distance we could see Him standing there under the tree. Jan asked us to look closely and tell him what we could see. We saw His hands with the nail scars in them and across the cleansing stream we saw a cross on a hill. Jesus was calling to us to come to Him. He stretched out His arms to us but we were afraid.

Jan said, "Just keep looking at Jesus. What is He doing?"

We saw Him coming toward us, coming to bring us to the meadow. We thought He didn't understand about us. We thought when He got closer He would see the River of Shame at the bottom of the canyon and He would know we didn't belong in the meadow. He walked straight to us. He walked right across the chasm as if it wasn't there! He reached down and took our hand. He touched our face and smiled.

We stood and walked with Him on one side of us and the Lioness on the other. Together we all crossed over the River of Shame as if it wasn't there. We didn't look down. We just held on tight and walked all the way to the maple tree where we sat down next to Jesus and leaned in close to His heart. His arm was around us. He doesn't think we are ugly and dirty. He says we are clean and beautiful. He knows where the slime came from and He let it fall off into the black river when we crossed over into the meadow.

From the safety of the tender arms of Jesus we entered the earliest memories of molestation. I remembered how desperately I wanted my father to stop, even then. How I wanted to cry out, "No! Please don't do this! Don't make me... I don't want to!"

I didn't want him to do it. I knew there was something very wrong and I wished so much he would just be my daddy, touch my face, hold my hand, hug me—but not this!

It was my body! Mine! My body! He stole it. He acted as if it belonged to him. It was supposed to be my body! And, yes! I was angry. Of course, I was angry. He stole my body!

3:30 PM — There is so much NO in me that needs to come out. So many screams and cries of protest that need to be heard. I have a right to be angry! I should have been able to scream and cry when he was raping me! I should have been able to shout, "No! No! No! Nooooooo!" and push him away. All of it was locked up inside of me. Fear of death held it in so tightly. I couldn't scream. I couldn't shout. I couldn't even cry—didn't dare to let a tear fall from my little girl's eyes.

Get out of here! Get away from me! Get out of me! Get off of me! Get off of me!

January 30, 1996 — Anger. After nearly four decades of running at breakneck speed away from it, and two years of talking about it and playing cat and mouse with it, I have at long last begun to face and feel my anger. And you know what? It feels good!

I am letting the Lioness roar at last, and oh, what a powerful and righteous roar she has. The "No!" within me, the "I don't wanna!"—The "Leave me alone! Get off of me!" are finally being released. All through the years of my childhood these words reverberate. Time and again I was forced to do things with my body against my will. Deep, deep within, a fierce and growing anger dwelt, locked in a cage of fear. I believed if I allowed the anger to have a voice, to have a body, I would be killed or abandoned.

My arms wanted to push. My legs wanted to kick. My voice wanted to scream and shout. My eyes wanted to shed tears of anger and frustration. A little girl, weak, powerless, no way out, no way to fight, no way to flee, frightened and confused, no one to rescue me. The anger became my enemy. I had to hold everything in, tightly squeezing, stiffly, silently enduring. No pushing arms, no kicking legs, not one single tear allowed. All held excruciatingly in check, while he stole my body, my innocence, my joy, my life.

Mommy only loved the babies. Daddy wanted a big girl. I just wanted to be a little girl and for that to be okay. I never got to be a little girl. It was wrong. So wrong. I didn't choose it. He chose it. He stole my choice away from me. He stole my power away from me. I'm taking back my power. I'm taking back my choices. I taking back my life, my joy, my anger, and even my innocence.

I am discovering an innocent infant child within me, the original child. She has no words, she's too young for that, but she has a sense of belonging in this world that I have never known. She is not an alter. She is who I really was before the damage was done. God is restoring her to me. I thought it was too late to go back to the innocence, but with God as my Father, nothing is impossible.

I thought the baby I tried so desperately to save was lost to me forever. Time after time, my dreams told me the Nazis had killed her or the bad men had taken her away, but it was a lie. My heavenly Father never took His watchful, loving eyes off of His precious child—not for a single moment. He preserved and protected her, nurturing her all through the years. God knew I needed to make peace with the anger and to let go of the shame and the fear to really make room for the infant in my heart. So He held her gently, patiently waiting for me to be ready to receive her.

One day soon He will hand her over into my care, but He will never stop watching over her—over me. He will always walk beside me on the journey, and He will carry me when I can walk no more. When the journey gets hard and I again grow weary and wounded, He will bring me into the meadow where I will find rest and healing once more.

One day, when the time is right, He will lead me across the cleansing stream, that sparkling river that runs along the edge of the meadow, into the Promised Land and I will be completely free. On that day, I will run confidently into His arms and He will look me in the eyes and say, "Well done, my beloved child," and my heart will sing for joy to the Lord forever, because that's what it's like to be loved by a God called Father.

Epilogue

September 17, 1997 — Every book must come at last to those final words "the end." Though my book, too, must come to an end, the story itself goes on. The journey to healing and wholeness takes a lifetime to complete. I chose to finish this work at the point when I finally realized I was going to get well! That moment of awareness, of absolute certainty, came to me with crystal clarity the first time I allowed myself to fully remember the depth and breadth of my anger at my father. That day I was able to fight him off and push him away from me in my mind, to peel his toxic shame away from my body and soul. I was finally able to say, "No!"

One final alter came to the surface in the months following the completion of the manuscript. She was an older version of Angel and we called her "Angel Too". She carried the parts of the worst memories that the younger Angel couldn't bear. Eventually Merriel and Angel Too joined together and I now use the middle name MerriAngela to honor the memory of all the brave little girls who were once within me.

My father continues to deny all and states that he will have nothing to do with me unless I tell everyone I made it all up—something I cannot do with integrity. I have not seen him since I started to remember. But I have let go of the anger, forgiven him and been set free.

Paul and I are planting a new church in a major city in Europe and loving each other and our ministry together. There is more work yet to be done but I am getting well!

Jesus left the earth with these final words: *"...the Messiah must suffer and die and rise again from the dead...that this message of salvation should be taken... to all the nations."* (Luke 24:46-48 Living New Testament)

Christ crucified. Christ risen. Christ proclaimed. Without the suffering of the Cross, there would be no resurrection. Without the resurrection, there would be no proclamation. Without the proclamation, there would be no salvation! The fact that Christ suffered and died is Good News! That's the paradox of the gospel. And we are called to follow Christ. We are appointed to suffer, to take up our cross daily, that we might be resurrected by the power of Christ to redeem, heal and sanctify us. And then we are to proclaim our testimony of resurrection! The paradox of our individual lives is that it is in our suffering that we can rise again to proclaim the good news of Jesus Christ.

There comes a time in each of our lives when we finally come up against the wall—when our self-protective strategies for survival start to fail us. A time when we have to choose. It's a matter of life and death. To really live, we first have to die—to take up our cross. To drink the cup of our own legitimate suffering, enter the Tomb and embrace what we find there, dying to the fantasies, illusions and false hopes we have held so dear. There in the darkness of the Tomb a transformation takes place.

In the midst of my anguish, I reached out in the darkness and found my true Father's hand was reaching in. By His hand the Pit of Longing—my loneliness, isolation and abandonment—became a Meadow of Peace where Jesus waits and watches over His little Lamb. By His hand the River of Shame became a cleansing stream of Living Water, purifying me from my own sins and the sins committed against me.

By His hand the Cave of Anger—once home to a boundless, murderous rage—became the dwelling place of a powerful Lioness whose anger is tempered by God's righteousness. By His hand my Glittering Image was shattered, revealing a broken and fragmented soul. And by His hand, piece by piece, He put me back together again and breathed new life in me. The Lioness laid down with the Lamb as God restored both my power and my vulnerability and made me whole.

By His hand, He raised me up from the Tomb and gave me a place in this world—and a place in the world to come—making me his own beloved child. The death. The resurrection. And now, through the voice of this book, the proclamation. This is my testimony to the glory of God.

Father God, I am amazed. Behind our glittering images, we human beings are all so small and weak and helpless and needy—sinful creatures desperately hungry for love and acceptance. Yet in your power and might and purity, You do not turn away from us in disgust or scorn. You take the broken fragments of our lives and restore us, reuniting us with ourselves and with you. You draw near to us in love and graciously meet our needs for forgiveness and healing. Help me to give that same kind of gracious love to those who are hurting as I once was. Help me find a way to reach them, Lord, to share with them the joy of experiencing the mothering love of a God called Father.

The Beginning

Words of Acknowledgement

Many people have contributed to the development of this book. Daral Boles believed that my story should be told and encouraged me to keep going when I wanted to give up. Kathleen Istudor turned her screenwriter's eye to the storyline in the final editing process. The help of both of these women was immeasureable in shaping the book as it stands today.

My friend Carolyn Gregware was the first to suggest that it might be time to give some attention to "Judy, the little girl" – as always, her advice was honest and good. My American therapist Sandy Sanders was a great support and a very present help during my trips to the States when I felt alone and afraid. Her hugs fed my hungry heart and her prayers fed my soul when "Jan" couldn't be there for me. My Dutch therapist "Jan" was not only brilliant but also incredibly patient and unfailingly honest. I know I will miss him forever.

Above all, I want to thank my husband. He surrounded me with his loyal love and gave me all the space I needed as I swung back and forth on my pendulum, until I finally settled down to rest with satisfaction at his side. I love you, honey.

About the Author

Judith Machree had no memories of her youth and for many years she was not conscious of the fact that she had split into multiple personalities in order to survive the traumatic events of her childhood. When as an adult her survival techniques began to work against her, leaving her lonely, confused and suicidal, she embarked on a journey of discovery of her past and of her inner world. Supported by her trust that a heavenly Father would help her on this difficult path of remembering, she faced her pain, her fear, her anger, her doubts — opening the door to the truth.

Working as a Christian missionary in Europe along with her husband, Judith's life began to fall apart and her glittering image came shattering to the ground when memories of childhood sexual abuse surfaced. Determined to reclaim her life, Judith worked intensely with an excellent Christian psychologist. In this book, she shares honestly and intimately both her trials and her triumphs and offers hope to all who must walk the treacherous path that leads to freedom and victory.

Her book was originally translated into the Dutch language and published in Europe under the title "Ik Zal een Vader voor je zijn..." (I Will Be a Father for You).

Judith continues her work in Europe where she and her husband give leadership to a growing international church. She is also working on her Master's Degree in Clinical Psychology. She has three married children, three grandchildren, three cats and two birds. She loves going to the movies, singing and walking in the forest.

Printed in the United States
106580LV00003B/237/A